THE ROAD TO BATEMANS BAY

SPECULATING ON THE SOUTH COAST
DURING THE 1840s DEPRESSION

THE ROAD TO BATEMANS BAY

SPECULATING ON THE SOUTH COAST DURING THE 1840s DEPRESSION

ALASTAIR GREIG

ANU PRESS

ANU PRESS

Published by ANU Press
The Australian National University
Canberra ACT 2600, Australia
Email: anupress@anu.edu.au

Available to download for free at press.anu.edu.au

ISBN (print): 9781760466053
ISBN (online): 9781760466060

WorldCat (print): 1392434965
WorldCat (online): 1392434929

DOI: 10.22459/RBB.2023

This title is published under a Creative Commons Attribution-NonCommercial-NoDerivatives 4.0 International (CC BY-NC-ND 4.0) licence.

The full licence terms are available at creativecommons.org/licenses/by-nc-nd/4.0/legalcode

Cover design and layout by ANU Press. Cover map: 'A Plan of 40 Suburban Allotments at St Vincent [Cartographic Material] on the North Shore of Bateman's Bay … 1841, R. Clint, Lith', NLA, digitised item, MAP F 87 copy, catalogue.nla.gov.au/Record/1105999.

This book is published under the aegis of the Humanities and Creative Arts editorial board of ANU Press.

This edition © 2023 ANU Press

Contents

List of illustrations	vii
Dramatis personae	ix
Acknowledgements	xi
1. Introduction	1
2. The first land purchasers on Batemans Bay	11
3. Puffing St Vincent	23
4. Competing for southern pre-eminence	49
5. Clint the engraver and his survey of St Vincent	71
6. John Staple and the trials of speculation	111
7. Long Beach and Australia's first lottery	133
8. Mercantile chicanery: 'It's a way that they have in Australia'	145
9. The PS *Clonmel* and the southern shipping lane	171
10. Conclusion	193
Bibliography	213
Index	229

List of illustrations

Figure 1. Northern Batemans Bay, looking west from the Pacific Ocean.   xiii

Figure 2. Cullendulla Creek, Square Head and Long Beach, looking east towards the Pacific Ocean.   2

Figure 3. Hughes & Hosking land purchase, 1840.   10

Figure 4. John Hosking, n.d.   13

Figure 5. Fire at Albion Wharf and Mill, March 1841.   16

Figure 6. Edward Lord land grant, 1840.   17

Figure 7. Detail from William Kellett Baker's map of the County of St Vincent, 1843–46.   25

Figure 8. Thomas Stubbs, c. 1860–69.   28

Figure 9. Advertisement selling last allotments at St Vincent, March 1841.   37

Figure 10. Samuel Thomas Gill, 'Wool Drays', 1865.   50

Figure 11. Raphael Clint, late 1820s.   72

Figure 12. Lithographic map of the township of St Vincent, 1841.   87

Figure 13. Lower George Street, 1848.   106

Figure 14. Detail from Benandra Parish Map showing St Vincent street names, 1907.   115

Figure 15. John Staple's superior, Sheriff Thomas Hyacinth Macquoid, 1836.   122

Figure 16. Bank of Australia lottery ticket no. 10,140, 1848.   137

Figure 17. Detail from 1861 indenture showing George Rattray bought Long Beach in 1851.   141

Figure 18. John Hosking, c. 1860.   148

Figure 19. John Terry Hughes's Albion House and Albion Brewery with church, c. 1840.   155

Figure 20. Edward Lord, n.d.   160

Figure 21. Detail of map showing R.J. Campbell's subdivision of Stubley Park, 1884.   162

Figure 22. The *Clonmel* postage stamp, 2017.   172

Figure 23. Detail from NSW Department of Lands map showing 'Conmel Wharf', 1964.   178

Dramatis personae

Raphael Clint—(b. 1797) English engraver, lithographer and surveyor who emigrates in 1829. A polymath whose erudition and behaviour provoke widespread public reaction in the press. Performs many roles in the sales campaign for St Vincent at Long Beach, Batemans Bay. Wearing different hats, he makes an appearance in every chapter. Insolvency in 1847.

John Hosking—(b. 1806) influential merchant born in England. Marries into the family of ex-convict Samuel Terry, the 'Botany Bay Rothschild'. Inaugural elected mayor of Sydney. Personal and business insolvency in 1843.

John Terry Hughes—(b. 1803) member of Terry family who emigrates in 1824. With partner John Hosking, purchases 320 acres at Batemans Bay in 1840. Becomes the 'scapegoat' of the 1840s depression. Personal and business insolvency in 1843.

Edward Lord—(b. 1812) born in Lancashire and emigrates in 1835. Invests in a merchant business, sales agency, squatting stations and land titles from the Monaro to Batemans Bay, where he is the largest landowner. Insolvency in 1842.

John Staple—solicitor who emigrates in 1839, becoming the under sheriff of New South Wales. One of the few identifiable purchasers of auctioned allotments at St Vincent, Batemans Bay. Leaves Sydney for Patrick Plains prior to insolvency in 1842 and is allowed to quit the colony at the end of 1843.

Thomas Stubbs—(b. 1802) 'currency lad' who becomes Sydney's most celebrated auctioneer by 1841, as well as a respected musician, composer and cricketer. Orchestrates the auction campaigns at St Vincent and writes the scripts.

THE ROAD TO BATEMANS BAY

John Jenkins Peacock—merchant, alderman, developer and joint owner of Long Beach in 1841.

Aeneas Macdonell (Glengarry)—Highland chief who lands at Long Beach in 1840.

Thomas Macquoid—sheriff of New South Wales (1828–1841) and southern-interior landowner.

William Oldrey—landowner, commissioner of Crown land and promoter of Broulee.

William Henry Wells—one of many surveyors and map-makers who feuds with Raphael Clint.

The *Clonmel*—Birkenhead-built steamship that arrives in 1840; grounded in Bass Strait in 1841.

Acknowledgements

I am grateful to the following individuals, services and organisations, whose images were invaluable for setting the scene: Geoff Payne, Australia Post, Graeme Bartlett, NSW Land Registry Services, City of Sydney Civic Collection, State Library of NSW, the 'Friends and Relatives of the Descendants of Edward Lord' collection in the State Library of Queensland, the National Library of Australia, the National Museum of Australia, State Library Victoria and the British Museum. All effort has been made to ensure no copyright has been breached, but should any issue be identified then the author welcomes any correspondence at alastair.greig@anu.edu.au.

At Long Beach, the following people helped inspire this project: the late David Lambert, who first suggested to me that a history of Long Beach should be written and generously donated his resources; Colleen Kristensen, who organised the 2017 historical soapbox at which members of the community recounted their memories of Long Beach, and who, along with Ian Kummer, enriched my appreciation of Long Beach; Robin Eckersley, who initiated the Long Beach website and not only prompted me to start writing but also offered ongoing technical and editorial support; Sue and Rodger Middlebrook from the Long Beach Community Association, who were unfailing in their encouragement and their knowledge of precious resources; Mariannia de Rocco and Jim Nairn, who pointed me in the right direction with their earlier archival diggings; Evan Holt, who was writing this before me and whose extracts of research I had the honour to read at the 2017 historical soapbox; Dave and Dee Martin, our neighbours who have always looked out for us.

Joe McCarthy was unstinting in commenting on earlier versions of the manuscript, while Nicholas Brown encouraged me to broaden the focus of the research by asking the most pertinent question: 'What were the promoters' intentions?' I am indebted to the Humanities and Creative Arts editorial board at ANU Press for supporting the manuscript, in particular its chairperson, Nic Peterson. I am also grateful to the two anonymous referees who provided generous feedback and helped me to reconsider the presentation of my argument. The staff at ANU Press could not have been more supportive and helpful in the production stage of the book.

I am the beneficiary of an ANU publication subsidy, and I thank the committee for their important contribution towards copyediting and indexing costs. At this stage, I was blessed to find Rani Kerin, who improved the manuscript beyond recognition. Her copyediting eye, along with her rigour in style guidance, was much appreciated.

Richard Baker, Jamie Pittock and Peter Kanowski from the Fenner School at The Australian National University pushed me, and our students, to connect the storylines of Indigenous history, European settlement and resource management. The university's Kioloa Advisory Board was a dedicated and inspiring group that provided me with a better understanding of the relationship between environmental management and history. In particular, I am indebted to Steve and Robin van Berkhout. I was privileged to work with Bruce Hamon and Marg Hamon. Bruce's work provided me with a model for researching the history of the South Coast. The helpful staff of the NSW Archives at Kingswood accommodated all my requests and guided me patiently through the numerical mysteries and labyrinthine world of land records.

Finally, I became absorbed in this story during the pandemic lockdowns, and I compensated for travel restrictions by transporting myself back to the 1840s. I am grateful to Sallyann Ducker, not only for allowing me this absence but also for her careful reading of the manuscript that I brought back from my time travels. Now travel restrictions are over, Sallyann and I (along with Nellie and Clyde) undertake our regular journeys from the Limestone Plains along the modern road to Batemans Bay, knowing that no amount of hyperbole from the renowned 1840s auctioneer Thomas Stubbs can match the reality of Long Beach.

ACKNOWLEDGEMENTS

Figure 1. Northern Batemans Bay, looking west from the Pacific Ocean.
Detail from Graeme Bartlett, 'Batemans Bay Aerial', 23 August 2008, en.m.wikipedia.org/wiki/File:Batemans_Bay_Aerial.JPG.

1

Introduction

Between 1842 and 1846, Joseph Phipps Townsend took the advice of his London doctor and sojourned in New South Wales, residing with relatives four miles inland from Ulladulla. After a brief expedition to 'the Pigeonhouse', he joined a party on horseback to visit settlers north of the Moruya River. Their journey took them over what later became known as Durras Mountain and then along the rocks under the cliffs south of what is now Depot Beach. Following the coast, they reached the northern shore of Batemans Bay (see Figure 1).

Approaching the mouth of the Clyde River at Batemans Bay, an Indigenous guide piloted their horses through a body of water. This would have been Cullendulla Creek (middle right of Figure 1 and centre of Figure 2). As they forded the water, Townsend recorded that they were 'greeted by a number of the Aborigines, who were running about in the shallows, spearing fish, and who carried on their operations amid much noise and laughter'.[1] This anecdote corroborates oral testimony and archaeological evidence that Cullendulla Creek was an important cultural site for the Walbanja people, who gathered shellfish, mussels and mud oysters from around its mangrove-flanked banks.[2]

---

1   Townsend, *Rambles and Observations*, 65–6.
2   Donaldson, 'Stories about the Eurobodalla by Aboriginal People', 40, 134; NSW National Parks and Wildlife Service, *Cullendulla Creek*, 14; Goulding and Waters, 'Eurobodalla'.

Figure 2. Cullendulla Creek, Square Head and Long Beach, looking east towards the Pacific Ocean.
Photo by Geoff Payne.

Townsend did not mention that he was on Walbanja Country, but neither did he mention that this fleeting encounter was on the site of the recently proclaimed 'Great Southern Township of St Vincent'. Over the previous two years, the government had auctioned and sold the land before it became subject to a prominent advertising campaign in the Sydney press that foresaw that ships would soon be anchored at the mouth of the creek servicing a private town predicted to become a commercial hub second only to Port Jackson.

This book tells the story of these land sales on the northern shore of Batemans Bay in the early 1840s. It explores the promoters' intentions in marketing this township and describes the fate of the St Vincent venture at Long Beach.

A real estate plan of the township and surrounds of St Vincent still exists, in the form of a cadastral map produced for an auction in April 1841 (see Figure 12). It identifies its streets, suburban allotments, moorings and the town boundaries, which stretched from the village reserve on the eastern bank of Cullendulla Creek to the Pacific coast. Further, NSW Land Registry Services holds the land-title deeds relevant to the venture. This makes it possible to link the lives of the key participants with the prevailing

1. INTRODUCTION

conditions within the colony, thereby making the story of St Vincent more intelligible. In this way, the following chapters are an attempt at 'sociological research informed by human understanding'.[3] The book recounts the story of the endeavours of landowners, their agents and southern woolgrowers to improve mercantile access to Sydney, thereby encouraging settlement on the South Coast.

Land-settlement patterns in NSW in the first four decades of the nineteenth century were dominated by the demographic and commercial centrality of Sydney, by the gradual movement of settlers inland after 1820 in search of pastureland, along with the administrative decision to impose boundaries on the spread of Crown land sales. As the following chapters show, the period around 1840 also witnessed the earliest attempts to establish coastal towns on the southern edges of these limits of colonial settlement. The purpose of these ports was to transport commodities from the Southern Tablelands to Sydney.

Over the past 50 years, various researchers have explored why no such prominent commercial port south of the Illawarra was established during the nineteenth century. In 1968, J.A. Clements and W.H. Richmond had queried why the dominance of Sydney and Melbourne on the south-eastern coast had not provoked more research on 'the competitive failure of the rival ports'.[4] To remedy this neglect, they studied Port Albert near Corner Inlet, Gippsland—founded in 1841—and described its brief competition with Gippsland Lakes up to the mid-1860s.

More recently, the rise, decline and readjustment of Port Albert has been subjected to more detailed assessment in Cheryl Glowrey's environmental history of Corner Inlet, while Wayne Caldow has analysed squatter diaries and ship logs associated with early Port Albert. Jane Lennon has provided an even more comprehensive analysis of the movement of livestock from Port Albert to Van Diemen's Land, showing how the viability of southern port settlements was subject to turbulent economic, demographic and administrative changes.[5]

---

3   Hancock, 'A Note on Mary Kingsley', 177–83. Hancock called this 'perspective' or 'span', which he defined as an appreciation of the 'relationship of things' and also 'historical or sociological work as an awareness of background'. See also Low, 'Introduction', 8–9.
4   Clement and Richmond, 'Port Albert', 129.
5   Glowrey, *South of the Strzelecki Ranges*; Caldow, 'The Early Livestock Trade'; Caldow, 'Gippsland and Van Diemen's Land Livestock Trade'; Lennon, *Across Bass Strait*.

On a more general scale, soon after Clements and Richmond called for more research on the competition between southern ports, Peter Rimmer advanced an ideal-type model to explain the historical development of a 'port hierarchy' on Australia's south-eastern coastline.[6] Adding empirical weight to Rimmer's model, in 1997 Gordon Waitt and Kate Hartig explained why the 'grandiose plans' for Twofold Bay between the 1840s and 1900 achieved such 'insignificant outcomes'. Marion Diamond has also described the rationale behind Benjamin Boyd's failed speculative interest in Twofold Bay during the 1840s.[7]

The following chapters contribute further to this history of early southern-coastal settlements and the motives for their establishment. It adopts a wider comparative perspective through exploring the reasons behind the 'competitive failure' of St Vincent, Batemans Bay, along with its rival ports at Jervis Bay and Broulee. All three were engaged in a challenge for the title of 'Great Southern Township' during the early 1840s, immediately before Boyd's venture at Twofold Bay.

Rimmer's model indicated that a successful port depended on the opening of a road from the interior to its harbour. In the 1830s, the main obstacle to transporting goods to Sydney through a southern port—rather than over the existing inland Goulburn route—was the absence of a dray road over the mountain ranges that separated the inland woolgrowers from the coast. Proponents of southern coastal townships claimed that the 'discovery' of such a road would reduce producers' costs and time considerably. This suggested the title of the book, *The Road to Batemans Bay*.[8]

Economic historians have debated the importance of carting costs for nineteenth-century woolgrowers and farmers.[9] The following chapters add another dimension to this debate by describing the hope that was invested in competing projects for dray roads to the coast. Many Southern Tablelands producers were subscribers to these schemes. Indigenous communities used long-established routes from the interior to the coast for their annual

---

6 Rimmer, 'The Search for Spatial Regularities'.
7 Waitt and Hartig, 'Grandiose Plans'; Diamond, *Ben Boyd*.
8 In turn, the title was also inspired by Paul Carter's book *The Road to Botany Bay: An Exploration of Landscape and History*. Given that the following chapters deal with a route for a prospective dray road (that had yet to be surveyed) to a prospective township (that was yet to be settled), my story appears, *quite literally*, to support Carter's advocacy for a history 'where discovery and settlement belong to the same exploratory process' (xxiv).
9 Jackson, *Australian Economic Development*, 77, 83–4.

1. INTRODUCTION

movements,[10] and many early colonial routes would appropriate such Indigenous knowledge, but the construction of roads for bullock drays carting wool bales and other produce would demand surveying, labour, capital and earthmoving on an unprecedented scale. This process continues today.

More locally, a number of researchers have alluded or referred to the St Vincent land sales at Long Beach, Batemans Bay, in 1841. In particular, Allison James noted that 'Long Beach once seemed set to become the major commerce centre of the district, outdistancing the village of Bateman'.[11] Given that so many local historians have made reference to these sales, it is legitimate to explore why the venture failed and the conditions under which it might have succeeded.

It is understandable that local historians have focused on 'what happened' rather than 'what might have been'. At the end of the story of St Vincent, the value of the land at Long Beach collapsed dramatically, caught up in the great depression of the 'Hungry Forties'—aggravated by drought, the collapse in the price of livestock, financial stringency in Britain, a contraction of the money supply and high interest rates, among other factors. The sales campaign for St Vincent had reflected the air of optimism that was prevalent in the more buoyant and expansionist economic conditions of the mid to late 1830s.

This exuberant atmosphere had promoted land speculation and an over-inflated property market. Regardless of the efforts of auctioneers, the St Vincent sales campaign could not have been initiated at a more inauspicious time. In 1841, the land market began softening considerably and competition intensified with other projected townships for the status of the dominant southern port. In the end, the main characters appearing in this book would find themselves insolvent and the 'Township of St Vincent' would become another of the many speculative ventures of the period that vanished without a trace, swallowing up the money of unfortunate punters. The following chapters chart the fate of these people and their properties and suggest that the period set the scene for institutionalising what Leonie Sandercock later described as 'the national hobby of land speculation'.[12]

---

10 The most comprehensive work in this area is Blay, *On Track*.
11 James, *Batemans Bay*, 125. The following researchers make a passing mention of the venture: Odgers, *Our Town*, 6; Bayley, *Behind Broulee*, 18 (this was first published in 1952 as *History of the Central South Coast*); Turner, *Thematic History*, 27; Biosis, 'Batemans Bay', 13–14; Aplin, Foster and McKernan, 'South Coast and Southern Tablelands', 258; Gibbney, *Eurobodalla*, 30–1.
12 Sandercock, *The Land Racket*.

The 1840s depression has been the subject of much debate among economic historians and political economists, especially over the relative importance of local and external causes.[13] The rival ventures at St Vincent, Jervis Bay and Broulee were undertaken between 'a golden decade of optimism and unexampled prosperity' and the 'desperate years of economic depression which demoralised colonial society and shook, and fractured, its foundations'.[14] The story of St Vincent, therefore, presents an opportunity to trace individuals' lives through this depression and helps us understand how they framed their circumstances and defined and reacted to their situation during this tumultuous period.[15]

The following chapters provide insight not only into the land use plans for Long Beach in 1841—and the tribulations of the individuals who purchased property there—but also into the social, legal, political, cultural and economic conditions prevailing in NSW during the early 1840s. In order to understand what happened at Batemans Bay in 1841—or, more accurately, what did not happen—it is necessary to draw together these milieux.

By intersecting the fate of the people involved in the Long Beach venture with the events and processes they lived through, these chapters reinforce the observation made by an earlier historian of Batemans Bay, Frank Johnson, that many of the colonists who explored and developed Batemans Bay were also 'hopelessly enmeshed in the settlement of N.S.W. as a whole'.[16] Both Jane Lennon and Wayne Caldow have used portraits of particular individuals to great effect in their research on the Port Albert livestock trade in the 1840s, and, in so doing, they link trading and maritime statistics with 'the intentions of squatters, merchants and mariners'. Given the oft-forgotten fate of 'the best laid schemes', this approach can help 'recover the possibility of another history'.[17] The following chapters adopt a similar approach when assessing the St Vincent venture at Batemans Bay, taking advantage of the possibility of identifying the chain of people involved in the scheme, from sellers, surveyors and auctioneers through to buyers. This in turn adds greater understanding to 'social facts' such as property-speculation bubbles and mass insolvency.

---

13   For a summary, see Dyster, 'The 1840s Depression Revisited', 589.
14   Broadbent, 'Aspects of Domestic Architecture', 518.
15   On 1 August 2022, the *Australian Dictionary of Biography* added Barrie Dyster's essay entitled 'The Depression of the 1840s in New South Wales' to its website. This essay also approaches the depression drawing on biographical portraits. See Dyster, 'The Depression of the 1840s'.
16   Johnson, *Where Highways Meet*, 1.
17   Lennon, *Across Bass Strait*, 5. 'The best laid schemes' refers to Robert Burns's observation in his poem 'To a Mouse' that they 'gang aft agley', or often fail to go as planned.

1. INTRODUCTION

Only one of the six dramatis personae in this tale of the depression has received comprehensive biographical treatment: Edward Lord, in Janet Spillman's *Queensland Lords*.[18] Two others, John Hosking and Raphael Clint, are subjects of brief entries in the *Australian Dictionary of Biography*.[19] However, all six were well-known public figures at the time of the depression, meaning that their movements have been captured in publicly available documents, including newspaper articles, court reports, published letters, advertisements, insolvency files, contemporary guidebooks and travel accounts as well as property-related documents held with the State Archives and Records Authority of NSW. This story draws together these individual lives into a wider colonial context.

Chapter 2 introduces the first landholders on the northern shore of Batemans Bay, the merchants John Terry Hughes, John Hosking and Edward Lord. Both the firm Hughes & Hosking[20] and the recent emigre Lord were large landholders throughout the colony. The chapter explores their business strategies, showing that they were both left holding an expansive portfolio of land as the market crested in 1840. The chapter concludes with an assessment of the scale of land-market speculation at this time.

Chapter 3 then sets the scene for the land sales at Batemans Bay. It starts by describing property developers' responses to the growing demand for land on the eve of the depression. This era witnessed the first major expansion of 'manufactured' suburbs and private townships. It then examines the auctioneering system and the sales techniques employed by auctioneers, profiling the celebrated Thomas Stubbs, who orchestrated the sales at St Vincent. The chapter then presents a detailed account of his advertising campaign for the St Vincent allotments, noting how it targeted speculators through emphasising the commercial potential of Batemans Bay. It concludes by returning to the broader concern among the public that the colonial market was softening, leading to a growing presentiment of 'the badness of the times'.

---

18 Spillman, *Queensland Lords*. Edward Lord is the principal character in this family history.
19 Parsons, 'Hosking, John (1806–1882)'; Gray, 'Clint, Raphael (1797–1849)'. A summary of Clint's life also appears in Worms and Baynton-Williams, 'Raphael Clint'. For a website devoted to references associated with Thomas Stubbs's musical life and other useful biographical information, see Skinner, 'Thomas Stubbs'.
20 When the two individuals John Terry Hughes and John Hosking are referred to together in this book, 'Hughes and Hosking' will be used. When their company is mentioned, 'Hughes & Hosking' will be used. Direct quotes are transcribed as found in documents.

Chapter 4 adopts a broader regional perspective, describing how the St Vincent venture faced rival port projects on the NSW South Coast that were making similar claims to those made for Batemans Bay. This context helps explain the wider rationale for establishing a great southern seaport and adds further intelligibility to the St Vincent venture. The chapter ends with a reflection on whether woolgrowers' freight costs were as important as claimed by proponents of these port schemes.

The most enigmatic and mercurial personality in the drama of St Vincent was the engraver, lithographer, surveyor, map-maker, hydrographer, draftsman and inventor Raphael Clint. Chapter 5 recounts his career in Australia, centring on his multiple roles in the St Vincent venture, in particular his production of its surviving cadastral map. The evidence suggests that his involvement with St Vincent was a personal turning point in his fortunes from which he never recovered. More broadly, this biographical portrait presents an opportunity to reflect on the role performed by surveyors and map-makers in the process of colonisation.

Chapter 6 investigates the available data on purchasers of the subdivided land at St Vincent. One of the purchasers, John Staple, was also the NSW under sheriff in 1840–41 and his brief colonial legal career provides insight into the workings of the administrative office most closely associated with the consequences of the mass insolvencies that characterised the period. John Staple himself becomes a case study in speculation-induced insolvency and the information presented in his insolvency schedule adds further clarity to Clint's cadastral map of St Vincent.

The personal misfortunes of Clint and Staple were overshadowed by the insolvency of the firm Hughes & Hosking, which shook the financial foundations of NSW. At the local level, it left the ownership of Long Beach unresolved until the early 1850s. At the broader level, the property became entangled in controversial legal wrangling associated with the long-anticipated 'Bank of Australia lottery' in 1848–49—an 'equitable' plan of partition of the properties mortgaged to the failed bank. The conclusion of Chapter 7 reflects on this enduring phenomenon of 'land mania' and the broader activity of land speculation.

In Chapter 8, the perspective returns from the corporate, legislative and legal milieux to the fates of John Hosking, John Terry Hughes and Edward Lord, recounting how they responded to their insolvencies. Sydney's merchants were a diverse group, and while they faced many threats during the depression some still availed themselves of opportunities. With the aid of the recently passed *Insolvency Act*, they were able to protect much of their personal property. While both Hughes and Hosking argued that they were made scapegoats for the depression, many colonists felt that insolvency law benefited the wealthy and powerful. The chapter draws on popular songs, poetry, novels and newspaper reports to illustrate these conflicting views on justice, power, wealth and capital accumulation.

Chapter 9 completes the story of the fate of the competing southern-port projects, symbolised by the wreck of the luxury paddle-steamer *Clonmel*. While Chapters 3 and 4 explore the terrestrial roads to the ports, this chapter focuses on maritime lanes. The *Clonmel* was a symbol of hope for proponents of the rival port schemes, all of which emphasised steam navigation when promoting their vision. Details from the vessel's unscheduled visit to Batemans Bay add further insight into the sales campaign at St Vincent and subsequent mapping of Long Beach. Further, the story of the *Clonmel* inadvertently triggered interest in another southern port, at Port Albert on Bass Strait. While this port was too far south to emerge as a rival to Batemans Bay, a comparative analysis with Batemans Bay, Broulee and Jervis Bay sheds additional light on the possibilities of southern-port development during the 1840s. The concluding section of the chapter explains how the terrestrial employment of steam finally scuppered the hopes for a great southern maritime township.

The last chapter reflects on the nature of the history produced in this research, in particular its relationship to 'local history'. It also assesses the scheme to establish South Coast townships in relation to other colonial ventures. When it comes to answering the questions posed earlier in this chapter regarding the rationale and subsequent failure of St Vincent, the conclusion is reached that timing—especially the prevailing speculation in export staples, land and steam navigation—made the venture momentarily intelligible. It would have made less sense a decade before, and it was redundant a decade after.

No history involving Long Beach in 1841 can be considered complete without paying attention to the role of the Walbanja people, who continued to be the most significant population around the district at this time, as the opening two paragraphs of this introduction testify. Yet, their voices are absent in available records in the early 1840s and they are rarely spoken of. This is a silence that needs to be rectified in a separate project. However, it is fundamental to the subject of this book—which deals with the transfer of Walbanja land into Crown land and then into private ownership—to pay respect to the Walbanja people upon whose ancestral lands St Vincent was envisaged and on which the suburb of Long Beach was eventually built, and to acknowledge their custodianship of Country.

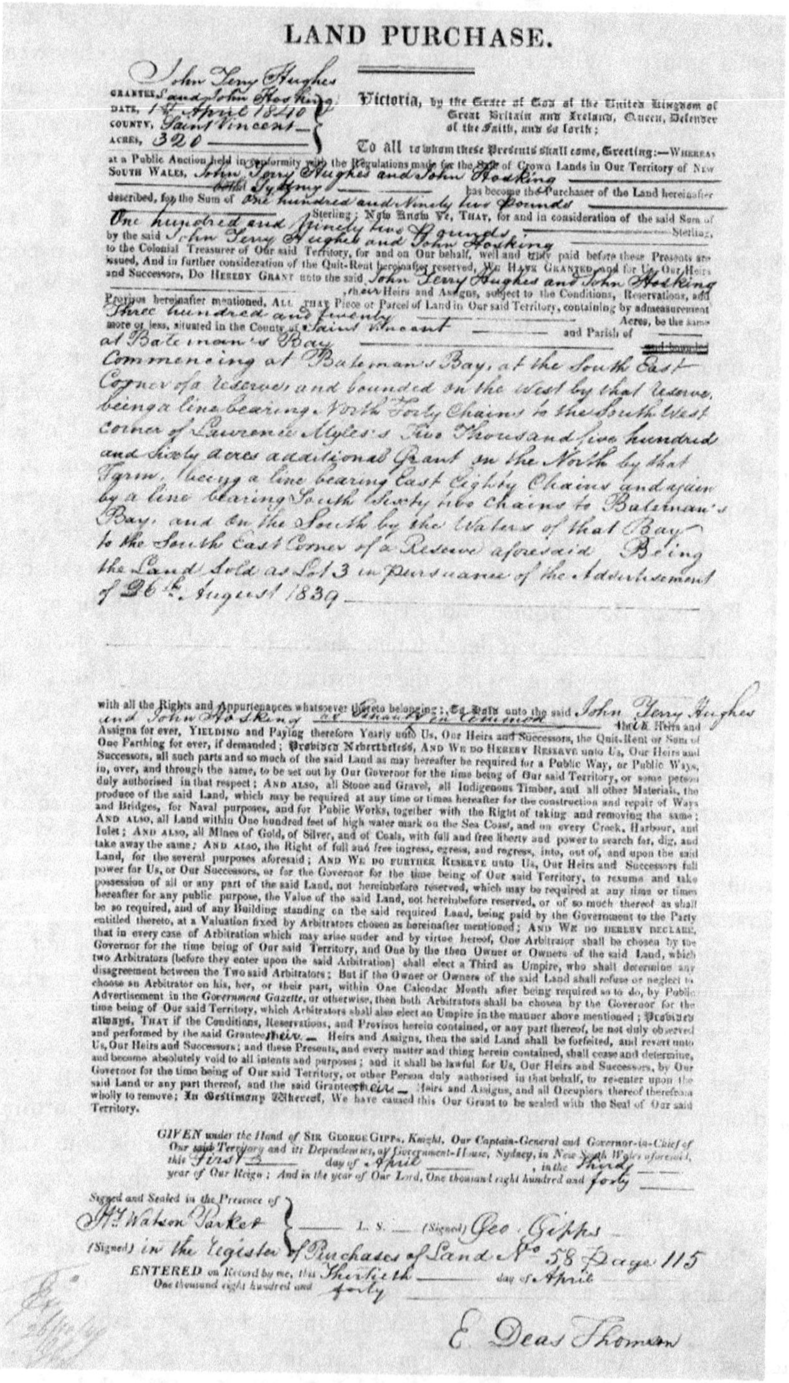

LAND PURCHASE.

GRANTEE, John Terry Hughes and John Hosking
DATE, 1st April 1840
COUNTY, Saint Vincent
ACRES, 320

Victoria, by the Grace of God of the United Kingdom of Great Britain and Ireland, Queen, Defender of the Faith, and so forth;

To all to whom these Presents shall come, Greeting:—Whereas at a Public Auction held in conformity with the Regulations made for the Sale of Crown Lands in Our Territory of New South Wales, John Terry Hughes and John Hosking both of Sydney has become the Purchaser of the Land hereinafter described, for the Sum of One hundred and Ninety two Pounds Sterling; Now Know Ye, That, for and in consideration of the said Sum of One hundred and Ninety two Pounds Sterling, by the said John Terry Hughes and John Hosking to the Colonial Treasurer of Our said Territory, for and on Our behalf, well and truly paid before these Presents are issued, And in further consideration of the Quit-Rent hereinafter reserved, We Have Granted, and for Us, Our Heirs and Successors, Do Hereby Grant unto the said John Terry Hughes and John Hosking their Heirs and Assigns, subject to the Conditions, Reservations, and Provisos hereinafter mentioned, All that Piece or Parcel of Land in Our said Territory, containing by admeasurement Three hundred and twenty Acres, be the same more or less, situated in the County of Saint Vincent and Parish of ~~and bounded~~ at Bateman's Bay Commencing at Bateman's Bay, at the South East Corner of a reserve, and bounded on the West by that reserve, being a line bearing North Forty Chains to the South West corner of Lawrence Myles's Two Thousand five hundred and Sixty acres additional Grant on the North by that Farm, being a line bearing East Eighty Chains and again by a line bearing South Sixty two Chains to Bateman's Bay, and on the South by the Waters of that Bay to the South East Corner of a Reserve aforesaid. Being the Land sold as Lot 3 in pursuance of the Advertisement of 26th August 1839

with all the Rights and Appurtenances whatsoever thereto belonging: To Hold unto the said John Terry Hughes and John Hosking as Tenants in Common their Heirs and Assigns for ever, Yielding and Paying therefore Yearly unto Us, Our Heirs and Successors, the Quit-Rent or Sum of One Farthing for ever, if demanded; Provided Nevertheless, And We do Hereby Reserve unto Us, Our Heirs and Successors, all such parts and so much of the said Land as may hereafter be required for a Public Way, or Public Ways, in, over, and through the same, to be set out by Our Governor for the time being of Our said Territory, or some person duly authorised in that respect; And also, all Stone and Gravel, all Indigenous Timber, and all other Materials, the produce of the said Land, which may be required at any time or times hereafter for the construction and repair of Ways and Bridges, for Naval purposes, and for Public Works, together with the Right of taking and removing the same; And also, all Land within One hundred feet of high water mark on the Sea Coast, and on every Creek, Harbour, and Inlet; And also, all Mines of Gold, of Silver, and of Coals, with full and free liberty and power to search for, dig, and take away the same; And also, the Right of full and free ingress, egress, and regress, into, out of, and upon the said Land, for the several purposes aforesaid; And We do further Reserve unto Us, Our Heirs and Successors full power for Us, or Our Successors, or for the Governor for the time being of Our said Territory, to resume and take possession of all or any part of the said Land, not hereinbefore reserved, which may be required at any time or times hereafter for any public purpose, the Value of the said Land, not hereinbefore reserved, or of so much thereof as shall be so required, and of any Building standing on the said required Land, being paid by the Government to the Party entitled thereto, at a Valuation fixed by Arbitrators chosen as hereinafter mentioned; And We do hereby declare, that in every case of Arbitration which may arise under and by virtue hereof, One Arbitrator shall be chosen by the Governor for the time being of Our said Territory, and One by the then Owner or Owners of the said Land, which two Arbitrators (before they enter upon the said Arbitration) shall elect a Third as Umpire, who shall determine any disagreement between the Two said Arbitrators; But if the Owner or Owners of the said Land shall refuse or neglect to choose an Arbitrator on his, her, or their part, within One Calendar Month after being required so to do, by Public Advertisement in the *Government Gazette*, or otherwise, then both Arbitrators shall be chosen by the Governor for the time being of Our said Territory, which Arbitrators shall also elect an Umpire in the manner above mentioned; Provided always, That if the Conditions, Reservations, and Provisos herein contained, or any part thereof, be not duly observed and performed by the said Grantees their Heirs and Assigns, then the said Land shall be forfeited, and revert unto Us, Our Heirs and Successors; and these Presents, and every matter and thing herein contained, shall cease and determine, and become absolutely void to all intents and purposes; and it shall be lawful for Us, Our Heirs and Successors, by Our Governor for the time being of Our said Territory, or other Person duly authorised in that behalf, to re-enter upon the said Land or any part thereof, and the said Grantees their Heirs and Assigns, and all Occupiers thereof therefrom wholly to remove; In Testimony Whereof, We have caused this Our Grant to be sealed with the Seal of Our said Territory.

GIVEN under the Hand of Sir George Gipps, *Knight, Our Captain-General and Governor-in-Chief of Our said Territory and its Dependencies, at Government-House, Sydney, in New South Wales aforesaid, this* First *day of* April, *in the* Third *year of Our Reign: And in the year of Our Lord, One thousand eight hundred and* forty

Signed and Sealed in the Presence of
H. Watson Parker — L. S. — (Signed) Geo. Gipps

(Signed) in the register of Purchases of Land No 58 Page 115

ENTERED on Record by me, this Thirtieth day of April One thousand eight hundred and forty

E. Deas Thomson

Figure 3. Hughes & Hosking land purchase, 1840.

NSW Land Registry Services, Book V, no. 73.

2

The first land purchasers on Batemans Bay

In the 1830s, the County of St Vincent was at the southernmost reaches of the New South Wales Government's 'limits of location', the term used for the area within which the government surveyed and released land in the colony of NSW. Squatters did operate outside these limits, but land sales were restricted within the limits of location, which ended on the County of St Vincent's southern border at the Moruya River.[1]

In 1838 and 1839, the government advertised its first releases of land on the shores of Batemans Bay in the southern part of the County of St Vincent. Two blocks were released on the northern side of the bay, running from Cullendulla Creek to the Pacific Ocean (see Figures 1, 2 and 7). These properties would become the township of St Vincent. This chapter introduces these two blocks of land and their purchasers.

Messrs Hughes and Hosking

The merchant firm Hughes & Hosking purchased 320 acres at Long Beach, Batemans Bay, in 1840. An application to purchase the land had originally been submitted by Alexander Kinghorne Jr in early 1839. In accordance

---

1 These limits of location were also known in official correspondence as 'the boundaries of location'. The land outside was known as 'districts beyond the boundaries' or 'unlocated districts'. The area inside these limits was known as the 'Settled Districts', which, in 1829, was divided into 19 counties. This helped the government limit the dispersal of population and the surveying department catch up with the issuing of new grants and sales of land.

with the land regulations, the surveyor James Larmer then surveyed the property, submitting his report and Crown plan on 17 June 1839.[2] The lot was then advertised by the government on 26 August 1839. Hughes & Hosking successfully bid at £192 and received their land purchase title on 30 April 1840 (see Figure 3).[3] They paid 12s. an acre, the minimum that government was instructed by the Colonial Office to sell Crown land. This suggests either that there was little competition for the property or that there was collusion among 'land-jobbing' auction attendees to keep the price at its minimum.[4]

The property, on the northern shore of Batemans Bay in an 'unnamed parish' (later 'Benandra', now Benandarah), was flanked on the east by a village reserve that extended from Square Head north along Cullendulla Creek.[5] The south-western corner of the 320-acre block commenced halfway along Long Beach at the modern boundary of Longbeach Estate. It then ran northward for 800 metres along the border of the village reserve to its north-western corner, then east for 1.6 kilometres to its north-eastern border, before running south for 1.25 kilometres back to the shore of Batemans Bay at what today is Wrights or Maloneys Creek.

Hughes & Hosking had already shown interest in the southern reaches of the County of St Vincent. The company was one of the largest landholders at the port of Broulee, purchasing land immediately south of Candlagan Creek in 1839 as well as the headland now known as Mossy Point (1,170 acres combined) for £468. It also bought town allotments when land was released

---

2   James Larmer Field Book, vol. 14, folio 101, see State Archives and Records Authority of NSW (hereinafter State Records Authority NSW), Crown plan 62-787 (V62 787).
3   NSW Land Registry Services, Book V, no. 73. The advertisement appeared in the *NSW Government Gazette*, 28 August 1839, 954.
4   A minimum price, otherwise known as the 'upset price', of 5s. per acre was imposed in 1831, and revised to 12s. in 1838, taking effect from 16 January 1839. Given that Kinghorne had requested that the land be advertised, an explanation is required for why there was no competition at the auction. For an 1837 example of 'land-jobbing' or 'combination' among auction attendees, involving John Terry Hughes (known as 'the land conspiracy case'), see Mann, *Six Years Residence*, 168–203; Chapter 8, this volume. Mann also provides a description of the conduct of government auctions. See also Burroughs, 'The Fixed Price'.
5   The village reserve was selected by Thomas Florance, who surveyed the coast from Jervis Bay to Moruya in 1828 and 1829. See Square Head in Figure 2 and 'VR' in Figure 7, this volume; see also Turner, *Thematic History*, 27. Florance also acknowledged the local Indigenous name 'Yangary' for the bay that Captain Cook had named 'Bateman Bay'.

at Broulee headland on 9 January 1840. It was reputedly one of the largest landholders in NSW and had recently made substantial investment in land at the newly established settlement at Port Phillip.[6]

Both Hughes and Hosking were related to the 'Botany Bay Rothschild', Samuel Terry, an ex-convict who became one of the richest men in the colony.[7] John Terry Hughes was his nephew, as well as his son-in-law. He had arrived in the colony in 1824 with £13,000 worth of merchandise and an order from Earl Bathurst for a grant of land, before marrying Samuel Terry's stepdaughter, Esther.[8]

Hughes's business partner was John Hosking (see Figure 4), who came to Sydney as a three year old. His father had been invited by the Reverend Samuel Marsden (the 'flogging parson' and sheep breeder) to run the colony's orphan school. The family returned to Britain in 1819, where Hosking finished his schooling before returning to NSW in 1825. He obtained a land grant and set himself up as a merchant, before marrying Samuel Terry's daughter, Martha Foxlowe Terry, and forming a business partnership with John Terry Hughes.

Figure 4. John Hosking, n.d.

Alderman John Hosking, mayor of Sydney (1842–43), by an unknown artist, presented by the Liverpool and District Historical Society and the City of Sydney as a sesquicentennial gift in 1992. City of Sydney Civic Collection, accession no. 1992.012.

---

6   Magee, *All Broulee*, 68. Like Long Beach, the land at Mossy Point had initially been subject to an application that it be advertised by William Barnard Rhodes. In this case, Hughes & Hosking outbid Rhodes, paying £2 10s. per acre (*Sydney Herald*, 16 November 1841, 3; Magee, *All Broulee*, 147). Their earliest Melbourne allotment was on the south-east corner of the intersection of Swanston and Little Bourke streets.
7   A.L.F., *Samuel Terry*, 5–11; Rubenstein, *The All-Time*.
8   Reported by John Terry Hughes in the *Sydney Morning Herald*, 27 June 1846, 1.

'Those enterprising individuals, Messrs Hughes and Hosking' expanded their operations during the 1830s,[9] running a wharf, a brewery, a whaling station, a shipping agency, warehouses, a steam flour mill, an inn and Sydney's largest hotel—as well as their extensive landholdings, some of which they began subdividing. The firm was also a significant contractor for the Commissariat, the government office responsible for buying and distributing provisions.

On the death of the men's emancipist father-in-law Samuel Terry in 1838, the *Sydney Times* claimed that 'there are not in the Colony two more enterprising merchants, or two gentlemen who have already done so much to improve our metropolis, as Messrs. Hughes and Hosking'.[10] John Terry Hughes became one of three executors of Samuel Terry's will, the largest deceased estate the colony had produced. As Hillary Golder notes, their status as members of Sydney's mercantile elite 'seemed unassailable'.[11] Hosking also had political ambitions. In November 1842, after Sydney had been incorporated as a city, he successfully ran for the ward of Bourke, before becoming Sydney's first elected mayor.[12]

Hughes & Hosking did not hold onto its 320 acres at Long Beach for long. The first private sale of the property was initiated only four months after the company received its land title from the government. The firm instructed the Australian Auction Company to sell a substantial number of country lands and town allotments on 28 October 1840.[13] The Long Beach

---

9   The accolade is from the *Australian*, 24 September 1830, 3.
10 *Sydney Times*, 26 February 1838, 2. A pro-emancipist paper, the *Sydney Times* was also conspicuous in defence of John Terry Hughes's conduct in the 1837 'land conspiracy case'.
11 Golder, *Politics*, 6.
12 On the day the Sydney Council was to elect the mayor, the *Sydney Morning Herald* (9 November 1842, 2) opposed the expected election of Hosking in an article entitled 'This is the Day!'. It warned that 'there should not be the slightest tinge of convictism' belonging to the mayor—an allusion to John Hosking's family connection to Samuel Terry. Manning Clark argued that Hosking was elected mayor in a wave of democratic and egalitarian rejection of conservatism; however, in dress and speech, Hosking conducted himself in a manner that mimicked the style and customs of the British aristocracy. Clark also argued that, despite buying 'a run among the gentry of the Limestone Plains' (Foxlow Estate), Hosking would never be received in the 'drawing rooms of the country gentry' due to 'his marriage to the daughter of a wealthy ex-convict'. See Clark, *History*, 212. Clark referred to Hosking as 'Australian by birth', when in fact he was born in England. Clark presumably was misinformed by Hosking's supporters in the pro-emancipist paper the *Australian* (9 October 1842, 2) who made this claim in favour of Hosking's election over the merchant and chairman of the Bank of New South Wales, Richard Jones.
13 *Sydney Monitor and NSW Advertiser*, 12 and 18 August 1840, 4; 2 and 17 September, 1840, 4; 28 October 1840, 4. See also *Australasian Chronicle*, 8 October 1840, 4.

2. THE FIRST LAND PURCHASERS ON BATEMANS BAY

property was one of 44 lots listed under 'country lands'—properties that the auctioneer boasted 'cannot fail to arrest the attention, excite the curiosity, and command the interest of a discerning public'.

The Sydney engraver, lithographer and surveyor Raphael Clint and the merchant seaman John Jenkins Peacock jointly purchased the Long Beach lot at this auction, or soon thereafter, for £800, showing that the land market was continuing to rise. The property deed was transferred to Clint and Peacock on 6 February 1841. As the following chapters reveal, Clint was the active partner. During 1841, Peacock was primarily engaged in developing other subdivisions, along with his many other commercial activities, as well as mourning the death of his 11-year-old son in February of the same year.[14] As will be discussed more in Chapters 3 and 5, Clint sold the property back to Hughes & Hosking nine months later.

The firm of Hughes & Hosking would soon become forever associated with the early 1840s depression. In the small hours of 3 March 1841, the bakehouse attached to its Albion Mill, inn and warehouses on Sussex Street and West Market Street at Cockle Bay (Darling Harbour) caught alight. It was referred to as 'one of the most serious and destructive fires that ever occurred in New South Wales'. Within hours, the entire premises had been destroyed (see Figure 5). According to the *Sydney Herald*, 'nothing was saved' and it estimated that stock beyond the value of £100,000 had been lost, including 500 tons of coal that would fuel the fire for days.[15]

It soon emerged that the wharf was massively underinsured.[16] As trading conditions worsened, Hughes & Hosking turned to the Bank of Australia, which lent a substantial proportion of its paid-up capital to the firm on the surety of the firm's extensive landholdings. Later, questions would be asked about the soundness of the bank's decision, the consequences of which will become evident in Chapter 7, as it also affected the future of the property at Long Beach.

---

14 Clint and Peacock's title is held at State Records Authority NSW, NRS-17513-8-34-PA 20438, vol. 2781, folio 34. For Clint, see Chapter 5, this volume. For Peacock, see Reynolds, 'Peacock', 14–16; Chapter 8, this volume.
15 *Sydney Herald*, 4 March 1841, 2. See also *Sydney Gazette and New South Wales Advertiser*, 4 and 6 March 1841, 2; *Australian*, 6 March 1842, 2. In 1846, John Terry Hughes reported that the losses amounted to £200,000 (*Sydney Morning Herald*, 27 June 1846, 1).
16 *Australian*, 4 March 1841, 4, claimed it was insured to the tune of £12,000.

Figure 5. Fire at Albion Wharf and Mill, March 1841.
George Roberts, 'The Mills Ablaze', State Library of New South Wales.

Edward Lord

The property surrounding Hughes & Hosking's 320 acres at Long Beach had been granted to Edward Lord—also in 1840. This large, 2,650-acre block was initially promised to Lawrence Myles, a Hunter Valley settler near Dungog, on 23 February 1838 by the acting governor of NSW, Colonel Snodgrass, on his last day in office. However, in February 1840, the Colonial Secretary's Office announced that Myles had requested that the land be readvertised for Edward Lord, who obtained the grant at a quit rent of £16 sterling per annum backdated from 1 January 1839 (see Figure 6).[17]

The south-westernmost corner of the property began at the north-western point where Hughes & Hosking's property met the village reserve. It ran north for 1.5 kilometres, then east for 3.2 kilometres, south for 1.5 kilometres again, then east again for 1.6 kilometres to the Pacific Ocean at what is now named Oaky Beach within Murramarang National Park. From here, the property ran south along the shore and beaches around North Head back to Wrights Creek within Batemans Bay, where its border ran north, then west, abutting Hughes & Hosking's property (see Figure 7).

---

17 NSW Land Registry Services, Book V, no. 99. See also *NSW Government Gazette*, 12 February 1840, 154. For the quit-rent system, see Campbell, 'The Quit-Rent System'.

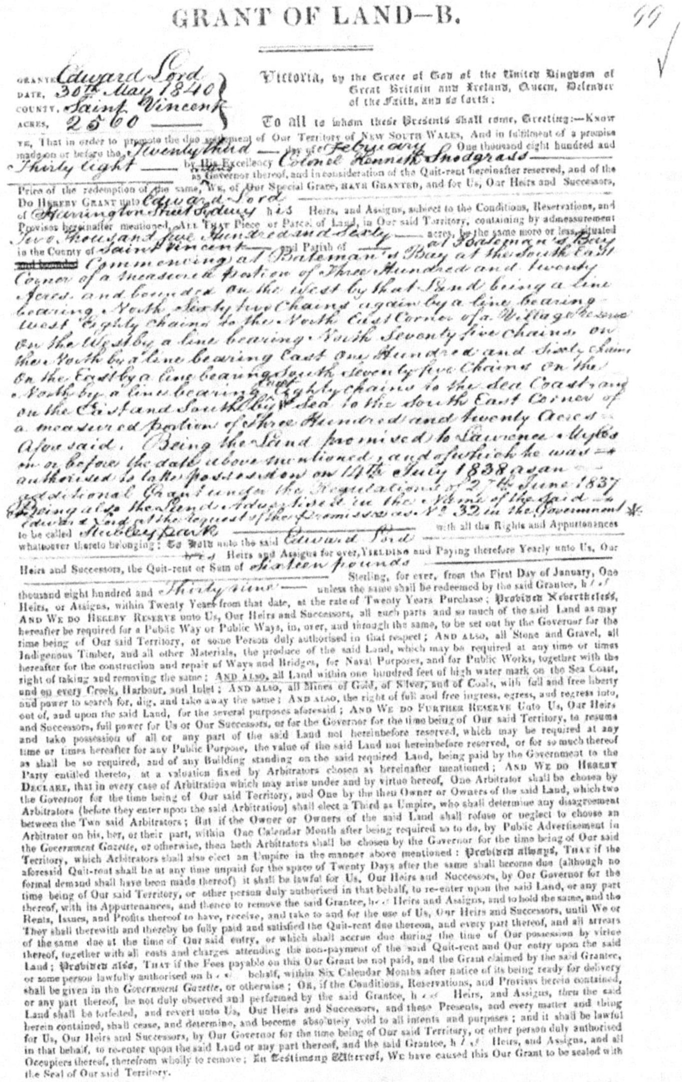

GRANT OF LAND—B.

99

GRANTEE, Edward Lord
DATE, 30th May 1840
COUNTY, Saint Vincent
ACRES, 2560

Victoria, by the Grace of God of the United Kingdom of Great Britain and Ireland, Queen, Defender of the Faith, and so forth;

To all to whom these Presents shall come, Greeting:—Know ye, That in order to promote the due settlement of Our Territory of New South Wales, And in fulfilment of a promise made on or before the Twenty third day of February One thousand eight hundred and Thirty eight by His Excellency Colonel Kenneth Snodgrass as Governor thereof, and in consideration of the Quit-rent hereinafter reserved, and of the Price of the redemption of the same, We, of Our Special Grace, have Granted, and for Us, Our Heirs and Successors, Do Hereby Grant unto Edward Lord of Harrington Street Sydney his Heirs, and Assigns, subject to the Conditions, Reservations, and Provisos hereinafter mentioned, All That Piece or Parcel of Land, in Our said Territory, containing by admeasurement Two thousand five hundred and Sixty acres, be the same more or less, situated in the County of Saint Vincent and Parish of at Bateman's Bay Commencing at Bateman's Bay at the South East Corner of a measured portion of Three Hundred and twenty Acres and bounded on the west by that Land being a line bearing North Sixty two Chains again by a line bearing west Eighty chains to the North East Corner of a Village Reserve On the West by a line bearing North Seventy five chains on the North by a line bearing East one Hundred and Sixty Chains On the East by a line bearing South seventy five Chains on the North by a line bearing East Eighty chains to the Sea Coast and on the East and South by the sea to the South East Corner of a measured portion of Three Hundred and twenty Acres Aforesaid. Being the Land promised to Lawrence Myles on or before the date above mentioned, and of which he was authorised to take possession on 14th July 1838 as an additional Grant under the Regulations of 27th June 1837 Being also the Land Advertised in the Name of the said Edward Lord at the request of the Promissee as No 32 in the Government to be called Stubley Park with all the Rights and Appurtenances whatsoever thereto belonging; To Hold unto the said Edward Lord his Heirs and Assigns for ever, Yielding and Paying therefore Yearly unto Us, Our Heirs and Successors, the Quit-rent or Sum of Sixteen pounds Sterling, for ever, from the First Day of January, One thousand eight hundred and Thirty nine unless the same shall be redeemed by the said Grantee, his Heirs, or Assigns, within Twenty Years from that date, at the rate of Twenty Years Purchase; Provided Nevertheless, And We do Hereby Reserve unto Us, Our Heirs and Successors, all such parts and so much of the said Land as may hereafter be required for a Public Way or Public Ways, in, over, and through the same, to be set out by the Governor for the time being of Our said Territory, or some Person duly authorised in that respect; And also, all Stone and Gravel, all Indigenous Timber, and all other Materials, the produce of the said Land, which may be required at any time or times hereafter for the construction and repair of Ways and Bridges, for Naval Purposes, and for Public Works, together with the right of taking and removing the same; And also, all Land within one hundred feet of high water mark on the Sea Coast, and on every Creek, Harbour, and Inlet; And also, all Mines of Gold, of Silver, and of Coals, with full and free liberty and power to search for, dig, and take away the same; And also, the right of full and free ingress, egress, and regress into, out of, and upon the said Land, for the several purposes aforesaid; And We do Further Reserve Unto Us, Our Heirs and Successors, full power for Us or Our Successors, or for the Governor for the time being of Our said Territory, to resume and take possession of all or any part of the said Land not hereinbefore reserved, which may be required at any time or times hereafter for any Public Purpose, the value of the said Land not hereinbefore reserved, or for so much thereof as shall be so required, and of any Building standing on the said required Land, being paid by the Government to the Party entitled thereto, at a valuation fixed by Arbitrators chosen as hereinafter mentioned; And We do Hereby Declare, that in every case of Arbitration which may arise under and by virtue hereof, One Arbitrator shall be chosen by the Governor for the time being of Our said Territory, and One by the then Owner or Owners of the said Land, which two Arbitrators (before they enter upon the said Arbitration) shall elect a Third as Umpire, who shall determine any disagreement between the Two said Arbitrators; But if the Owner or Owners of the said Land shall refuse or neglect to choose an Arbitrator on his, her, or their part, within One Calendar Month after being required so to do, by Public Advertisement in the *Government Gazette*, or otherwise, then both Arbitrators shall be chosen by the Governor for the time being of Our said Territory, which Arbitrators shall also elect an Umpire in the manner above mentioned: Provided always, That if the aforesaid Quit-rent shall be at any time unpaid for the space of Twenty Days after the same shall become due (although no formal demand shall have been made thereof) it shall be lawful for Us, Our Heirs and Successors, by Our Governor for the time being of Our said Territory, or other person duly authorised in that behalf, to re-enter upon the said Land, or any part thereof, with its Appurtenances, and thence to remove the said Grantee, his Heirs and Assigns, and to hold the same, and the Rents, Issues, and Profits thereof to have, receive, and take to and for the use of Us, Our Heirs and Successors, until We or They shall therewith and thereby be fully paid and satisfied the Quit-rent due thereon, and every part thereof, and all arrears of the same due at the time of Our said entry, or which shall accrue due during the time of Our possession by virtue thereof, together with all costs and charges attending the non-payment of the said Quit-rent and Our entry upon the said Land; Provided also, That if the Fees payable on this Our Grant be not paid, and the Grant claimed by the said Grantee, or some person lawfully authorised on his behalf, within Six Calendar Months after notice of its being ready for delivery shall be given in the *Government Gazette*, or otherwise; Or, if the Conditions, Reservations, and Provisos herein contained, or any part thereof, be not duly observed and performed by the said Grantee, his Heirs, and Assigns, then the said Land shall be forfeited, and revert unto Us, Our Heirs and Successors, and these Presents, and every matter and thing herein contained, shall cease, and determine, and become absolutely void to all intents and purposes; and it shall be lawful for Us, Our Heirs and Successors, by Our Governor for the time being of Our said Territory, or other person duly authorised in that behalf, to re-enter upon the said Land or any part thereof, and the said Grantee, his Heirs, and Assigns, and all Occupiers thereof, therefrom wholly to remove; In Testimony Whereof, We have caused this Our Grant to be sealed with the Seal of Our said Territory.

GIVEN under the hand of Sir George Gipps, *Knight, Our Captain-General and Governor-in-Chief of Our said Territory and its Dependencies, at Government House, Sydney, in New South Wales, aforesaid, this* Thirtieth *day of* May *, in the* third *year of Our Reign; and in the year of Our Lord One thousand eight hundred and* forty

Signed and Sealed in the Presence of
M. Watson Parker — L. S. — (Signed) Geo Gipps
(Signed) In the Register of Lands of Land No 59 page 204

ENTERED on Record by me this Twenty Second *Day of* June *One thousand eight hundred and* forty

E. Deas Thomson
COLONIAL SECRETARY AND REGISTRAR.

Figure 6. Edward Lord land grant, 1840.

NSW Land Registry Services, Book V, no. 99.

Following his grant of land title, Lord named the property 'Stubley Park' after a manor near his Lancashire home. Edward Lord was born in 1812 at Rochdale into a family with a long connection to the wool trade. Generations of Lords had been engaged in wool cleaning and processing. The first fulling works had been established at Stubley in the sixteenth century. Edward had received an inheritance as a result of the division of the family estate and acquired an education in Germany where he advanced his knowledge of the wool trade.[18]

In 1835, Lord, now aged 23, visited Sydney looking for business opportunities in which to invest his inheritance; subsequently, he announced a partnership with the merchant company Kenworthy & Son on 1 January 1836. After Lord returned to Rochdale to marry Eliza Fletcher, the couple emigrated to Sydney, taking rooms in Kenworthy & Lord's Harrington Street premises at The Rocks. These premises were also the headquarters for the firm's export and import activities.

The partnership with Kenworthy was dissolved in late September 1838 due to financial losses. By 1839, Edward's brother James had also migrated to the colony, purchasing land and a store on Paterson River in the Hunter Valley.[19] Edward and James acted as joint commission agents using Harrington Street as their business address.

Lord also set up large squatter stations in the High Country beyond 'the limits of location' that were selected and managed by Edward Bayliss. The government, from 1836, attempted to control such squatting by imposing annual 'depasturing licenses' on squatters.[20]

By 1840, Lord possessed an extensive portfolio of land, including properties he had purchased in 1839 and 1840 along the upper reaches of the Clyde River at Burooman (Brooman) and land beside Cyne Mallowes Creek, the long eastern arm of the Clyde River immediately north of Nelligen Creek. After receiving another readvertised 1,030-acre grant promised to his brother James on the northern shore of the Clyde River, and an adjacent

---

18   Spillman, *Queensland Lords*, ch. 1. The choice of Germany for studying wool was logical. German wool imports to Britain were eight to 10 times higher than that of Australia in 1831, and still higher than Australia in 1842. See Burrows, *Britain and Australia*, 383; Huf, 'Making Things Economic', 246.
19   *NSW Government Gazette*, 3 October 1838, 806; Spillman, *Queensland Lords*, ch. 2.
20   See 'Depasturing Licenses Index 1837–1851', Museums of History News South Wales, mhnsw.au/indexes/land/depasturing-licenses-index/, accessed 27 January 2023. The licence, or fee, was introduced by Governor Bourke and embodied in a statute by Governor Gipps. See also Roberts, *History*, 161–204. Lord's properties were named 'Aston' on the Maneroo and 'Kilantby' further south.

2. THE FIRST LAND PURCHASERS ON BATEMANS BAY

1,010 acres to the west of Hughes & Hosking's property, he then owned all the land westward from Cullendulla Creek to the land due north of Budd Island. He was also grazing cattle at Batemans Bay.[21]

Like John Terry Hughes and John Hosking, Edward Lord never visited his Batemans Bay properties. However, he envisioned a day when Batemans Bay would become the favoured NSW harbour south of Sydney, where ships would receive goods that had been carried down the Clyde Mountain from Braidwood and the Southern Tablelands. This would open up a quicker route from the southern interior to Sydney, compared with the costly and slow inland route through Goulburn and Marulan.

The further south-west that settlers and squatters moved from Sydney—through Braidwood, the Limestone Plains and the Maneroo (Monaro)—the more urgent such a coastal route became.[22] As Chapter 4 will show, Batemans Bay was one of a handful of potential ports that could alleviate this transportation problem facing settlers, squatters and vertically integrated mercantile farmers. In order to compete as a maritime township, a location required a safe harbour and a dray road through the mountains that separated the southern inland settlements from the sea.[23] The demand for a southern port would encourage a number of speculative ventures in the early 1840s, including Batemans Bay, Broulee, Jervis Bay and Twofold Bay.

Lord's investments on the Clyde River from Brooman to North Head—along with property at Bungendore, his squatting stations in the High Country and his commercial store in Goulburn—suggest that he was financially committed to this vertically integrated vision, which required a road to Batemans Bay, or even nearby Broulee. The problem he faced was that by 1840 his inheritance was spent and he was purchasing additional

---

21 Hamon, *They Came*, 30. Lord also purchased land at Kiama and at Bungendore, connecting lines between the High Country and the coast. Spillman, *Queensland Lords*, 39. For the 1,010 acres at Cullendulla Creek and 1,030 acres at the mouth of the Clyde River, see *NSW Government Gazette*, 16 October 1839, 1161.
22 For the occupation of the Monaro, see Hancock, *Discovering Monaro*, part 2, 'New Arrivals'. For the Limestone Plains, see Robinson, *Canberra's First*, 1–19, 68–71; Brown, *A History*, ch. 1.
23 Christopher Pemberton Hodgson took up squatting after arriving in the colony in 1840: 'When a "new chum" is about to form a New Station in a new country, he has four grand objects constantly in view:—First, an open and sound country; Secondly, a good supply of water; Thirdly, a neighbouring port for shipment of goods; and, Fourthly, a road to that port' (Hodgson, *Reminiscences*, 94–5). The last two conditions were a source of frustration for settlers and squatters in the counties of Murray, Argyle and King at this time. For this reason, Lord, Hughes and Hosking supported ports along the southern coastline. See Chapters 3 and 9.

properties through mortgaging his existing landholdings, using other people's money.[24] Still, he remained hopeful that British demand for wool would remain strong and land values would continue to increase.[25]

However, by late 1840, lending was tightening and creditors were beginning to call in their accounts. Lord was short of liquid capital and relinquished his Maneroo squatting stations. In December 1840 he placed Stubley Park on the market without attracting a buyer.

The following two tables illustrate that 1840–41 was a turning point in the land market. Table 1 presents the revenue from the sale of Crown land and Table 2 presents total sales from NSW auctions, which attracted a 1.5 per cent auction duty paid to the Colonial Treasury.

Both tables indicate that the market for land became increasingly heated until it reached its peak in 1840. In the press, this was sometimes referred to as 'land mania'. To emphasise the scale of this land mania, government auction sales by acreage peaked at just under 389,547 acres in 1836 before declining to around 178,993 acres in 1840.[26] Table 1, therefore, does not adequately reflect the substantially higher prices per acre. Both tables also show that the sale of Crown land and auction sales declined significantly after 1840.

Table 1. Revenue from government land grants, NSW (including Port Phillip), 1838–43[27]

1838	£116,324 16s. 0d.
1839	£152,962 16s. 4d.
1840	£316,626 7s. 5d.
1841	£90,387 16s. 10d.
1842	£14,574 10s. 4d.
1843	£11,297 3s. 9d.

Source: Braim, *A History*, vol. 1, 137. See also Golder, *Politics*.

---

24 See, for instance, NSW Land Registry Services, Book S, no. 419; Book Q, no. 800.
25 See letter forwarded by Lord to *Sydney Herald*, 15 July 1840, 1, from a Liverpool merchant.
26 Butlin, Ginswick and Statham, 'Colonial Statistics', 34. Sales other than by auction were relatively insignificant. The series only starts in 1840, but follows the same post-1840 downward trend as the other tables. See Butlin, Ginswick and Statham, 'Colonial Statistics', 35, Table B 13.
27 Braim, *A History*, vol. 1, 137. See also Golder, *Politics*, 7. While this table plots a dramatic decline in Crown land sales that correlates with the onset of the depression, Braim (*A History*, vol. 1, 88–139) identified other factors that affected the sale of Crown lands. First, in 1839, the minimum price of Crown land was raised from 5s. to 12s. per acre. Second, by the late 1830s there was a perception that the best land within the limits of location had been sold. Third, the rise in sales around 1840 was aided by the release of land in the Port Phillip District.

Table 2. Total sales from auctions, NSW, 1834–43[28]

Year	Amount
1834	£155,156 2s. 2½d.
1835	£209,503 17s. 9½d.
1836	£313,171 7s. 9½d.
1837	£321,246 7s. 9½d.
1838	£409,166 18s. 10½d.
1839	£513,388 1s. 1½d.
1840	£1,246,742 15s. 6½d.
1841	£963,696 18s. 10½d.
1842	£686,088 17s. 9½d.
1843	£454,565 0s. 0d.

Source: Balfour, *A Sketch*, 134.

The steeper decline in the sale of Crown land after 1840 reflects the government's ability to suspend much of its land-release program as the depression worsened (it also increased the upset price to £1 per acre).[29] In contrast, many private landowners were forced to sell their properties at a discount as their financial position deteriorated, often leading to insolvency. The effects of insolvency on people and property will become increasingly evident as the following chapters unfold.

Conclusion

Lord, like Hughes & Hosking, was operating inside a speculative bubble. The buoyancy of the previous decade was ending. Soon, land prices would start dropping and the colony's economy would enter recessionary times. This would present a severe test to the business models of merchants and landowners such as Edward Lord and Hughes & Hosking. It was under these conditions in early 1841—in which the market was beginning to soften,[30] and in which surveyors were searching for a route from the southern interior to a seaport—that plans were initiated to transform the northern side of Batemans Bay into the 'Great Southern Township of St Vincent'.

---

28 Balfour, *A Sketch*, 134.
29 The total number of NSW land grants declined from 413 in 1840 to 34 in 1843. See Balfour, *A Sketch*, 32–3.
30 For accounts of the origins and onset of the 1840s depression, see Butlin, *Foundations*, 318; Sykes, *Two Centuries*, 589–607; McMichael, 'Crisis in Pastoral'. For a general account of the prevailing economic conditions in the period 1820–50, see Morrissey, 'The Pastoral Economy'.

3

Puffing St Vincent

> A city auctioneer, one Samuel Stubbs,
> Did greater execution with his hammer,
> Assisted by his puffing clamour,
> Than Gog and Magog with their clubs.[1]

The previous chapter introduced the first two land purchasers on the northern shore of Batemans Bay. It was on their land that an attempt was made to establish the township of St Vincent. This chapter describes the promotion associated with their land auctions. In order to contextualise this sales campaign, the chapter begins with an explanation of the 'auctioneering system' in Sydney along with trends within the property market in early 1841 as the campaign began. It concludes with an assessment of the state of the colonial economy at the end of 1841.

The rage for suburban allotments and private townships

By the mid-1830s the Government of New South Wales faced a land supply problem. There was a perception that there was a shortage of good available land within the limits of location.[2] At the same time, the British Government instructed Governor Gipps to increase the minimum price of land per acre from 5s to 12s. This took effect in January 1839.

---

1 Anon., 'Professional Duties', *Commercial Journal and Advertiser*, 10 October 1840, 4.
2 This point was often stressed by squatters to justify why they proceeded beyond the 'limits' 'to the far interior' (see, for instance, Brodribb, *Recollections*, 6–7). For a useful summary of the land market in Van Diemen's Land and New South Wales at this time, see Boyce, *1835*, chs 3 and 4. For Van Diemen's Land, see Lennon, *Across Bass Strait*, ch. 2, esp. p. 16.

Closer to Sydney, there was 'a scramble for town allotments' as the incentive to buy marginally cheaper land on the periphery of settlement, far from the towns, had declined due to its increased price.[3] The release of land at Port Phillip from 1838 signalled that demand for town land was still strong. To compound matters, record numbers of free and assisted immigrants were arriving at the expanding towns.[4] Revenue from land sales had helped subsidise emigration as the colony moved towards a convict-free future.

Private landowners sought to benefit from this demand for town land through subdividing properties on the edge of Sydney, in areas such as Balmain, Newtown, Bourke Town (Five Dock Estate) and Paddington. This led to the beginnings of 'suburbanisation'.[5]

A content analysis of available Australian newspapers from 1820 to 1850 shows that the term 'suburban' was used only twice in the 1820s. It was used sparingly up to the mid-1830s, but then regularly from 1838. By 1840, its use peaked at 1,094 mentions, before dropping to 727 mentions in 1842, then between 277 and 416 mentions per year for the rest of the decade. Further, from 1839, the adjective 'suburban' was often associated with the noun 'allotments'. Thus, its vogue during this period followed the fortunes of the property market quite faithfully (see Tables 1 and 2). Reflecting on the historical growth of Sydney, in 1848 Joseph Fowles noted that 'the suburbs have, during the last few years, steadily increased in size and importance'.[6]

---

3   Braim, *A History*, vol. 1, 127–9. In the late 1830s, the British Government attempted to fix all non-town land at £1 per acre, provoking a further scramble for valuable land surrounding towns. This was successfully opposed by Governor Gipps. See Braim, *A History*, vol. 1, 130–6; Scott, *A Short History*, 178–81. Samuel Sidney wrote that this 'land mania' began on the eve of Governor Bourke's departure in 1837. See Sidney, *The Three Colonies*, 106.
4   The year 1841 was known as 'the great year' for emigration. Approximately 28,000 migrants arrived in Australia from Britain alone. See McDonald and Richards, 'The Great Emigration', 337. See also Golder, *Politics*, 5; Morrissey, 'The Pastoral Economy', 53–4, 57.
5   Both John Hosking and J.J. Peacock released subdivided estates in Balmain during 1841. As Reynolds ('Peacock', 13) notes: 'Suburbs were about to be made. "Suburbanisation" was about to begin.' For a more general discussion of the early process of suburbanisation around 1840, see Dyster, 'Inventing the Suburbs'; Golder, *Politics*, 6. The increase in the rate of Sydney's growth (excluding the suburbs) is evident in the following census returns for the non-Indigenous population: 1828, 10,815; 1833, 16,232; 1836, 19,729; 1841, 29,973 (*Fisher's Colonial Magazine and Commercial Maritime Journal*, December 1842, 581).
6   The content analysis was derived from the search engine Trove. Fowles, *Sydney*, 5–6. Among the suburbs listed were Woolloomooloo, Paddington, Surry Hills, Redfern, Chippendale, Camperdown, Newtown, Glebe, Balmain and St Leonards (the last also referred to as a 'township').

Encouraged by the ready availability of British capital, and competition between local banks seeking outlets for their funds, other landholders began promoting regional 'private towns', boasting that one day they would either rival Sydney as a centre of commerce or become a node funnelling traffic to the metropolis.⁷ Advertisements for these towns sought to attract a range of customers, including speculators, merchants and immigrants, along with settlers and pastoralists from surrounding districts. The township of St Vincent was conceived within this context.

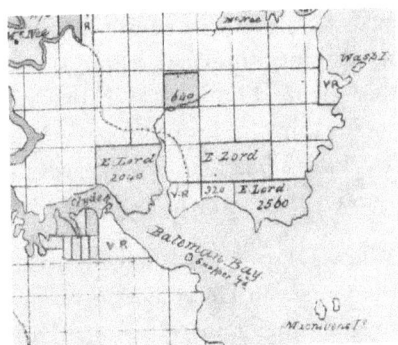

Figure 7. Detail from William Kellett Baker's map of the County of St Vincent, 1843–46.

Baker's Australian County Atlas: Dedicated by the Publisher to Sir T.L. Mitchell … Showing the Various Parishes, Townships, Grants, Purchases and Unlocated Lands (Sydney: W. Baker, 1843–46). NLA, catalogue MAP RaA 8.

There is no evidence that the government commissioned or sanctioned the township of St Vincent. The announcement in January 1841 of an auction for the sale of township allotments was made after the property was sold by the government. It involved the 'Township of St. Vincent' (Hughes & Hosking/Clint and Peacock's 320 acres) and, a few months later, included '40 suburban allotments' surrounding the township (most of Lord's Stubley Park) and 'land reserved for the extension of the Township' (a 251-acre portion of Lord's Stubley Park abutting Hughes & Hosking's property at today's Maloneys Beach) (see Figure 7 and Lot E on Figure 21).

Even though at this time there was no obligation for landholders to deposit proposals for private subdivisions with the registrar-general, a plan for the 320-acre portion of the private township of St Vincent was drawn up and catalogued as 'Plan 359(A)' in 1841, presumably superimposed on James Larmer's 1839 Crown plan (see Chapter 2).⁸ The only surviving 1841

---

7   See also Earl, *Enterprise*, 158–9. Another proposed private township was laid out by the surveyor James Larmer at O'Hara Head, Kioloa, in 1843 at the initiative of William Carr, who purchased the Murramarang and Willinga properties 15 miles north of Batemans Bay in 1838 for £4,500. See Hamon, *They Came*, 19–21. Other private towns discussed in the following chapters include South Huskisson, Jervis Town, Central Jervis Town and New Bristol on Jervis Bay, Boyd Town at Twofold Bay, along with Brecon and Singleton.

8   While this plan was subsequently referred to by a supervising surveyor in 1917, it was not found, or accessible, for my research. The mapping of St Vincent will be discussed in greater detail in Chapters 5, 6 and 9.

plan for the whole of the township of St Vincent is a lithograph for the advertising campaign selling subdivisions of Edward Lord's Stubley Park (see Figure 12).[9] However, that campaign began in April 1841, after the lots within the township of St Vincent on the land owned by Hughes & Hosking/Clint and Peacock began to be advertised on 4 January 1841, presumably on the basis of Plan 359(A).

When Edward Lord had first placed his 2,650 acres at Stubley Park on the market in December 1840, there was no mention of St Vincent. This suggests that Lord was not originally involved in the township scheme. The auctioneer Samuel Lyons had marketed Lord's property as a pastoral venture, selling the land in three lots described as 'admirably adapted' for the establishment of a dairy farm, not 'suburban allotments'.[10]

This suggests that the name St Vincent and the plan for its development originated either with Hughes & Hosking or with Raphael Clint and J.J. Peacock. Hughes & Hosking was a firm experienced in subdividing land at Port Phillip and, during 1841, it was arranging subdivisions at Shoalhaven, while Hosking was subdividing land at Balmain.[11]

Raphael Clint was a surveyor and producer of cadastral maps used by auctioneers to advertise subdivided estates. He had produced maps and charts for a 29 April 1840 auction of four of Hughes & Hosking's suburban sections in Melbourne. The advertisement stated that 'maps of the property obtained, by applying to Mr. R. Clint, Engraver, George-street'. Thus, a relationship between Hughes & Hosking and Clint can be established before their Long Beach transaction. In the mid-1830s, J.J. Peacock operated out of Market Wharf, making him the southerly neighbour of Hughes & Hosking at Darling Harbour. Like Hosking, he purchased land in Balmain in 1836 and subdivided it in 1841. It is possible, then, that the scheme for the township of St Vincent took advantage of synergies between Hughes & Hosking and Clint and Peacock.[12]

---

9   This lithograph is discussed in more detail in Chapter 5. See Figure 12: 'A Plan of 40 Suburban Allotments at St Vincent [Cartographic Material] on the North Shore of Bateman's Bay ... 1841, R. Clint, Lith', National Library of Australia (hereinafter NLA), digitised item, MAP F 87 copy, catalogue.nla.gov.au/Record/1105999.
10 *Sydney Herald*, 4 December 1840 – 21 December 1840, various pages.
11 See Reynolds, 'From Johnson', 23–53.
12 *Colonist*, 21 March 1840, 1. See also Clint's advertisement in *Sydney Gazette and New South Wales Advertiser*, 17 March 1840, 3. However, if any evidence of cooperation did exist between Hughes & Hosking and Raphael Clint it was probably destroyed in the Albion Wharf fire of 3 March 1841, which took the 'whole of Messrs. Hughes and Hosking's books, together with their documents of every description, including a large sum in promissory notes'.

Regardless of who named and laid out the town, confusingly they adopted the county name of St Vincent for their settlement. This was possibly to suggest to buyers its future 'capital' status as a significant port settlement within the county.[13]

The inimitable auctioneer: Mr Stubbs

Advertisements for the township of St Vincent appeared throughout the first half of 1841 in the Sydney press, including in the *Sydney Herald*, the *Australian*, the *Sydney Gazette and New South Wales Advertiser* and the *Australasian Chronicle*. Advertisements for Lord's Stubley Park portion of the town reappeared in 1842. These advertisements provide the clearest picture of how the land was intended to be subdivided, and a chronological account helps gauge the progress of the sales campaign. The advertisements also indicate how auctioneers profiled their targeted market, as their descriptions of the properties were designed to lubricate the clasps of buyers' purses.

Thomas Stubbs (see Figure 8) was the auctioneer who published the initial advertisements in 1841. The auctioneer who followed Stubbs, Samuel Lyons, copied or paraphrased his original text. The epigraph at the beginning of this chapter is from an 1840 poem that presented a composite caricature of Samuel Lyons and Thomas Stubbs, the two most renowned auctioneers in Sydney at the time.

Born in Sydney in 1802, Stubbs was the son of a Third Fleet convict. He joined the British Army at the age of 10 (later claiming to be the first 'native born' to do so) and spent part of his service in a regimental band before returning to Sydney at the age of 23. He became a respected musician during the 1830s and 1840s, accomplished on the flute, violin, French horn and bugle. He also taught pupils 'among the best families'.[14]

---

13   To compound confusion, in June 1840, the colonial secretary announced the auction of three lots of land at a place called 'St Vincent' in a 'parish unnamed' near Crookhaven, south of the Shoalhaven River. This other place named St Vincent was close to the northern boundary of the County of St Vincent. However, the name for this northerly location fell from use. There was one auction held on 24 February 1841 by Samuel Lyons for 10 cows, 10 bullocks, a mare and a foal 'running at Saint Vincent, near the Shoal Haven River' (*Sydney Gazette and New South Wales Advertiser*, 23 February 1841, 3).
14   State Records Authority NSW, Colonial Secretary's papers, no. 61, fol. 119 (reel 6062; 4/1782, 12 November 1825); J.B.M., *Reminiscences*, 41.

THE ROAD TO BATEMANS BAY

Figure 8. Thomas Stubbs, c. 1860–69.
Photographer: Batchelder. State Library of Victoria, handle.slv.vic.gov.au/10381/311519.

Stubbs wrote music as well. His 'delightful' piece 'The Jubilee Waltz' was composed for the fiftieth anniversary of the colony, while 'The Corporation Waltz' was commissioned for the official dinner celebrating the fifty-fifth anniversary of the founding of the Colony of NSW in January 1843 at Mr Sparks's new Royal Hotel, rebuilt by John Terry Hughes. The composition was described as 'a very pretty air', performed immediately after the toast to the mayor, Mr John Hosking.[15] Stubbs also arranged musical recitals for gatherings of the Australian Cricket Club. Along with his younger brother George, he was an active member of this club, which consisted principally of 'currency lads' like himself, in the 1830s. He was also the club's opening bowler and a middle-order batsman.

Stubbs commenced his career as a general commission agent in 1832, working initially on his own account then as an assistant and auctioneer for James & Co. and then Isaac Simmons & Co. (a company in which Hughes & Hosking had an interest). In October 1838, shortly after news reached him that his brother George had drowned while working on a US whaling boat in the South Seas, Stubbs set sail on a year-long Asian buying tour for Simmons that reaped profits back in Sydney while the market remained buoyant.

After the Australian Auction Company briefly secured his services, Stubbs announced on 1 April 1840 that, henceforth, he would be practising 'upon his own account', initially operating from the Auction Bazaar in George Street. On 1 September 1840 he established his New Auction Mart in King Street and from this location he earned his reputation as Sydney's leading auctioneer.[16] The US writer Herman Melville, author of *Moby Dick* and *Billy Budd*, recalled in his account of his South Seas voyages that when lameness forced him off-duty on board the whaling ship *Julia* in 1842 he killed time by reading the Sydney papers. He found that 'the rhetorical flourishes of Stubbs, the real estate auctioneer, diverted me exceedingly'.[17]

---

15 *Australian*, 16 January 1838, 3; *Australasian Chronicle*, 28 January 1843, 2. See also Skinner, 'Toward a General', 39, 144.
16 *Sydney Herald*, 11 June 1832, 2; 3 April 1837, 1; *Australian*, 16 October 1838, 2–3; 17 December 1839, 3; *Colonist*, 21 December 1839, 2; *Sydney Herald*, 1 April 1840, 2. Stubbs's Auction Mart previously belonged to Isaac Simmons & Co. It was two blocks north of Stubbs's home, Rose Cottage, in Druitt Street.
17 Melville, *Omoo*, 39.

The *Sydney Morning Herald* later described Stubbs as 'compact, portly and well-balanced', with an uncanny facial resemblance to George IV: 'As an auctioneer of the ornate order, he had no rival.'[18] The *Australasian* called his advertisements an 'exceptional kind of literature'.[19] Writing for a British audience, Alexander Marjoribanks likened Stubbs to the famous London auctioneer George Robins, claiming he would 'eclipse his master altogether were his sentences a little more grammatical and a little more intelligible'.[20] Indeed, the language used in his real estate advertisements often reads like a script from *Blackadder the Third*.

Marjoribanks's description of the typical atmosphere at a Sydney auction house in 1841 helps to set the scene for the campaign at St Vincent.[21] What Marjoribanks found 'most extraordinary' about the colonial auction system was how people would bid sight unseen for everything from land to livestock, so that 'it might be said that they actually buy a pig in a poke'. He had witnessed land auctions where hundreds of bidders based their knowledge of a town solely on a survey plan.

Mounting his rostrum, the auctioneer would then deliver a speech 'to his admiring audience, mustering ... all the eloquence which he happens to possess, and describes the locality of the place, and its numerous advantages, in the most glowing colours'.[22] This address would be followed by questions from the floor, such as whether it was close to a major road or the ocean, the distance from the nearest town with a post office 'and other questions of a similar nature, all indicating that those who are about to become purchasers actually know no more about it than the man in the moon'.[23]

Bidders could also find themselves befuddled by the champagne lunch provided by the auctioneer 'to elevate the spirits of the company'. As a consequence, 'a few glasses of that exhilarating wine produces a wonderful effect, some of the bidders after that being apt to forget whether it is land

---

18 *Sydney Morning Herald*, 13 March 1878, 5. Stubbs's death was reported across Australia.
19 *Australasian*, 23 February 1878, 17. The Leichhardt conservation historian Peter Reynolds also noted how the 'redoubtable' Stubbs was 'famous for the seductiveness of his land-sale advertisements'. Reynolds, 'From Johnson', 24.
20 Marjoribanks, *Travels*, 25. See also *Colonial Observer*, 14 October 1841, 12. Townsend also compared Stubbs to Robins. See Townsend, *Rambles and Observations*, 6–7.
21 Marjoribanks, *Travels*, 23–5. While this book was published in 1847, the examples Marjoribanks used on pages 26–9 are all identifiable from auctions conducted in 1841.
22 Marjoribanks, *Travels*, 24.
23 Marjoribanks, *Travels*, 24.

or cattle they are purchasing', let alone the location of their purchase.[24] Marjoribanks noted that, in some cases, the uninhibited mood of the auction house was followed by the more sober atmosphere of the courtroom, when successful bidders 'brought actions of restitution against the auctioneers, after they had seen the place with their own eyes'.[25]

One well-publicised, drawn-out legal controversy of buyer restitution throughout 1841 involved *Lyons v. Isles*, *Lyons v. Reynolds*, *Lyons v. Lefevre* and *Dent and Another v. Lyons*. In each case, buyers argued that land at Berkley Estate, Chittaway Bay, sold by the auctioneer Samuel Lyons on 27 May 1840, 'was not of the description advertised' and that they were 'induced to purchase by a fraudulent description of the property'. When some buyers later viewed their land, they found that it was far more remote from settlement than advertised, the land was less productive than claimed, the advertised road to the nearest town did not exist and the front blocks were under water at high tide.[26]

Lyons's defence was that he was merely an agent acting for his vendor. His duty involved reading out the description supplied to him by the owner before conducting the sales.[27] In *Lyons v. Isles*, the chief justice explicitly rejected this defence, arguing that where 'the auctioneer mixed himself up with the vendor ... the former should be held responsible'. Later in the year, in his summing up of *Dent and Another v. Lyons*, the chief justice directed the jury to 'lay out of consideration' the 'poetry and puffing of an auctioneer's advertisement' and 'simply try whether the representations made, were materially false'. However, this left the jury with the awesome responsibility of distinguishing the line between 'puffing' and 'misrepresentation'. The court found against Lyons in each case.

---

24   Champagne lunches were also an 'institution' in Port Phillip during 'the insane spirit of speculation at that time'. See Curr, *Recollections*, 4–19. For a poem reminiscing on better auctioneering days, see 'The Glorious Days of Melbourne: Air—A Long Time Ago', *Port Phillip Patriot and Melbourne Advertiser*, 12 September 1842, 2.
25   Marjoribanks, *Travels*, 23–5.
26   Among other major Sydney papers, see *Sydney Herald*, 11 and 13 March 1841, 2; 9 June 1841, 2; 10–13 November 1841, 2. See also *Omnibus and Sydney Spectator*, 13 November 1841. The solicitor-general told a special jury on 9 November for *Dent and Others v. Lyons* that 'he was afraid the repetition of the words Berkley Estate would not be very pleasant to their ears, but both he and the jury must endeavour to overcome their disgust at the sounds, and look steadily to the facts of the case'.
27   Given its publicity and its timing, this is possibly the case Marjoribanks drew on in his remarks about restitution. The case continued into 1843, involving retrials, damages, expenses, libel cases and the jailing of a witness. See W.H. Wells, 'Plan of the Berkeley Estate Divided into 59 Farms', lithograph, 1840, nla.gov.au/nla.obj-230001377.

A case shortly after involved *Sheehan v. Stubbs*, where the plaintiff brought an action against Thomas Stubbs for 'misrepresentation' of a Wollongong property. Stubbs's clerk at the time was called as a witness and claimed that Stubbs's advertisements were usually written by a Mr Richard Stubbs.[28] Whether or not this was true, Stubbs—like Lyons—was using the 'don't shoot the messenger' defence. However, it was also alleged that Stubbs had used a fictitious bidder to raise the price of the property. Further, when Sheehan subsequently inspected 'his purchase, he found he had been grossly deceived, the property falling far short of realising the descriptions given of it'. Stubbs was ordered to reimburse the defendant. He accepted the court order, unlike Lyons, who appealed.

In March 1841, as Lyons appealed the verdicts against him, the *Sydney Herald* editorialised on the Berkley Estate affair, claiming that 'land quackery' was symptomatic of the colony's deepening economic malaise. It also condemned 'the growing rage for manufacturing townships'. Regardless of the quality of a property, estate holders would hire a surveyor, parcel out allotments, draw up streets and public squares, borrow an evocative name from Britain, then offer their captivating vision to a public that was 'weak enough to risk their money upon these mere day-dreams of sordid vendors'. This 'chicanery' would be supported by

> the descriptive pens of our George Robins's, who, in terms glowing with poetic conceptions, have expatiated upon the matchless advantages possessed by the embryo town, and upon the splendid fortunes which could not fail to be realised by the lucky purchasers of the allotments.[29]

While the editorial claimed that vendors and auctioneers 'gulled' buyers, it failed to mention that newspaper advertisements were the main conduit through which the public was made aware of these schemes.[30] Newspaper

---

28 *Sydney Herald*, 27 January 1842, 2. There was a Richard Stubbs in Elizabeth Street (no relation to Thomas) cognisant of property issues. This is likely the same Richard Stubbs who held the position of Sydney's inspector of nuisances (1847–64) and was known for his quick wit.
29 *Sydney Herald*, 17 March 1841, 2.
30 *Sydney Herald*, 17 March 1841, 2. In 1836, the same paper had 'assailed the New South Wales "Auctioneering System"', calling auction houses the 'Dens of Thieves'. The principal issue in this case was the consignment of goods from Britain, in which the paper accused auctioneers of being in combination with convicts. Lyons, who had stopped advertising in the *Herald* over the previous year, took offence and successfully sued the paper for defamation. See *Sydney Herald*, 20, 23 and 30 June 1836, 2; 4 July 1836, 2. The *Sydney Monitor* (2 July 1836, 2) replied to the 'Tory' *Herald*, claiming: 'Gold formerly induced you to puff Mr Lyons; its absence induces you to abuse him!' By 1841, Lyons was again advertising in the *Herald*.

editors might plausibly respond that they merely printed the information supplied by auctioneers, but this was the same defence used by auctioneers when buyers accused them of 'misrepresentation'.

There is every reason to assume that Marjoribanks's description of a Sydney auction house resembled the scene within Stubbs's Auction Mart at King Street when the land in the 'manufactured town' of St Vincent went on sale in January 1841. There is even strong circumstantial evidence that Marjoribanks was present at and was, in fact, describing Stubbs's auction of St Vincent.[31]

Selling the Hughes & Hosking township allotments

Lengthy advertisements—1,100-word essays—for the subdivisions within the 'Great Southern Township of St Vincent' heralded the beginning of its sales campaign. The initial advertisement appeared on 4 January 1841 and was reprinted over the following weeks in readiness for the public auction at Stubbs's New Auction Mart, King Street, at 12 pm on Monday 25 January 1841. Interested parties could view a plan of St Vincent in advance at the Auction Mart. The advertisements did not mention who 'instructed' auctioneer Stubbs to bring the allotments under the hammer, whether Hughes & Hosking or Clint and Peacock.[32]

Stubbs targeted southern settlers and farmers beyond the mountain range as the audience 'about to be benefited by this Advertisement'. This included 'the whole of the Wealthy Proprietors of Land and Stock &c. in Argyle, St. Vincent, and in the South West Country generally', mentioning, in

---

31   Marjoribanks presented five examples of Stubbs's oratory skills in *Travels in New South Wales*. Four of the examples (from Kingsgrove [*Sydney Herald*, 14 May 1841, 3], Rushcutters Bay [*Australasian Chronicle*, 3 August 1841, 3], Brecon [*Sydney Monitor and Commercial Advertiser*, 27 January 1841, 4] and Ashfield [a short sentence on Stubbs's standard mention of a liquid lunch]) are identifiable from newspaper advertisements. The fifth and final example was from St Vincent, but the speech attributed to Stubbs did not appear in any newspaper. This suggests that Marjoribanks might have attended the January St Vincent auction in person, drawing his description from this auction scene as well as making a verbatim transcript of Stubbs's presentation—which will be reproduced in Chapter 9. See Marjoribanks, *Travels*, 26–9.

32   *Sydney Herald*, 4 January 1841, 3. It was reprinted, among various other papers, in the *Australian*, 9 January, 14 January and 16 January 1841. Presumably, the plan was the one catalogued as Lands Title Plan 359(A). There are two references to 'the proprietor', but this could refer to either the individuals Clint and Peacock or the company entity Hughes & Hosking. The initial advertisement is cited in Bayley, *Behind Broulee*, 18.

particular, the 'Wealthy Proprietors of Braidwood, Lake Bathurst, Lake George, Molonglo, Limestone Plains, Bungendore, Maneroo, Yass, Murrumbidgee, Jembecumbean, Goulburn, Marulan, Bungonia and the whole of the respectable inhabitants of the South West Country'.[33]

Stubbs also sought a hearing from 'the enterprising Emigrant and Speculatist of the Colony', claiming that the harbour 'cheers the sight and excites the hopes of the emigrant sailing around its shores'. His diction always left his audience with the impression that he was merely repeating well-known colonial truths.

Stubbs's introduction also presented the fashionable vision of steamships berthing in the harbour, taking advantage of public knowledge that 'the Magnificent Steamer CLONMEL landed her passengers and took in Wood and Water' at Batemans Bay only a fortnight beforehand. Even though the landing was for emergency purposes, referencing the *Clonmel* allowed Stubbs to describe the location as an accessible port used by Sydney's most acclaimed ship (see Chapter 9).

This idea of Batemans Bay as a southern transportation axis was central to Stubbs's narrative. Drawing on the 1797 survey by George Bass and the 1822 soundings from 'Lieutenant Johnson', he continued the maritime theme by describing the bay as 'an eligible Port of Refuge for vessels bound along the coast with adverse winds, and as it offers many secure anchorages, protected in every direction'. Over-inflating its population density, he called Batemans Bay 'a closely settled district' and predicted that it

> must shortly become the grand outlet of the Southern interior: its waters presenting the busy aspect of commerce, under which the value of adjacent lands will soon be on a par with those of Sydney.[34]

The plan on show at the Auction Mart identified a 'natural Wharf', claimed to be the same one that the passengers and crew from the *Clonmel* used to disembark. In addition, the proprietor had contracted a shipowner to lay down moorings capable of securing ships of all classes. This task had been assigned to 'a competent and duly qualified officer' who would also 'make minute surveys of the whole Bay'. The proprietor also proposed to erect a 'conspicuous Flag Staff' on North Head with a published code of signals in order to assist marine traffic.

---

33 *Sydney Herald*, 4 January 1841, 3.
34 *Sydney Herald*, 4 January 1841, 3.

Addressing the woolgrowers of the southern counties, Stubbs observed that Batemans Bay was only 20 hours' sail from Sydney, 'while the interior transit of produce occupies nearly as many days'. He then drew attention to the communication between Batemans Bay and the interior, again quoting George Bass's prediction that this 'was the part of the Blue Mountain range which would ultimately afford the best line of communication'. Stubbs predicted that Kinghorne and Green's recent 'discovery of a Dray Road' from Braidwood to the Clyde River would 'ensure to this port at an early day … the best line of transit for interior productions, and give it a commerce little short of Port Jackson'.[35]

In November 1839, the press had reported that Kinghorne and Green had charted a 35-mile path from Braidwood to the Clyde River that was 'passable by a dray', apart from a 1-mile stretch. The explorers considered the road 'as good as the present road between Sydney and Goulburn'. Despite an 'understanding' that it would be discussed in the Legislative Council on 19 November 1839, nothing more was heard of this road to Batemans Bay.[36]

It was Alexander Kinghorne Jr who had initiated the land sale at Long Beach earlier in 1839 by applying for it to be surveyed and advertised. If he was the member of the Kinghorne family involved in the mountain road expedition with Green, then it is not clear why he chose Long Beach on the northern side of Batemans Bay, when a Clyde Mountain dray road to Batemans Bay would have to terminate on the southern side. This problem would occupy the new owner, Raphael Clint, in 1841 (see Chapter 5).

This also might have been why Stubbs's lengthy advertisement did not specify whether the township lay on the northern or southern side of Batemans Bay. Despite this, Stubbs asserted that instead of going to neighbouring Broulee, the dray road over the mountain now 'must come to Bateman's Bay, making it … the principal outlet &c. of the Industry of the country south of Port Jackson'.[37]

Further, Stubbs assured readers that land transportation from the township of St Vincent to the north had also been secured with a road marked out through 'thickly settled' country, with gangs 'stationed from Cook's River

---

35 *Sydney Herald*, 4 January 1841, 3.
36 *Sydney Herald*, 15 and 18 November 1839, 2; see also *Sydney Gazette and New South Wales Advertiser*, 19 November 1839, 2. The road Kinghorne and Green discovered was likely another well-established Indigenous route.
37 *Sydney Herald*, 4 January 1841, 3.

down to Ulladulla, to carry the object of communication into effect'.[38] However, like the western route over the mountain, this road remained aspirational.

After this fulsome report, Stubbs pondered the obvious question of why such fine country had 'been allowed to remain so long without exciting public attention'.[39] He offered two reasons: first, the same 'public apathy' that allowed the now-booming Port Phillip 'to remain in a state of nature for thirty-five years'; and, second, the interests of landed proprietors in the west who sought to keep public attention off the Crown land on which they were squatting. Indeed, he claimed that the land on which St Vincent would be built had been 'picked out for a long time as a squatting station' and, as a consequence, the freehold purchasers would enjoy the advantages of their 'many improvements'. These property enhancements remained unnamed. This claim that the property had been used as a squatting station remained unsubstantiated—although it cannot be ruled out.[40]

Stubbs's advertisement also remained vague on the topographical and environmental properties of the town, apart from the claim that it was 'fertile country', 'alluvial' and situated on an 'extensive plain', the 'open verdure of which is the first object of admiration (never to be forgotten)'. The property was also 'watered by creeks and lagoons, which have never failed'.[41] Stubbs was also far from expansive in his description of the nature of the allotments offered or other features of the township plan (see Chapters 5 and 6).

The advertisement concluded by assuring readers that the description had avoided 'all remarks of a puffing nature, geographical facts alone having been adduced'. Even so, Stubbs blurred the line between puffing and misrepresentation, as his claims of road building and population density show. When he had announced in 1840 that he was striking out on his

---

38 *Sydney Herald*, 4 January 1841, 3.
39 *Sydney Herald*, 4 January 1841, 3.
40 One copy of James Larmer's 1839 Crown plan (1831–3040) of the property held in the NSW State Records Authority NSW does indicate 'Kerr's Hut and Stockyard' south-east of the lagoon (close to where Gibraltar Way is now situated). However, the feature appears to have been written over the plan, making it difficult to determine whether it existed in 1839–41. John Ryan, who had lived at Cullendulla since 1871 and recalled the property being owned by Harrison and Llewelyn (1884–89), provided a statutory declaration in 1916 stating that landowners during the late nineteenth century occasionally leased the land or paid royalties for various purposes, including timber-getting and pasturage, but he never mentioned a hut and stockyard. See Augustus Edmund Blair's Primary Application, held at State Records Authority NSW, NRS-17513, item 17513-8-34-PA 20438, vol. 2781, folio 34. James described Kerr's hut and stockyard as being in place when the land was surveyed in 1839. James, *Batemans Bay*, 125.
41 *Sydney Herald*, 4 January 1841, 3.

own as an auctioneer, Stubbs had proposed 'personally to survey all Landed Property that may be confided to him for sale previous to advertising'.[42] This promise was issued to reassure buyers that his advertisements would not misrepresent the properties he offered. However, it is doubtful that Stubbs, or any other person associated with the sale of the property, set foot on Long Beach prior to the commencement of the advertising campaign. It was also difficult for potential buyers to check the veracity of any claims, given that the auction was held at Mr Stubbs's rooms on King Street, Sydney, where the plan was available for viewing.

This characteristic vagueness was precisely what Marjoribanks found 'most extraordinary' about the atmosphere within Sydney auction houses. Yet, Stubbs's text becomes more intelligible when considering the types of buyers he sought to attract: first, landholders in the interior who would benefit from a foothold at a future port in which they would have an interest; second, speculators in Sydney who banked on the value of the land rising once the town linked the interior with the metropolis. Stubbs's advertisement focused attention on the mercantile potential of Batemans Bay. The township was admired principally as a node connecting a future dray road with an emerging shipping lane. The town lots themselves were of secondary consideration. The yet-to-be-built road to Batemans Bay was the promise on which speculators banked their money.

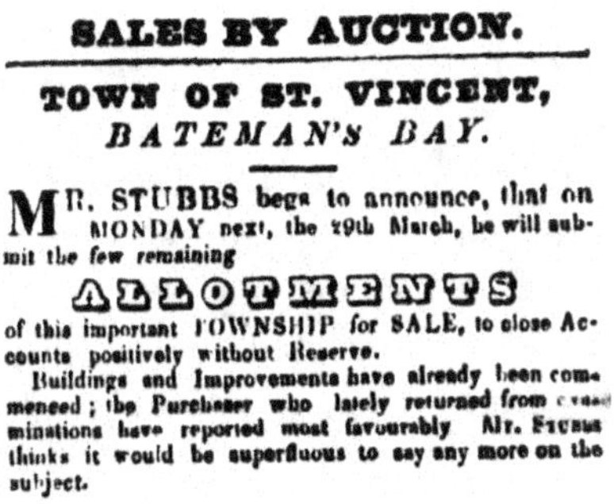

Figure 9. Advertisement selling last allotments at St Vincent, March 1841.
Sydney Gazette and New South Wales Advertiser, 25 March 1841, 3.

The extent to which Stubbs had read the market correctly can be judged from the results of the 25 January auction for the allotments at St Vincent. Originally, Stubbs had announced that the town would be sold in quarterly stages, with purchasers required to put down a 25 per cent deposit, and the remainder due over three to five years. Two months after the January auction, he announced that he would auction 'the few remaining'

42 Sydney Herald, 1 April 1840, 2.

unsold allotments within the township of St Vincent on 29 March (see Figure 9), confirming the claim that he had sold three-quarters of the town's allotments on 25 January.[43]

Stubbs also announced that 'Buildings and Improvements have already been commenced' and that 'the Purchaser who lately returned from examinations [has] reported most favourably'.[44] He did not elaborate on 'the building and improvements' made in the two months since the initial sales, and the 'purchaser' who visited their new property at St Vincent was not identified. Development in the township was so self-evident that 'Mr. Stubbs thinks it would be superfluous to say any more on the subject'.[45]

However, on the day of the auction (29 March), Stubbs published an unrelated advertisement for another Hughes & Hosking property at Shoalhaven that gave some insight into how the 'purchaser' might have visited St Vincent. Stubbs offered to 'facilitate the arrangement for the hire of a vessel' to carry purchasers down to their Shoalhaven property along with a surveyor 'as was carried into effect so satisfactorily to the parties interested, immediately subsequent to the sale of the township of St Vincent'.[46] Chapter 5 will consider whether the identity of the 'purchaser' and 'surveyor' who visited St Vincent after the January auction was the same person—the one and only Raphael Clint.

Selling Edward Lord's suburban allotments

From early April 1841, attention turned to the sale of the surrounding 'suburban allotments' on Edward Lord's Stubley Park property. Again, Thomas Stubbs was the auctioneer. The real estate language in the advertisement for Lord's 'suburban farms' remained bullish and there appears to have been every expectation that this auction would yield results similar to those in January.

---

43 *Australian*, 28 January 1841; *Sydney Gazette and New South Wales Advertiser*, 25 March 1841, 3; 27 March 1841, 1. Were these the few remaining allotments of the first quarterly stage, or the few remaining allotments left in the township? The wording in Figure 9 suggested the latter. For an analysis of the sales at St Vincent, see Chapter 5.
44 *Sydney Gazette and New South Wales Advertiser*, 27 March 1841, 1.
45 *Sydney Gazette and New South Wales Advertiser*, 27 March 1841, 1.
46 *Sydney Herald*, 29 March 1841, 4. This offer from Stubbs would not have diminished Marjoribank's bemusement over the conduct of colonial auctions, as punters were still viewing their properties after they completed their transactions. They were not only purchasing on spec; they were also doing it on trust.

Announcing the upcoming 26 April auction of Lord's 'judiciously selected' Stubley Estate—now the suburban surrounds of St Vincent—Stubbs anticipated

> the pleasure of enjoying the most lively competition he has witnessed during his professional exertions, based on the fact that the first sale held on the 25th January last, of the township adjoining, has produced important results.[47]

Further, in an advertisement for a cottage at Wollongong, Stubbs said it would be auctioned 'immediately before the great Land Sale, at Batemans Bay', amplifying the importance of the auction of Lord's allotments.[48]

Raphael Clint, who was now the joint owner of the Long Beach land on which the adjoining township of St Vincent was situated, was listed as the contact for further information about Lord's property. The one surviving lithograph for the sales campaign was designed and produced by Clint for this April 1841 auction and any subsequent auctions of Lord's land (see Figure 12). While the lithograph leaves the specific auction date open ('_____ 1841'), the focus of the plan is clearly the 40 suburban allotments belonging to Lord's estate, rather than the township of St Vincent, suggesting this was not the same plan referred to earlier by Stubbs that was drawn up for the auctions in January and March 1841.

Whether Clint and Peacock coordinated their advertising campaign with that for Edward Lord's property remains unclear. However, given that they both initially used the auctioneering services of Thomas Stubbs, that the advertisements often used much of the same text and that Raphael Clint was associated with both estates, it is highly likely that the campaigns involved some degree of cooperation between both parties.

Regardless, Edward Lord's own active role in events had ended on 28 January 1841 when he 'assigned and conveyed … all his Property and Effects, in trust for the benefit of his Creditors'.[49] Having already mortgaged many of his landholdings—most heavily to Alexander Park for the sum of £3,000—

---

47 *Australian*, 10 April 1841, 4 (reprinted 8 and 17 April 1841); *Sydney Herald*, 5 April 1841, 2; 21 April 1841, 4 (with a reminder in the *Australian*, 24 April 1841, 2). In terms of advertising rates, the version of this advertisement placed by Stubbs in the *Sydney Herald* on 5 April cost 17s. 3d. *Sydney Gazette and New South Wales Monitor*, 8 April 1841, 2.
48 *Australian*, 22 April 1841, 4.
49 *Sydney Gazette and NSW Monitor*, 16 March 1841, 3.

he was unable to service his debts.[50] During the entire period in which Stubley Park was advertised—April 1841 through to June 1842—Lord had no control over the disposal of the real estate assets held in his name. It is possible that his trustees were aware of the impressive January and March sales in the township of St Vincent and saw an opportunity to recover some of Lord's debts.

Consistent with his January strategy, Stubbs targeted settlers in the inland counties of Argyle, Murray and King, in addition to coastal interests at Broulee, Braidwood and Ulladulla. He also claimed that the land had been subdivided at the request of those who had earlier purchased land in the township of St Vincent. Again, he claimed that the first purchasers at St Vincent had already been 'settled', giving assurance that the township was a hive of activity.[51]

More broadly, he boasted of 'this port said to possess the highest order of maritime advantages'. Once more, the passive language gave the impression of well-known truths. Stubbs also repeated his earlier assertion that the 'most superficial observer' could see that 'at no distant period Bateman's Bay will become the grand outlet for the Colonial produce of the Southern Countries'.[52] He reinforced this claim by predicting that the bay would also become an important embarkment point for livestock destined for New Zealand. There was substance to his trans-Tasman link. One pastoral lessee at Broulee, William Barnard Rhodes, was organising for his herd of cattle to be transferred to the developing New Zealand market after he was outbid by Hughes & Hosking at the Broulee land auctions in 1839.[53]

---

50   Spillman, *Queensland Lords*, 40–1.
51   Stubbs claimed that the 'Express, Captain Clinton, has just returned from locating the first settlers, and brought up wool on freight'. Captain Clinton sailed the Schooner *Express* out of Sydney on 8 March for Bateman's Bay carrying 'sundries', but there is no record of the passengers. The *Express* is mentioned departing from Wollongong to Sydney with a cargo of wheat. See *Sydney Herald*, 16 March 1841, 2. It is possible that Clinton made the trip from Batemans Bay to Wollongong before heading for Sydney, but there is no record of wool on board, or the passengers. On 1 April, the *Express* sailed again for Batemans Bay and Broulee. See *Sydney Herald*, 31 March 1841, 1. Sydney papers published monthly summaries of inward and outward shipping. For the month of March, for the first and only time, a separate column was added for traffic to and from 'St Vincent' (one vessel 'whence' and two 'where to'). This was not a generic county label, as the ports of Batemans Bay, Ulladulla, Jervis Bay, Broulee and Shoalhaven were also listed in the 'whence' and 'where to' columns. See *Sydney Herald*, 2 April 1841, 2.
52   *Australian*, 10 April 1841, 4.
53   *Sydney Herald*, 16 November 1841, 3; *New Zealand Gazette and Wellington Spectator*, 29 June 1842, 2; *Sydney Morning Herald*, 27 October 1842, 2.

3. PUFFING ST VINCENT

Because the larger allotments on Lord's Stubley Park were advertised as 'suburban farms', more space was devoted to the agricultural potential of the land that, it was claimed, was 'particularly adapted to the growth of wheat or the vine'. The low-lying grounds on the estate abounded 'in rich decayed vegetable matter' forming an 'inexhaustible deposit of the best character for agricultural purposes'. Further, if 'properly attended to', the low-lying wattle and she-oak woods could be put to 'great profitable account'. While the higher land away from the beach was also 'adapted to the vine', it was equally suitable for 'ship building and carpenter's work', being 'covered with the finest and best grown timber'. Some of these immense-girthed trees (spotted gum) reportedly reached 60 feet before 'throwing out a branch'.[54]

Given that the properties for sale contained 3 miles of water frontage and 'delightfully curved' bays with 'white sandy beaches', Stubbs also envisaged 'marine villas' becoming eagerly sought after among the more affluent proprietors in the district, who 'will ere long gladly leave the perpetual succession of forest and brush, the wild bush and sunburnt paddock, for the all reviving and invigorating breeze of the deep deep Sea!' Nature had 'gifted this attractive spot with facilities' both restorative and productive.[55]

Clint's plan of the 40 suburban allotments was available at Stubbs's auction rooms and interested parties could also approach Mr Clint, who would address any inquiries and 'afford all the information required'. Clint was, therefore, possibly the source of the intelligence about the agricultural potential of the allotments (see Chapter 5). The terms on which the land was sold would be announced at the time of sale but were promised to be 'very liberal'. Like in January, the advertisement ended with the reminder that Stubbs had studiously avoided 'all remarks of a puffing name'.

On 11 May, without reporting the results of the April auction, Stubbs announced that the remainder of Lord's estate would be auctioned on 19 May. This consisted of that portion adjoining the 'Township of St Vincent' (the land on which Maloneys Beach now sits), comprising 'twenty-seven sections of land, subdivided into Building Allotments, and fronting Bateman's Bay'.[56] It was again 'expressly advertised' by order of Lord's trustees.

---

54 *Australian*, 10 April 1841, 4.
55 *Australian*, 10 April 1841, 4.
56 *Australian*, 11 May 1841, 4 (reprinted 13 May 1841, 3).

Stubbs adopted a different narrative for this auction, avoiding the agricultural detail from the previous advertisements. This time he targeted the 'speculator', emphasising the reluctance of the proprietor to sell an estate that would 'turn the channel of its prosperity into the pockets of strangers'. Stubbs asserted that the speculator would 'complete a pretty good day's work on the day of competition, and close his list with a few hundreds on his purchases of the day'.[57]

As the market tightened, the terms were eased, with a mere 10 per cent deposit on purchases, but the remainder due at the tighter schedule of three, six and nine months, without interest.

Stubbs felt that it was 'unnecessary to dilate more upon the general merits and beauty of this favourite spot'. Instead, he eulogised the location with overblown generalities. Apart from its 'positive locality' and its shipping and mercantile advantages, it possessed 'all the subordinate benefits that are always belonging to well selected and defined allotments'. Compared with other properties, St Vincent was 'decidedly superior'.[58]

Stubbs also referred to St Vincent in a contemporaneous advertisement, giving the town greater substance than it deserved. When promoting allotments at Kingsgrove, south of Sydney, he described its location as situated 'near the new line of Road leading from Cook's River Dam—to Wollongong, Jervis Bay, Shoalhaven, Ulladulla, St. Vincent, and the great Southern Interior'.[59]

Unlike the January 1841 sales within the township of St Vincent, there were no subsequent notices by Stubbs announcing the volume of sales from either the 26 April or 19 May auctions of Lord's allotments, suggesting that interest in land at St Vincent was waning. Indeed, land sales were softening throughout the colony. On the April advertisement of Lord's Stubley Estate, Stubbs had used an epigraph from Shakespeare's *Julius Caesar*, where Brutus exclaims: 'There is a tide in the affairs of Men, which taken at the flood leads on to Fortune.' But the tide of speculation on Batemans Bay, as elsewhere, was ebbing.

---

57 *Australian*, 11 May 1841, 4.
58 *Australian*, 11 May 1841, 4.
59 *Sydney Herald*, 14 May 1841, 3.

3. PUFFING ST VINCENT

The badness of the times

As 1841 advanced, steadily more attention turned to the tightening money crisis, the bursting property market bubble, collapsing livestock prices and rising insolvencies. Surveying the smoking ruins of Hughes & Hosking's Albion Wharf in early March, one paper lamented that the 'disastrous' fire compounded the 'rickety state of our financial affairs'.[60] At the end of April—almost simultaneously with Stubbs's first auction for Edward Lord's Stubley Park—an article by 'Veritas' warned in more apocalyptic tones that:

> We have certainly seen signs; wonders; and appalling sights in the mercantile-sky; but these, I fear, are merely the shadow of coming events ... We have to pass through scenes still darker than any thing we have hitherto witnessed, we have yet to experience destruction in its wildest form.[61]

The previous month, an editorial in the *Sydney Morning Herald* reflected on 'the violent panic which, during the last five or six months, has seized upon all classes of our community'. It offered 'over-speculation' as the explanation for 'the whole of our late financial difficulties'. It blamed 'this rage for buying land as so much merchandise' and 'this consequent practice of chalking out townships, dividing and subdividing, and puffing off without the slightest regard for truth or common honesty'. In ominous tones, the paper spoke of stalking bankruptcy, burst bubbles, monetary embarrassments and 'overwhelming disaster'.[62]

The 'badness of the times' was a popular euphemism for these omens hanging over the colony. The phrase emerged in the colonial press in late 1840. By November 1841, the *Sydney Free Press* wrote:

> It requires no research or sagacity to discover, and there is no use in denying—that the Colony is at present in a very depressed and critical condition. Money is extremely scarce—the value of property is depreciated—trade of every description is languishing—and everybody, from the highest to the lowest, complains of the badness of the times.[63]

---

60 *Sydney Gazette and New South Wales Advertiser*, 4 March 1841, 2.
61 See Veritas's two articles in *Free Press and Commercial Journal*, 28 April 1841, 2; 1 May 1841.
62 *Sydney Herald*, 17 March 1841, 2.
63 *Sydney Free Press*, 11 November 1841, 2. Benjamin Franklin used the phrase in his 1758 'The Way to Wealth' (reprinted in Franklin's edited works, published in Boston in 1836).

However, the phrase quickly became a cliche and, before long, it tended to be prefaced in the press by the words 'notwithstanding', 'despite' or 'proverbial' and 'the vaunted badness of the times' or simply used inside inverted commas.[64]

In response to this prevailing sentiment, auctioneers sought to reassure speculators and investors that purchasing land remained the key for opening the doors to wealth in the colonies. In September 1841, in a preface to one of his real estate advertisements, Thomas Stubbs announced in bold and capital letters: 'Land at a premium in New South Wales. Good news at last! Parliamentary and Colonial!! Confidence restored!!!' Australian securities were rising, he claimed, due to (unspecified) actions taken by influential parliamentarians and to the 'discovery' of Gippsland (see Chapter 9). As a consequence, the 'Landed interests will hail with joy ... it will be like— Gold breaking out of the Miser's Bag—there will be no keeping pace with its overwhelming influence.' In November, the same paper reported that it was 'truly astonishing that notwithstanding the badness of the times, land still retains its high price, as fully exemplified by the late sales effected by Mr. Stubbs of King Street'. Stubbs was not alone in puffing the property market (see Chapter 4).[65]

The Reverend Dr John Dunmore Lang penned an article in November calling upon the press to avoid characterising the colony as a picture of hopeless, unremitting doom. Despite this, he still admitted that there was 'no subject that is so frequently in every person's mouth at present as the badness of the times'. This sentiment pervaded all classes and all parts of the colony, so much so that throughout the colony 'there is such general depression ... that one would almost be tempted to believe that the colony is on its last legs'.[66]

---

64 It was still used in the late 1840s. An 1848 article in the *Sydney Daily Advertiser* on 'the state of the colony' complained that: 'The principal topic for conversation, now and for some time past, appears to be the "badness of the times".' *Sydney Daily Advertiser*, 4 September 1848, 2. Golder states that the depression had reached its lowest point in 1842. Golder, *Politics*, 5.
65 See *Sydney Gazette and New South Wales Advertiser*, 18 September 1841, 3; 6 November 1841, 3.
66 *Colonial Observer*, 4 November 1841, 1. However, as Chapter 7 shows, some of the largest financial shocks came after 1841. Depressed conditions persisted well into the 1840s, especially during 1847. Braim (*A History*, vol. 2, 325–6) described the atmosphere at the end of 1844 in the following terms:
   Storms of adversity are now howling around the land. Fear and trembling have seized upon her merchants and bankers, her tradesmen and mechanics, her agriculturists and graziers. Many are ready to give up all for lost. A panic has seized upon her people, and under its maddening influence, everybody is anxious to sell, and nobody willing to buy. The inevitable consequence is, that property of all kinds has become already depreciated. Three years ago, the colonists were drunk with exaggerated joy; they are now just as drunk with exaggerated despondency. And as the elation of their spirits then caused property to mount far, far beyond its intrinsic value, so their present dejection has caused it to fall as deeply below what it is fairly and honestly worth.

Reflecting this general depression, on 1 November 1841 Raphael Clint had sold the 'undivided moiety' of Long Beach, the site of the township of St Vincent, back to Hughes & Hosking for £200. This was a significant discount on the £800 he and Peacock had handed over for the property only nine months before. The reason Clint sold the property will be considered in Chapter 5. On 1 January 1842, Hughes & Hosking mortgaged the property to the Bank of Australia and the consequence of this transfer will be discussed in Chapter 7.[67]

By this time, Stubbs's role as an agent for property owners at St Vincent was over and no more advertisements appeared for allotments on the 320-acre block. Yet, this did not signal the end of the sales campaign for the township of St Vincent. The trustees of Edward Lord's estate, after waiting a year, again tested the market for Stubley Park. It was in the midst of this 'badness of the times' that a second series of advertisements was organised for Lord's estate, in June 1842. The auctioneer on this occasion was Samuel Lyons, who offered at auction on 24 June the same 18 town allotments and 40 farm blocks advertised in April and May 1841 by Thomas Stubbs.[68] This confirms that no sales for Lord's property were completed by Stubbs.

The advertisement borrowed most of Stubbs's text. A short alert informing readers of an upcoming 'favorable opportunity of laying out their unemployed capital' was followed by the main advertisement, issued, like the May 1841 advertisement, by order of Edward Lord's trustees.[69]

Samuel Lyons, like his predecessor Stubbs, could not generate much interest in Lord's subdivisions. It was telling that there was no description of the progress of the settlers whom Stubbs claimed had landed at the township of

---

67 For the transfer back to Hughes & Hosking, see NSW Land Registry Services, Book Y, no. 314. Peacock does not appear as a party in the transfer of the title back to Hughes & Hosking. See Augustus Edmund Blair's primary application, held at State Records Authority NSW, NRS-17513, item 17513-8-34-PA 20438, vol. 2781, folio 34.

68 In Marjoribanks, Samuel Lyons is the only other auctioneer described apart from Thomas Stubbs. However, unlike Stubbs, Lyons is distinguished by his wealth, his convict past and his religion rather than his professional skills: 'Mr Samuel Lyons, a Jew, and originally a convict, makes six or eight thousand a year as an auctioneer, driving about in his carriage and four, and his auction rooms are more like assembly rooms than anything else.' See Marjoribanks, *Travels*, 23. These auction rooms were designed by the in-demand architect John Verge.

69 *Sydney Morning Herald*, 30 May 1842, 4. Minor variations were reprinted in the *Australasian Chronicle*, 4 June 1842. See also *Sydney Gazette and New South Wales Advertiser*, 16 June 1842, 3 (also printed, for example, in *Sydney Morning Herald*, 24 June 1842, 4; *Sydney Herald*, 13 June 1842; *Australian*, 21 June, 24 June). The only new information was that the town extension comprised 116 half-acres, divided into sections of 6 and a half acres, subdivided into 24 building allotments each.

St Vincent the previous year. The fact that Lyons's advertisement reprinted verbatim so much of Stubbs's original text was testimony to the lack of development on the northern shore of Batemans Bay.[70]

Lyons's lot was more arduous than Stubbs's in the sense that, by mid-1842, the public's enthusiasm for land had diminished further. Contrary to Stubbs's optimism, the land market was in freefall and the depression had deepened. Further, the number of settlers with 'spare capital' was declining. 'Speculatists'—so coveted by auctioneers—were in retreat. The days when auctioneers would offer champagne lunches was past:

> Then a glass of prime Colonial rum to New South Wales we'll drain,
> For in such wretched times as these we can't afford Champagne.[71]

Conclusion

This chapter devoted extensive coverage to the real estate claims by the auctioneers involved in the St Vincent project for four reasons: first, to gain some insight into the 'auctioneering system' that prevailed in 1841; second, to understand how the sellers presented the township and its suburban farms; third, to appreciate the broader aspirations that its promoters had for Batemans Bay as a future commercial port; and, fourth, to trace the level of interest in the properties.

---

70 There is only one official document suggesting development at St Vincent. On 14 June 1841, John Mallon was granted Publican's Licence 128 by Captain Oldrey from the Broulee Magistrate Bench for a hotel named 'The Shamrock Inn'. The licence cost £30. The location recorded for Mallon's 'Shamrock Inn' was 'St Vincent'. See State Records Authority NSW, NRS 1440 [7/1501], reel 1236, Licence 128, Place: St Vincent. A publican's licence always listed the specific location of the establishment rather than the broader county. Mallon is mentioned in two November 1841 letters to the *Sydney Herald* (3 and 15 November 1841, 2) as the owner of a tavern and the builder of a boat at Batemans Bay. However, there is doubt whether Mallon's inn was located on the Long Beach property, the site of the private township of St Vincent. While Biosis ('Batemans Bay', 14) was unable to confirm any particular location for the inn, the report speculated that it might have been somewhere along what is now Beach Road, on the southern side of the bay. It is possible that in 1841 any settlement within the bay was referred to as St Vincent, given that the village of Bateman had yet to be laid out. Regardless, archaeological research has yet to uncover any evidence of the inn, and Mallon's licence remains the only official government document to acknowledge the town of St Vincent. The two *Sydney Herald* letters printed on 3 and 17 November 1841 presented contrasting reports on Batemans Bay. The first informant briefly mentions that it had only been a 'few months since this township was sold' (without mentioning the name St Vincent) and gave encouraging reports of the harbour, its communication and its resources. Apart from Mallon, it noted that a Mr Thomas had 'erected an excellent house' in his 'happy valley'. The longer, dismissive reply claimed the report contained 'scarcely one word of truth'.

71 Pastor Olim, 'A Yarn of the Colony', *Colonial Observer*, 6 June 1844, 78.

3. PUFFING ST VINCENT

Selling real estate was one of the 'manifest' functions of auctioneers and, in their role as agents, they presented their clients' properties in the most favourable light. Puffing and misrepresentation were occasionally used to facilitate this goal. Auctioneers also performed another 'latent' function: they fired the public's imagination with alluring visions of unfamiliar frontier land brought into the orbit of the colony's lifeworld.[72] Their grid plans of far-flung territory on the periphery of settlement gave comfort that 'what lay beyond resembled precisely what was already familiar'.[73] Thomas Stubbs performed this function admirably with St Vincent.

Further, as Huff noted, their advertisements 'were among the genres used to mediate and legitimate a new kind of economy'.[74] This legitimating genre simultaneously sanctified the private ownership of property while reinforcing the unspoken dispossession of its traditional custodians. Land buyers would not have been concerned with the legality of their new title,[75] but auctioneers still studiously avoided mention of the presence of First Nations people, maintaining the myth that the land was 'undeveloped', 'vacant', or 'waste', yet possessing commercial and agricultural potential as well as excellent communication with nearby colonial settlements.

Thomas Stubbs's St Vincent advertisements also appealed to settlers and squatters beyond the mountain through articulating aspirations to the transport of produce to Sydney through the coast rather than the existing lengthy overland route through Goulburn. In this context, his vision of a major commercial port at Batemans Bay in 1841 appears more intelligible. Indeed, Stubbs's advertisements almost exclusively promoted St Vincent as a maritime communication node serving this purpose, leaving the structure of the township itself as an afterthought. He seemed to presume that if this broader colonial purpose of St Vincent was appealing enough, settlers would follow, and the shape of the subsequent urban environment would spontaneously take care of social life within a time-tested and familiar town-grid template.

---

72 Merton, *Social Theory*, 60–9.
73 Carter, *The Road*, 227.
74 Huf, 'The Capitalist', 432.
75 As McKenna (*Looking*, 59) puts it more broadly, they would have been 'untroubled by any sense of obligation to Aboriginal people'. In 1841 there was more newspaper commentary on Indigenous conflict around Gippsland and Port Phillip, as that area was being 'opened up'. For the new settlements branching out from Port Phillip, see Boyce, *1835*, 161–3.

Considerable energy was spent on generating interest in this St Vincent venture at Long Beach in 1841 and early market interest was encouraging. However, by mid-year the land market throughout the colony was softening and by 1842 Edward Lord's trustees could not attract any buyers. Further, Hughes & Hosking had relieved Raphael Clint of his proprietorship of the entire 320 acres at Long Beach, suggesting that the purchases from January to March 1841 had fallen through.

However, the description in this chapter of the rise and fall of St Vincent is far from the end of the story. If anything, it is only the setting for the puzzle. A number of questions remain unanswered. First, who was Raphael Clint and why did he assume so many different roles in the development of St Vincent? Second, what happened to the claims of those buyers who purchased allotments within the township of St Vincent? Third, what happened to the Hughes & Hosking and Lord properties that constituted the township and suburbs of St Vincent? Fourth, what fate befell the merchants John Hosking, John Terry Hughes and Edward Lord? Fifth, what relevance does the 'magnificent steamer' *Clonmel*—mentioned twice by the auctioneer Thomas Stubbs in January 1841—have to St Vincent?

Before exploring these questions, it is necessary to describe the broader competitive South Coast environment, because the softening of the property market and the badness of the times outlined in this chapter were not the only reasons why land sales tapered off at Batemans Bay after the January and March 1841 sales. As noted in this chapter, auctioneers were promoting a broader vision of the colony that corresponded with many settlers' long-anticipated hope of founding a southern port that would challenge Sydney's maritime dominance and establish closer communication with Van Diemen's Land and more recent government settlements at Port Phillip and in New Zealand. The next chapter shows that Batemans Bay encountered stiff competition from other pretenders for the title of 'Great Southern Township'.

4

Competing for southern pre-eminence

> Any person, in the slightest degree acquainted with the Colony, must be perfectly aware that the difficulty of overland communication is the greatest drawback; and, until railroads can be established, good seaports, of easy access from the interior, must inevitably acquire the utmost importance.[1]

Parties had long endeavoured to find a route for a road from the south-west counties to a reliable harbour on the South Coast.[2] The renewed allure of a South Coast port by the late 1830s came from the growing south-western movement of settlers through the 'new country' of Argyle, Murray, King and the Maneroo (Monaro). They were producing wool and wheat that were increasingly significant to the colony's economy.

However, the only existing means of getting wool bales to Sydney was through Goulburn using bullock-pulled wool drays. This mode of haulage traversed between 3 and 15 miles a day, depending on weather and road

---

1   Messrs Falwasser and Rogers, 'Thirty Allotments at Broulee', *Australian*, 31 December 1840, 4.
2   In the late 1820s, Thomas Mitchell had proposed a line of road between Braidwood and the Clyde River; see State Library of NSW, www.sl.nsw.gov.au/collection-items/plan-proposed-line-road-braidwood-clyde-river-county-st-vincent. See also the *Sydney Herald* (16 April 1832, 2) editorial advocating a road from Argyle to the coast. Cynics in the press charged that Colonial Secretary Macleay, who claimed land at Batemans Bay, was attempting to feather his nest at government expense. For an example of a proponent of southern coastal ports, see *Colonist*, 23 March 1837, 4. Governor Bourke, in the mid-1830s, wrote to Lord Aberdeen expressing the hope that a port could be found with the aim of 'facilitating the intercourse between remote and more settled districts'. See Sidney, *The Three Colonies*, 100.

49

conditions. It was hoped that a dray road to a southern coastal port, where the wool bales could be transferred to ships, would reduce the length and the cost of carting produce considerably.[3]

The previous chapter described the case made for a road to Batemans Bay on these grounds. This chapter recounts how rising interest in competing ports also reached its zenith during 1841. There was one proposal with powerful backers that threatened to sabotage plans for the 'Great Southern Township of St Vincent'.

Figure 10. Samuel Thomas Gill, 'Wool Drays', 1865.
Gill, *The Australian Sketchbook*. See National Museum of Australia, collectionsearch.nma.gov.au/icons/piction/kaui2/index.html#/home?usr=CE&umo=44136224.

---

3   Samuel Thomas Gill depicted the tribulations of transporting wool to market along bad roads with his coloured lithograph 'Wool Drays'. See Gill, *The Australian Sketchbook*; Figure 10, this volume. See also Henzel, *Australian Agriculture*, 161. For a contemporary description of drays, see Marjoribanks, *Travels*, 63–4. Marjoribanks gives the daily distance of a wool dray as 10–12 miles. Brown (*A History*, 17) notes that as late as 1856 it took the Shumack family three weeks by a nine-horse dray to travel from Sydney to Canberry, some days travelling 7 miles, other days up to three times more. The journey could often take longer than anticipated, due to giving assistance to bogged vehicles. See Shumack, *Tales and Legends*, 2. Smith describes an 1839 journey from Sydney to Braidwood, noting that a bullock dray usually took six weeks on firm ground. See Smith, *The Clarke Gang*, ch. 2.

Jervis Bay and the Wool Road

The proposal that posed the greatest challenge to Batemans Bay involved a privately sponsored dray road connecting Braidwood with Jervis Bay through Narriga (Nerriga). What made this scheme a mortal threat to the future of the proposed township of St Vincent was the support it secured from some of the most prominent landholders in the southern districts. If they were to sponsor a road from their properties to a port on Jervis Bay, 90 kilometres north of Batemans Bay, then this would undermine the commercial rationale behind St Vincent.

Under the governorship of Lachlan Macquarie 20 years earlier, when the southern interior was more sparsely covered with settlers, it seemed only a matter of time before the capacious harbour of Jervis Bay became an important port. Yet, the surveyor-general, John Oxley, was left unimpressed with Jervis Bay after an inspection, and government attention eventually focused north towards the Hunter River that flowed into the ocean, while the southern districts remained more marginal, with the rivers there running away from Sydney south-westward into the Murray–Darling Basin.[4]

A scheme began receiving publicity in the Sydney press during 1839 when a group of notable southern landholders presented a 'memorial from the settlers in the southern districts, praying that a road might be formed between these districts and the harbour of Jervis Bay'. Governor Gipps responded by claiming that he did not possess the funds to assist with the project.[5] Undeterred, the landholders formed a committee to raise money

---

4   Perry, *Australia's First Frontier*, 116–19. However, writing to Macquarie in January 1820 after visiting Jervis Bay, Oxley conceded that 'the principal Object in Settling this Part must be the facility it would Afford in Conveying the produce of the Interior'. Perry, *Australia's First Frontier*, 117–18.
5   *Colonist*, 18 December 1839, 2. In September 1840, the governor officially expressed his hope for a route to Jervis Bay, as well as the possibility of routes further south. See 'Despatch from Sir George Gipps, Governor of New South Wales, to the Secretary of State for the Colonies, Transmitting a Report of the Progressive Discovery and Occupation of that Colony during the Period of His Administration of the Government (No. 139.) Government House, Sydney', 28 September 1840:
> To the south of Sydney the same or a similar ridge presents itself, running through the counties of Cumberland, Camden and St. Vincent though nearer to the sea. This ridge has hitherto cut off the western parts of these counties, as well as the counties of Murray, King, Georgiana and Argyle, from any communication with the sea, except by the way of Sydney; but I am happy to say, that a route has been discovered, which may be made practicable with little trouble or expense, from a place called Narriga, on the western side of the ridge, in the county of St. Vincent, to Jervis Bay which is a commodious harbour, in latitude 35 0. A similar route may, it is hoped, be opened to Bateman's Bay which lies 50 miles further south; and another perhaps, still further south, to Twofold Bay. At this latter place there is a very large cattle station belonging to Dr. Imlay (formerly a surgeon in the navy,) but the usual communication with it is by water.

51

privately for their scheme, based on a report by the surveyor James Larmer to the surveyor-general, Thomas Mitchell, identifying the most 'practicable' route and estimating the cost at £994.⁶

A convict labour gang was 'placed at the disposal' of the committee by the government and by early 1841 it had completed sections of the 35-mile route, including dynamiting difficult passes. In June 1841, the committee issued a plea in the Sydney press for more private subscriptions from landholders to complete the project, pointing to the benefits that pastoralists would derive from the construction of the road, which would ensure that 'the greater portion of the wool produced in those counties and districts will be conveyed by this road to the sea coast'.⁷

The road would make the Kinghorne–Green route to Batemans Bay redundant. It would also reduce traffic along the inland route. Regionally, it would promote greater decentralisation of colonial trading relations through expanding the local southern market.⁸ Distancing themselves from Sydney, the committee presented the southern producers as a collective with their 'own' regional future:

> The formation of a town on what may be called their own portion of the coast, whence they may obtain their supplies of foreign necessaries and luxuries, and to the increasing population of which they will in a very few years readily dispose of their surplus stock and grain; the consequent introduction of steamboats to run between that town and Sydney, whereby an uninterrupted intercourse with the metropolis will be greatly facilitated; the saving of distance as regards land carriage, a saving in many instances of about one hundred miles, and the superior feed for working oxen which the new route will afford to that which can be now obtained on the road to Sydney; all these advantages are so obvious that the committee confidently count upon obtaining the unanimous support of the inhabitants of the southern districts.⁹

---

6 For a report on Larmer's 'important discovery' of this 'practicable' route and its improvement over the inland road, see *Australasian Chronicle*, 11 July 1840, 2; *Sydney Herald*, 13 July 1840, 4.
7 *Sydney Herald*, 19 June 1841, 3; *Australasian Chronicle*, 1 July 1841, 1.
8 See also *Sydney Free Press*, 2 December 1841, 3. Speaking of the woolgrowers around Goulburn, the correspondent suggested that: 'The times are so bad ... that they are determined to look after themselves, and will not trust to the monopolists of the metropolis.'
9 *Sydney Herald*, 19 June 1841, 3.

4. COMPETING FOR SOUTHERN PRE-EMINENCE

Further subscriptions were required, as the estimated cost of this 'wool road' had increased to over £2,000. Leading members of this committee included Colonel John MacKenzie of Narriga, Thomas Braidwood Wilson of Braidwood, the Ryrie family at Arnprior (now Larbert), John Coghill of Bedervale at Braidwood and Terence Murray, who held grants at Lake George and the Limestone Plains. Among the list of subscribers were Jervis Bay landholders Alexander Berry, Archibald Campbell, George Thompson and Edward Deas Thomson (the colonial secretary), along with Thomas Walker, Robert Campbell and Thomas Macquoid of the Limestone Plains.[10]

Their grander plan for the venture was made clear in May 1841 when Samuel Lyons advertised that he would be auctioning 100 township allotments situated at the 'private township of South Huskisson', Jervis Bay, on 21 June. This was on 2,560 acres of land promised in 1830 to Edward Deas Thomson,[11] who took over from Alexander Macleay as colonial secretary in 1837. Thomson was also a subscriber to the Jervis Bay Wool Road. The advertisement for the town made the same claims that Stubbs used for St Vincent—safe anchorage for ships of any tonnage and a site destined to become of great significance to the colony—but with the added advantage over St Vincent of 'a new road which there is every reason to expect will be practicable for the wool drays of next season', running between Narriga and Jervis Bay, and 'terminating at the latter place, on the property now offered for sale'.[12]

Reinforcing the advantage of South Huskisson over St Vincent, Lyons informed readers that the road to the town was 'carried on at the expense of many of the most influential persons in the southern districts' and would open communication with the principal towns of the interior. Lyons foresaw that most of the produce of the southern interior would be shipped directly to England and other markets, and that imports would arrive directly to the port of South Huskisson.[13]

---

10   *Sydney Free Press*, 2 December 1841, 3.
11   *Sydney Gazette and New South Wales Advertiser*, 5 July 1834, 4. Edward Deas Thomson was former governor Bourke's son-in-law. He had explored Jervis Bay in 1832 with George Macleay, the son of the then colonial secretary Alexander Macleay. See Donaldson, *Colonial Mandarin*. Thomson was also a shareholder in the Australian Steam Navigation Company.
12   *Australasian Chronicle*, 20 May 1841, 3. The *Sydney Gazette and New South Wales Advertiser* (8 June 1841, 3; 12 June 1841, 1) presented an expanded description of the town and its potential. See also *Sydney Monitor and Commercial Advertiser*, 18 June 1841, 3. The *Sydney Herald* (21 June 1841, 2) reported that the *Tamar* had taken passengers down to Jervis Bay to view Jervis Town and South Huskisson and provided glowing accounts of the progress on the Wool Road.
13   *Australasian Chronicle*, 20 May 1841, 3.

Sales in June for the 100 allotments offered were strong (all lots were sold for a total of £3,519) and it was later claimed that they changed 'hands at a very high premium'. Encouraged by the 'great demand for Allotments in South Huskisson', and progress on the Wool Road, Lyons announced that a further 100 town allotments would be auctioned on 29 November.[14]

Also in May 1841, Thomas Stubbs was advertising allotments at the township of Jervis Town (now Callala Beach) further north within Jervis Bay. Even though the proposed town was not directly linked to the Wool Road, Stubbs reassured readers that the new road to Jervis Bay was almost complete, and that it would cut off 'about one hundred and forty miles of land carriage' compared with the inland route to Sydney.[15]

Forgetting claims he made in January and March that St Vincent possessed 'the highest order of maritime advantages', Stubbs now puffed Jervis Bay as an 'almost unequalled port; which nothing can prevent from becoming, in a very short time, the second place of importance to Sydney'. Now that the government had decided to release this 'valuable' port, settlers could be 'quite assured their grain, and next year's clip will be delivered to Jervis Bay'.[16]

Stubbs's advertisements for Jervis Town during May ran parallel with those for Lord's township extension blocks at St Vincent, often separated by one column, and it is notable that these May advertisements for Lord's estate underplayed the claims for Batemans Bay as a harbour when compared with his January/April advertisements described in the previous chapter. The auctions for Jervis Town and Lord's allotments were held four days apart and it is possible that 'speculatists' held back their 'spare capital' from Lord's property on 19 May to await lots at Jervis Town and South Huskisson. On 7 July 1841, Thomas Stubbs auctioned more sections of Jervis Town.

In October, Stubbs was also the auctioneer for Mr Stuart's adjoining private venture at Central Jervis Town, arguing that the project offered the 'most direct communication between the vast Southern Districts of the colony, and Mercantile Interests of Sydney'.[17]

---

14   *Australian*, 22 June 1841, 2, for sales figures. See also *Sydney Monitor and Commercial Advertiser*, 29 November 1841, 2; *Australasian Chronicle*, 7 October 1841, 4; *Sydney Herald*, 27 October 1841, 4; *Sydney Gazette and New South Wales Advertiser*, 27 October 1841, 3.
15   *Free Press and Commercial Journal*, 8 May 1841, 3.
16   See *Free Press and Commercial Journal*, 8 May 1841, 3; 19 May 1841, 1.
17   *Sydney Free Press*, 5 October 1841, 3. See also *Australian*, 6 July 1841, 2; *Australasian Chronicle*, 7 and 9 October 1841, 4. At the same time in October, Stubbs's former employer Joseph Simmons was offering 100 allotments at Jervis Town.

4. COMPETING FOR SOUTHERN PRE-EMINENCE

Other Jervis Bay landholders moved in the slipstream of the demand for South Huskisson allotments. On the same day of the November auction, Lyons also offered 16 farms on St Georges Basin.[18] On a grander scale of opportunism, in July 1841, the auctioneers Foss and Lloyd gave prior announcement that they had received instructions that allotments would shortly be submitted for public competition in the private township of New Bristol, south of South Huskisson and closer to the heads of Jervis Bay.[19] The auction took place on 22 October when some of the allotments went under the hammer for an impressive £160.[20]

The years 1841 and 1842 marked the halcyon days of the Jervis Bay Wool Road scheme. Supporters of the road were encouraged by the announcement from the Colonial Secretary's Office on 14 January 1842 giving notice that a site had been surveyed for the township of Narriga 'on the new line of road from Braidwood to Jervis Bay'.[21] This development appeared to give government imprimatur to the Jervis Bay Wool Road. In July 1842, the government also announced that it had surveyed an adjoining road from Braidwood to Narriga, giving a further fillip to the scheme.[22] Five months later, 'by His Excellency's Command', Thomson announced that sites had been fixed upon for three townships (Farnham at Jerrawongola, Marlow at Mongarlow and Larbert at Kurraducbidgee)—all described as 'on the road from Braidwood to Jervis Bay'.[23]

However, from 1842, there were reports of rising construction costs on the Wool Road, ongoing problems with its reliability, negligent supervision of the convict road gang, the lack of feed and water for draught animals en route and the high cost of freight from Jervis Bay. There were also logistical problems coordinating wool drays and ships, with reports of ships waiting in vain for wool drays.

---

18   *Sydney Herald*, 29 November 1841, 2.
19   *Sydney Herald*, 17 July 1841, 4; see also 22 September 1841, 4; *Sydney Gazette and New South Wales Advertiser*, 21 October 1841, 1.
20   *Sydney Monitor and Commercial Advertiser*, 25 October 1841, 2.
21   *NSW Government Gazette*, 14 January 1842, 54.
22   *Colonial Observer*, 13 July 1842, 327. While most of the previous work on the Wool Road was privately funded, this announcement left Colonial Secretary E. Deas Thomson open to the same cynical charge to which his predecessor, Macleay, was subjected in the early 1830s when supporting a Batemans Bay road.
23   *NSW Government Gazette*, 13 January 1843, 72.

Further, in the Legislative Council on 29 June 1842, Alexander Berry reported that when the Wool Road committee called upon their subscribers, many pleaded poverty 'and really were unable to pay them'. This hinted at the straitened times many southern landowners were facing as the depression tightened its hold on the colony. In October 1843, Mr Cowper presented a petition to the Legislative Council pleading for a grant of one-quarter of the £2,400 debt already incurred on the 'Southern Road' to Jervis Bay. This was rejected.[24]

Supporters of the Wool Road venture also complained of having to 'contend against the evil reports which have been so industriously circulated respecting them by interested parties'. These reports came from Sydney merchants as well as landowners along the inland route to Sydney, but landowners at rival coastal harbours such as Broulee also joined the criticism.[25]

Despite periodic reports from Dr Wilson and residents of the 'new country' that South Huskisson was 'at last likely to emerge from obscurity', and despite land sales in the government township of Huskisson in 1843,[26] the Wool Road and its Jervis Bay destination would soon be all but abandoned.[27] When Joseph Townsend travelled round Jervis Bay in the mid-1840s, he passed the site of five towns designed to 'be an outlet of the country in the interior'. However, 'amongst them all, are but two inhabited houses'.[28]

---

24   For Berry, see *Australasian Chronicle*, 2 July 1842, 2. A letter in the *Sydney Morning Herald* (2 August 1842, 3) called upon the 'narrow-minded' settlers of the Maneroo to subscribe to the Narriga Road, 'given the benefits they must eventually derive' from communication with Jervis Bay. For Cowper, see *Sydney Morning Herald*, 26 October 1843, 2. After travelling by horseback to Narriga, Terence Murray had already decided that while the Wool Road benefitted Braidwood farms, it was not practicable for the Limestone Plains (see Wilson, *Murray*, 120–1).
25   *Sydney Morning Herald*, 11 January 1843, 2. For four examples of such 'evil', see *Sydney Free Press*, 8 January 1842, 2; 22 January 1842, 3; *Sydney Gazette and New South Wales Advertiser*, 25 January 1842, 2; *Australian*, 14 December 1842, 2. See also the following section on Broulee.
26   *Sydney Herald*, 30 March 1842, 2; *Sydney Morning Herald*, 2 August 1842, 3; 10 September 1842, 2; 11 January 1843, 2. For the Huskisson sales, see *Sydney Morning Herald*, 18 January 1843, 4. By 1843, some earlier landholders were also offering their South Huskisson allotments on the depressed market (see *Sydney Morning Herald*, 8 and 10 April 1843, 3). Allotments at Central Jervis Town were again advertised in 1846 without mention of any existing settlers. See *Sydney Morning Herald*, 20 March 1846, 4. 'A labouring man' wrote to the *Sydney Morning Herald* (12 March 1856, 8) at a time when all hope for the government-initiated Huskisson scheme was lost, requesting information on the value of the land he had purchased from the government for his children's future back in 1843. Fearing that the land would remain worthless for generations, he queried whether the sales had involved collusion between the government and Colonial Secretary E. Deas Thomson to defraud unsuspecting workers such as himself.
27   In 1848, *Bell's Life in Sydney and Sporting Reviewer* (12 February 1848, 1) mocked the fate of South Huskisson. See also Hoskins, *Coast*, 171; *People's Advocate and New South Wales Vindicator*, 11 October 1851, 6.
28   Townsend, *Rambles and Observations*, 143. The five towns would have been the private towns described in this section: South Huskisson, Jervis Town, New Bristol, Central Jervis Town (all 1841) and the government town of Huskisson (1843).

4. COMPETING FOR SOUTHERN PRE-EMINENCE

The hopes of exporting wool directly to Britain from southern ports such as Jervis Bay, Broulee, Twofold Bay or Batemans Bay rather than through Sydney were dashed a few years later once growers accepted the centralised wool-auctioning system based in Sydney.[29] The opportunity to export wool to Britain directly from Jervis Bay had passed. Another blow was further competition from Benjamin Boyd, who had turned his attention in 1843 to establishing a port on Twofold Bay at his private township of Boyd Town, puffing this venture with what appeared to be limitless capital from the Royal Bank of Australia and three new steamships.[30]

The timing of the announcement of the Wool Road scheme and land sales at Jervis Bay in the first half of 1841 had the effect of taking more wind out of the sails of the St Vincent scheme. The influential backers of Jervis Bay had implicitly rejected the Clyde River and Batemans Bay as the location of the great southern township. St Vincent was at a disadvantage under such circumstances, especially in a softening land market.

Listed among the most generous subscribers of the Jervis Bay Wool Road in 1841 was John Terry Hughes, along with the firm Hughes & Hosking. Individually, and as a company, both men owned tracts of land at Jervis Bay, St Georges Basin and Shoalhaven.[31] The new co-owner of St Vincent, Raphael Clint, could not have felt too much betrayal when Hughes & Hosking aligned itself with the Jervis Bay venture. Clint himself prepared the lithographic plan for Samuel Lyons's auction of the South Huskisson township allotments in June 1841.[32]

---

29 Previously, wool sales tended to be conducted in London. T.S. Mort played a pivotal role in the transformation by establishing his Sydney broking and auctioning business in 1843. See Pearson and Lennon, *Pastoral Australia*, 66.
30 See Diamond, *Ben Boyd*. See also Chapters 9 and 10.
31 Hughes & Hosking had put its Jervis Bay holdings up for sale in the same October 1840 auction along with their Long Beach and Broulee properties (see Chapter 2). Its Shoalhaven property to the north was subdivided in April 1841 (see Chapter 3).
32 R. Clint, 'Sketch of the Township of South Huskisson', 1841, Lithog., Ferguson Collection, map 57, nla.gov.au/nla.obj-229901982. One of the two surviving lithographs contains a table with columns listing the purchasers, the sections and the numbers of their allotments. This will be revisited at the end of Chapter 6.

Broulee and 'the road to the moon'

Another harbour vying with Jervis Bay and Batemans Bay in 1841 for the title of the great southern port was Broulee, 20 kilometres south of Batemans Bay. This section tracks the efforts of its most prominent resident, Captain William Oldrey RN,[33] to promote a route from the Maneroo to Broulee. It also assesses the land market at Broulee in 1841. The evidence so far suggested that Batemans Bay was softening considerably, while Jervis Bay was still attracting interest.

In the four years since Broulee was officially surveyed and laid out in 1837, the village had witnessed slow but steady progress. Oldrey was appointed the village's first magistrate in 1839 and government land sales surrounding the harbour were held that year, followed by lively sales at the town-allotment auction. Further, vessels regularly stopped at Broulee Harbour.

On 26 February 1840, William Oldrey had been appointed commissioner of Crown lands. In addition, he also held depasturing licences beyond the limits of location on the Maneroo.[34] Along with his large landholdings at Broulee and his shareholding in the Australian Steam Navigation Company, he was strategically placed to influence the opening of a southern port, as well as an interested party in the outcome.

To maintain this momentum, on 29 August 1840, a deputation led by Edward Lord, and including John Hosking, waited on the governor with a petition drawn up after a meeting held at the Royal Hotel the previous week, which had been chaired by Lord.[35] The petition called on the government to make good its promise for a breakwater or wharf at Broulee Harbour, noting that this feature on the surveyor's plan had 'enhanced' prices at the recent government land auction at Broulee. This plea was an implied warning that the government might be accused of 'misrepresentation'. The improvements on the harbour were also necessary for developing the region's resources:

---

33   See Magee, *All Broulee*, 73–6; Sewell, 'Captain William Oldrey RN', 18–20.
34   *NSW Government Gazette*, 4 March 1840, 199; 19 February 1840, 172; 3 June 1840, 541; *Colonist*, 8 September 1840, 4.
35   *Sydney Herald*, 31 August 1840, 6. With Lord's vertically integrated interests in the County of Murray and at Batemans Bay, progress at Broulee would improve his lines of communication. He also possessed land on the Shoalhaven River, near Jervis Bay, and was a director of the Hunter River Steam Navigation Company.

4. COMPETING FOR SOUTHERN PRE-EMINENCE

> One of the advantages afforded will be the shortest road from Maneroo, &c., via Broulee to Sydney, &c., which voyage can be performed in three days; and also for transporting the large and increasing produce on the coast as far as Mount Dromedary.[36]

The governor sought more detail from the Survey Department without committing himself.

Unlike St Vincent at Batemans Bay and the Jervis Bay private towns, Broulee appeared to have the advantage of being a 'government town', laid out by a government surveyor and sold at the Colonial Treasury. This, however, did not necessarily raise its appeal over its competitors. In 1837, when the surveyor James Larmer was requested to lay out Bungendore, Braidwood and Broulee, he delivered supportive descriptions of the first two locations but a rather lukewarm assessment of Broulee.[37]

What the Broulee deputation needed most was evidence of a feasible route down the mountain to its harbour. In September 1840, a £100 reward was offered for the discovery of a 'practical dray road from Bradbo, Maneira' (Bredbo, Monaro) to Broulee, payable by the manager of the Sydney Bank.[38] Hopes in this direction were raised in May 1841 when an editorial in the *Australian* reported that it had received a letter announcing the 'discovery' of a 'practical dray road' from Broulee to the Maneroo and Limestone Plains. The editorial felt certain that settlers would soon be able to transport their produce by ship to Sydney through Broulee 'in less than one-half of the time, and expense now incurred'.[39] The letter (written on 6 May by Oldrey's superintendent and leader of the expedition Charles Nicholson) calculated that a squad of 50 men could make it 'an excellent road' in six months: 'There are no impediments in the way, in the shape of rocks to blast, as is the case in the Jervis Bay Road. Shovel and pick-axe will do it.'[40]

This challenge did not go unnoticed by Jervis Bay proponents. One respondent took offence to the Wool Road allusion:

---

36 *Sydney Herald*, 31 August 1840, 6.
37 See Magee, *All Broulee*, 79–80.
38 *Colonist*, 5 September 1840, 4. The reward was contingent on the road being approved by the surveyor-general or the commissioners of the district, one of whom was Oldrey.
39 *Australian*, 15 May 1841, 2.
40 *Australian*, 15 May 1841, 2

As it appears to me, from the tone of your correspondent's letter, that it was sought to throw the Jervis Bay line into the shade, I as a resident of the southern district, and one interested in the formation of the Jervis Bay road, from which, in common with all the 'southerners', I expect to derive great advantages, could not allow it to be thus disparagingly alluded to.[41]

Two days later, the *Australian* conceded that Nicholson 'was in error' and confirmed that the Jervis Bay Road was 'free from the obstacles incidentally alluded to' in Nicholson's letter.[42]

In a diplomatic gesture, the paper also commented favourably on the 'newly discovered road between Maneroo and Broulee', and published another letter from Nicholson, dated 16 May, after he had returned to Broulee.[43] Without mentioning the Narriga—Jervis Bay Wool Road, the letter repeated the prediction that this new road to Broulee could eclipse its Jervis Bay competitor. Nicholson was confident that, even in its present state,

> a dray might go to Maneroo, with the assistance of a cross-cut saw and axes, there being no necessity for gunpowder the whole of the way—nothing but pick-axe and shovel—to make it an excellent mountain road; and, I am confident that, was a party immediately placed on it, it might be made ready to receive January's clip of wool.[44]

In furtherance of this project, Captain Oldrey adopted the same strategy as the Jervis Bay Wool Road consortium. In July, he circulated a petition addressed to the governor pleading for the provision of government labourers to work on the route. Further, various establishments were listed where interested parties could subscribe to the private undertaking.[45] In September, Oldrey took his case to Sydney, hosting a meeting at Petty's Hotel to consider the means to improve 'the road recently discovered'. However, no assigned labour from the government was forthcoming for the Maneroo–Broulee road.[46]

---

41 *Australian*, 25 May 1841, 2.
42 *Australian*, 27 May 1841, 2.
43 *Australian*, 27 May 1841, 2. See also *Sydney Herald*, 27 May 1841, 2.
44 *Australian*, 27 May 1841, 2.
45 The petition was reproduced in, and supported by, the *Australian*, 1 July 1841, 2.
46 The government's budget was much tighter than when it assisted the Wool Road with labour power, but Oldrey must also have suspected that the government was not treating both projects equally, especially after it allocated funds to the Braidwood–Narriga road in mid-1842.

4. COMPETING FOR SOUTHERN PRE-EMINENCE

In the midst of these Sydney meetings, Oldrey published another letter from Nicholson, dated 16 September, informing Oldrey of the 'success of my trip from Broulee to Maneroo, over the heretofore considered impossible Coast Ranges'. Improving on his May adventure, this trip took 14 days with a dray laden with half a ton of tobacco, and he expected to return downhill with six bales of wool and three kegs of butter in eight days.[47]

Reinforced with this information, Oldrey chaired another public meeting, in early October, at the Exchange Rooms, Macquarie Place, where resolutions were passed that hailed Nicholson's discovery of the dray road; noted its significance to the colony; claimed that ships could sail direct from Broulee to London, Liverpool and Bristol; called for an adequate pecuniary remuneration to be presented to Nicholson; requested that the government assign labour to the task of completing the road; pleaded with settlers in the district to cooperate with the resolutions of the meeting; announced the subscription for the new road and another for its discoverer; and resolved to widely publish these resolutions.[48]

In July 1842, Oldrey changed course, holding another meeting, forming another committee and opening another subscription with the intention of cutting a route from Broulee through Ballalaba to the Limestone Plains. This route was 'neither half so tedious, hazardous nor expensive' as the 'present land carriage' to Sydney. Further, he claimed the path would increase population and regional trade through opening up Crown land along the route. The road construction cost was estimated at £500. Oldrey was the largest subscriber with £50 and three others provided £10, including John Terry Hughes, who attended the meeting.[49]

Five months later, an unsigned correspondent (but sounding much like the indefatigable Oldrey) in the *Australian* listed every laden dray and stock drive that had taken the Ballalaba–Broulee route as proof 'that the worthy resident magistrate of Broulee is not endeavouring "to find out a road to the moon," as rival interests are pleased to express'. Addressing sceptics, he acknowledged that the correspondence had been written 'for the purpose of

---

47 *Sydney Monitor and Commercial Advertiser*, 24 September 1841, 2; *Sydney Herald*, 27 September 1841, 2; *Colonial Observer*, 7 October 1841, 8.
48 *Sydney Herald*, 2 October 1841, 3; *Sydney Gazette and New South Wales Advertiser*, 23 September 1841, 3.
49 *New South Wales Examiner*, 27 and 29 July 1842, 3; 5 September 1841, 2; 19 September 1842, 4. A letter from Captain V. Wiseman was also read out reassuring subscribers of the safety of Broulee Harbour after the *Rover* capsized in the harbour with the loss of 12 lives in October 1841.

arousing the settlers from their present state of apathy and incredulity as to the proposed undertaking'. He also compared the Broulee route favourably to the Wool Road, which had 'never yet been practicable to drive even an empty dray from the Mountains down to Jervis Bay'.[50] 'Evil reports' from 'interested parties' were clearly still circulating around the Wool Road.

Yet, Jervis Bay was not the sole target of evil reports from rivals. Previously, on 6 February 1841, a letter had appeared in the *Sydney Gazette and New South Wales Advertiser* accusing Broulee's advocates of 'puffing'.[51] The author, using the pen name 'Lictor', could not have been more dismissive of progress around the settlement, describing the surrounding country as 'loose sand and rotten swamps'. The harbour was only fit for vessels under 100 tons, 'and I question whether a vessel of that tonnage would be safe in a N.E. gale of any strength'. Any use of public funds on, or roads to, 'such a miserable country' would constitute a 'complete misappropriation of money'.[52]

Lictor claimed that the town itself lacked potable water and was situated on a 'promontory of wretched land' that could not 'support a hamlet, to say nothing of even a village'. Further, due to the absence of a 'fit Bench of Magistrates', the community was left 'in a most lawless state', with Lictor proclaiming: 'I never saw or heard of such a perfect hell upon earth.'[53] The management of post office affairs at Broulee was also criticised, leading to the suggestion that a road from Braidwood to Batemans Bay was a better option than the Braidwood–Broulee route, and would also 'save a considerable time, expense and risk'. While it can only be speculated whether 'Lictor' was acting on behalf of parties associated with other proposed southern townships, each port proposal was clearly subject to puffing and 'counter-puffing'.

Lictor's dismissal of Broulee was written in the midst of numerous attempts to privately subdivide land surrounding the government-surveyed township. Like those at Jervis Bay and Batemans Bay, the Broulee schemes sought to take advantage of its location as a future harbour articulating Sydney with a road leading into the interior tableland.

---

50   *Australian*, 14 December 1842, 2.
51   *Sydney Gazette and New South Wales Advertiser*, 6 January 1841, 2.
52   *Sydney Gazette and New South Wales Advertiser*, 6 January 1841, 2.
53   A petition organised by Oldrey in September 1841 to the Legislative Council requesting a Court of Requests showed that even Oldrey recognised that the village was prey to sly grog sellers, cattle thieves, escapees from fraudulent insolvency and loss of property, and that the area was used as an asylum for bushrangers, 'endangering the peace and order of the community'. See *Sydney Free Press*, 21 September 1841, 3.

4. COMPETING FOR SOUTHERN PRE-EMINENCE

For instance, in June and August 1840, the auctioneers Hebblewhite and Vickery had advertised subdivisions of the 'magnificent estate' of Goodridge-Leigh as part of 'a continuation' of the town.⁵⁴ The land belonged to Oldrey. They hailed Broulee as the 'only shipping harbour for the immense produce brought down from the entire south and eastern district of the Colony', and predicted that its advantages would 'speedily give it a degree of importance far surpassing that of Wollongong and equally that of Newcastle'. They also highlighted roads 'marked out' on the route from Braidwood, and another 'under inspection' that would 'communicate with all the important inland grazing districts'.⁵⁵

At the end of December 1840, Messrs Falwasser and Rogers were instructed to sell 30 building allotments at Broulee, a location that they claimed had been 'forcing itself more and more prominently on the public mind', unlike 'the greater portion of the new townships that are daily advertised'. Like the advertisements for St Vincent, the auctioneers devoted the description to the commercial potential of Broulee, 'the only eligible harbour along the whole line of coast from Wollongong to Port Phillip', ensuring that it would soon become the 'grand centre' for exporting produce from all the surrounding pastoral and agricultural districts.⁵⁶

At the same time, Captain Oldrey placed his property at Mount Oldrey on the market, along with 70 town allotments. The advertisement drew attention to Oldrey's homestead and its attached four-acre garden—'in the course of construction'—that benefited from a climate resembling 'the genial south of Italy'. Despite its location close to the southernmost boundary of the limits of location, coastal vessels could reach Sydney in a day, while steamers would soon make the journey 'in less than 18 hours'. Their arrival would significantly increase the value of the property.⁵⁷

When buyers could not be found, Oldrey renewed his campaign to promote Broulee. Then, after the discovery of Nicholson's dray road, he again advertised the sale of part of his property, this time breaking it into smaller allotments of between 25 and 500 acres for up for three-, five- and seven-year leases.⁵⁸

---

54 *Sydney Herald*, 22 June 1840, 8; *Commercial Journal and Advertiser*, 24 June 1840; 12 August 1840, 4. A map of the subdivision is held at the NLA, Ferguson Collection, MAP F 447.
55 *Sydney Herald*, 22 June 1840, 8.
56 *Australian*, 31 December 1840, 4.
57 *Sydney Herald*, 24 November 1840, 4; *Australian*, 26 December 1840, 3; 9 January 1841, 1.
58 *Sydney Herald*, 19 June 1841, 3; 28 June 1841, 2; 29 June 1841, 1; 9 July 1841, 4.

A more ambitious sales campaign was announced in June 1841 for the estate of Captain Francis Charles Waldron, who had assumed the duty of clerk of the Bench of Magistrates at Broulee the previous year.[59] Waldron named his estate 'Frankville', subdividing it into 22 lots, including his own residence and farm, three small subdivisions 'calculated for Inns, Stores &c.', and 18 other farming lots suitable for agricultural purposes and timber harvesting.[60] An added inducement was that the proposed road to Twofold Bay ran through the property.[61] Similar to Lord's 'suburban allotments' at St Vincent, Frankville's and Goodridge-Leigh's allotments were 'extensions' of planned townships connected by roads that lay in the future.

Waldron's auctioneer Foss and Lloyd addressed the public's declining confidence in real estate by reminding readers that land was the bedrock of colonial fortune (see Chapter 2 on the 'badness of the times'). Without mentioning the descending financial gloom, they warned readers that too many people had purchased land rashly and without foresight. This was followed by lengthy sage advice on the characteristics required to become a discerning owner of property. The remainder of the advertisement described Frankville's proposed subdivisions in such a manner as to leave no doubt that they would appeal to a discerning buyer.

On 4 August, under a new auctioneer, Samuel Lyons, Waldron was offering 'eight farms near Broulee, varying in extent from twenty to thirty-three Acres'.[62] Unsuccessful in selling any of his subdivisions, he repackaged the offerings again in March 1842: 640 acres, a mile and a half from the town and port of Broulee, along with a cottage and farm buildings, with much of the land fenced and subdivided.[63] The property was to 'be sold very cheap'. Ten weeks later, it was reported that Francis Charles Waldron had become another of the 'new insolvents'.[64]

A similar fate befell Major James Frazer. In February and May 1841, he subdivided his property along Scarborough Beach immediately south of the township. The auctioneer Joseph Simmons described the offering as 'nine farms, containing from 50 to 60 acres each'.[65] Simmons's prediction of the likely monetary gain sat uncomfortably with the prevailing conditions—

---

59 Magee, *All Broulee*, 83.
60 *Sydney Herald*, 19 June 1841, 3; 28 June 1841, 2; 9 July 1841, 4.
61 *NSW Government Gazette*, 25 November 1840, 1252.
62 *Sydney Monitor and Commercial Advertiser*, 4 August 1841, 3.
63 *Australasian Chronicle*, 10 March 1842, 3.
64 *Sydney Herald*, 27 May 1842, 2.
65 *Sydney Monitor and Commercial Advertiser*, 24 May 1841, 3; *Sydney Herald*, 24 February 1841, 4.

4. COMPETING FOR SOUTHERN PRE-EMINENCE

'so rapidly are population and improvements increasing here, that it is fair to infer that a still greater advance will take place in the corresponding period to come'.[66] Even more problematic than this demographic misrepresentation, the 'farms' were not suited to their advertised agricultural pursuits as they were situated on the Bengello sand plain. A new auctioneer, Mr Barton, offered reconfigured allotments of Frazer's land in February 1842; in May, the entire parcel of land was auctioned by Samuel Lyons, but this time on behalf of R.T. Platt, the trustee of the insolvent James Frazer.[67]

These multiple reconfigurations of Broulee subdivisions reflected the difficulty of attracting buyer interest. Most of these properties were on the market around the middle of 1841, at the same time as Edward Lord's 40 suburban allotments at Stubley Park and the privately developed townships at Jervis Bay. By this stage the demand for land had softened considerably. Only the Jervis Bay properties were attracting any attention, suggesting buyers had more confidence in the progress of the Wool Road than the roads to Broulee and Batemans Bay. However, as noted in the previous section, even that buoyancy did not last into 1842. By then, the hopes for Broulee had diminished considerably, further dashed by a flood in 1841 that opened the mouth of the Moruya River leading directly into the settlement at Moruya.

Oldrey continued to promote Broulee until 1844, when he was also declared bankrupt. Stuart Magee's summary of Oldrey's predicament can be extended to that of Waldron and Frazer as well as Edward Lord, Raphael Clint and Hughes & Hosking: 'Alas, Captain Oldrey's grand plans, like most others connected with Broulee at the time, were swamped by the economic collapse of 1841.'[68]

Conclusion

Chapters 3 and 4 have shown that the sales campaigns for the private townships and subdivisions at Batemans Bay, Jervis Bay and Broulee all depended not only on the presence of a safe harbour but also on a reliable road from the Southern Tablelands to these projected coastal townships. The importance of a coastal road for these projects can be further emphasised by examining the case of Ulladulla.

---

66 *Sydney Monitor and Commercial Advertiser*, 24 May 1841, 3.
67 *Australasian Chronicle*, 8 February 1842, 3; *Sydney Free Press*, 24 May 1842, 3.
68 Magee, *All Broulee*, 75.

By 1841, Ulladulla (or 'Holy Dollar') was known as the 'Boat Harbour', servicing land grants and other properties settled from the late 1820s.[69] The harbour was not as capacious as Jervis Bay or Batemans Bay, but compared favourably with Broulee, and could accommodate vessels up to 200 tons. Ulladulla at this time appeared to be following a similar settlement trajectory as Broulee. In November and December 1840, the Colonial Secretary's Office announced that it had approved applications for the purchase by auction of 65 allotments at Ulladulla (including half-acre town allotments and 5-acre suburban allotments at South and North Ulladulla). Then, in May 1841, 194 half-acre town allotments at £20 per acre were put up for sale by the government.[70] By late 1841, government notices listed land-title transfers at Ulladulla and, in December, a correspondent for the *Sydney Herald* made the encouraging observation that 'several buildings' were 'springing up on the beach', and a licensed inn was in the process of construction.[71]

The high price tag reflected the value the government placed on the location in May 1841, but it might also have inhibited speculators, especially as the land market softened. By 1842, as the depression deepened, the government was finding it difficult to offload unsold blocks at £10 per acre, then £8 per acre (or 1s. per perch).[72]

However, another reason speculative interest in Ulladulla remained subdued at this time was the less realistic prospect of constructing a road over the mountainous terrain behind the township that would link it with producers. Given prevailing market conditions and topographical challenges, there was less appetite for speculative subdivisions and private townships at Ulladulla in the early 1840s. Ulladulla was not competing with South Huskisson, Jervis Town, New Bristol, St Vincent or Broulee.

When Thomas Stubbs auctioned the licensed George Inn at Ulladulla Harbour in February 1842, he listed among the main assets of the district the neighbouring cedar and the recent 'immigrants' engaged in agricultural and dairy pursuits. Despite noting its safe anchorage, he promoted the

---

69   Colonial Secretary Alexander Macleay had received a grant of land at Croobyar, north-west of Ulladulla, in the late 1820s, while the surveyor Thomas Florance was granted land at Narrawallee, north of the port. As noted in Chapter 1, Joseph Phipps Townsend was residing with relatives on a property 4 miles from Ulladulla.
70   *NSW Government Gazette*, 21 November 1840, 1247; 19 December 1840, 1373; 11 May 1841, 657.
71   See, for instance, *NSW Government Gazette*, 30 November 1841, 1647; *Sydney Herald*, 27 December 1841, 2.
72   See, for instance, *NSW Government Gazette*, 7 January 1842, 16; 5 April 1842, 518–19; 12 July 1842, 998.

4. COMPETING FOR SOUTHERN PRE-EMINENCE

promise of a pastoral future, without any hyperbole over the prospect of Ulladulla Harbour becoming a node connecting the south-western farmers with Sydney.[73]

Meanwhile, the combination of market conditions and competitive pressures eventually undermined plans for the 'Great Southern Township of St Vincent', featured in Chapter 3. This chapter has shown how powerful southern landowners and squatters were already investing in a scheme to cart their produce to Jervis Bay rather than Batemans Bay. Notwithstanding the 'badness of the times', there was ongoing interest in the various speculative town ventures at Jervis Bay between mid and late 1841. While these speculative Jervis Bay ventures served the same function as those at Broulee and Batemans Bay, they possessed the added advantage of a stronger coalition of influential sponsors with an interest in developing Jervis Bay.

Despite its more promising beginnings, the Jervis Bay Wool Road soon lost its advantage as its proponents faced financial difficulties and its builders experienced technical problems. By June 1852, when James Larmer was surveying a road from Braidwood to Broulee through Araluen for the government, one newspaper correspondent felt that the difficulties would prove 'insurmountable' and the costs 'too great'. Locals were 'more anxious to have a dray road formed to Bateman's Bay'.[74] From this report, it appears that, by 1852, the Jervis Bay Wool Road was no longer even considered a competitive option in the minds of Braidwood residents. Yet, this observation also reveals that no progress had taken place on 'the road to Batemans Bay' between the 1839 discovery of Kinghorne and Green's dray road and the 1852 report.

Then, in 1854, the government changed direction and gave preference to the road to Batemans Bay via 'Nilligan Creek'. One correspondent reported that inhabitants in the district considered it a 'better and more expeditious route to Sydney'.[75] Explaining the importance of the 'Clyde Road', the same correspondent asserted that:

> no portion of New South Wales could be more benefitted by the formation of a road, than the district of Braidwood, and the extensive country adjoining will be, by the completion of this line; nothing tends more to develope [sic] the resources of a country, than rapid and

---

73 *Sydney Herald*, 16 February 1842, 3. When describing the construction schedule of the George Inn, Stubbs wrote that it 'may be inferred to be complete'.
74 *Maitland Mercury and Hunter River General Advertiser*, 12 June 1852, 4.
75 *Sydney Morning Herald*, 25 May 1854, 3.

cheap communication—to the deficiency of that great commercial indispensable requisite, we may attribute that want of development in the unlimited resources of this portion of the country.[76]

As it stood, communication with Sydney remained 'tedious and expensive' and in wet seasons it was 'utterly impracticable'. The cost of transportation was aggravated by labour shortages, and the correspondent related an anecdote of a carter demanding £60 per ton for the carriage of goods to Sydney.[77] The logic of a road to Batemans Bay remained compelling. A decade after the 1858 completion of this road to Batemans Bay, the Braidwood–Araluen–Broulee road was eventually built.[78] Later chapters will explain why these roads came too late for visionaries of a great southern port.

Overall, the search for a great southern port in 1841 was premised on claims made by prominent squatters, graziers, landowners, auctioneers and press editorials that a route to the coast would benefit woolgrowers in the interior by reducing the haulage time and costs to Sydney. As noted above, these voices were still prominent in the mid-1850s. Their premises were later accepted by economic historians such as S.J. Butlin and Geoffrey Blainey, especially with respect to settlers near the limits of location and beyond.[79]

However, their assumptions did not go unquestioned. Drawing on G.J. Abbott's study of pastoral records, R.V. Jackson argued that:

> In all, it seems unlikely—though the available information is far from being conclusive—that a situation was reached before 1850 in which even a station on the fringes of the pastoral expansion could expect to have its wool income seriously eroded by the cost of the long haul to Sydney or Melbourne.[80]

He added the proviso that cartage costs 'varied with distance from the major ports', which could add to transport charges in remote regions.[81]

---

76 *Sydney Morning Herald*, 19 July 1854, 2.
77 *Sydney Morning Herald*, 19 July 1854, 2. Anticipation of a government town opening at the junction of Nelligen Creek and the Clyde River was rising and the correspondent claimed some locals had already named the future town Glasgow. For the debate about a road to the Clyde or Broulee from Braidwood in the early 1850s, see *Sydney Morning Herald*, 12 April 1853, 2.
78 While inspecting the progress of the Clyde Road in September 1855, Surveyor-General Thomas Mitchell caught a chill and died from bronchial pneumonia. For Mitchell, see Cumpston, *Thomas Mitchell*, ch. 14. A detailed account of this road to Batemans Bay can be found at: 'Dray Trail to Prosperity', accessed 20 January 2023, www.southcoast.com.au/batemans-bay/draytrail/index.html.
79 Butlin, *Foundations*, 316; Blainey, *Tyranny*, 130–1.
80 Jackson, *Australian Economic Development*, 84.
81 Jackson, *Australian Economic Development*, 83.

Overall, Jackson concluded that 'high land transport costs were not a significant barrier to the development of wool exports in the first phase of pastoral growth' because wool realised sufficient profit per unit of weight to bear the high cost of cartage. He again added the proviso that 'transport costs presumably rose for stations on the pastoral frontier'.[82] The previous two chapters can be considered an illustration of Jackson's proviso on southern remoteness, in the absence of a navigable river to the coast.

A March 1841 editorial in the *Sydney Gazette and New South Wales Advertiser* clearly felt that cartage costs were a significant factor that reduced woolgrowers' profits:

> Let the woolgrowers in the remote districts calculate the expense of sending their bales to Sydney for sale or shipment—let them estimate the wear and tear of drays and teams—the loss of time and cost of rations—the waste of money in the shape of interest by the delay of sales, and the frequent relapse of a favorable market, before the slow ox can drag his heavy load along.[83]

However, the solution offered in the editorial was not the development of sea ports but 'the establishment of rail-roads' that 'would more than double the amount that now really finds its way onto their pockets'. The challenge that railroads posed to the southern ports will be addressed in Chapter 9.[84]

If costs were not a primary issue for southern woolgrowers and squatters, it needs to be explained why many were petitioning Governor Gipps to open roads to the coast. These woolgrowers were also a force behind private subscriptions for such projects, including vertically integrated capitalists such as Hughes & Hosking, Edward Lord, William Oldrey and later Benjamin Boyd. In support of Jackson, the evidence from the previous two chapters shows that prime movers behind these schemes to create a great southern coastal township, apart from the woolgrowers of the southern interior, included coastal landowners and auctioneers, who were puffing the speculative mania for 'manufactured' town subdivisions.

However, it is possible to remain agnostic with respect to this debate on the significance of land transport costs. Even if Jackson's argument that such costs represented only a small proportion of woolgrowers' overall outlays is

---

82 Jackson, *Australian Economic Development*, 83. Nicholas Brown makes the additional point that the transportation of *perishable* goods was risky and expensive. See Brown, *A History*, 19.
83 *Sydney Gazette and New South Wales Advertiser*, 18 March 1841, 2.
84 *Sydney Gazette and New South Wales Advertiser*, 18 March 1841, 2; 17 April 1841, 2.

accepted, it is still possible that many southern woolgrowers considered their remoteness along with associated land haulage as a cost to be addressed and they therefore acted accordingly, avidly supported by coastal landowners and auctioneers. For the purpose of this chapter, it is sufficient to note that those promoting the various schemes for a southern port around 1841 framed land-transportation costs as a problem. This perception is enough to account for the reality of the southern-port schemes, if not their realisation.[85]

---

85 This argument corresponds with the Thomas Theorem: 'If people define situations as real, they are real in their consequences.' See Merton, *Social Theory*, 421.

5

Clint the engraver and his survey of St Vincent

> O'er the far-off plain we'll drag the chain,
> And mark the settler's way –
> Theodolite-tum, theodolite-ti, theodolite-too-ral-ay.[1]

To return to first question posed in the conclusion to Chapter 3, Raphael Clint (see Figure 11) has been introduced as the person who jointly purchased the title of Hughes & Hosking's block at Long Beach in February 1841, only eight months after the government released the land. However, he sold the land back to Hughes & Hosking in November 1841. According to auctioneer Stubbs, most of the subdivided lots in the 'Great Southern Township of St Vincent' had been sold at auction by the time Clint took possession of the land title in February. The reason Clint bought and held the title for such a short period remains a matter to be determined.

Clint was also the lithographer who produced the plan for St Vincent that accompanied the sales campaign of April 1841 (see Figure 12). His name also appeared on the lithographic plan for the competing scheme to sell town allotments in June 1841 at South Huskisson, Jervis Bay. Another role that Clint performed during this period involved acting as an agent for Edward Lord's trustees. As Lord's Stubley Park property came onto the market (both the 40 farm allotments and the 27 sections reserved for the extension of the town), Clint was mentioned by Stubbs as the contact for further information about the property.

---

1   Anon., 'The Old Survey', in Paterson, *Old Bush Songs*.

Figure 11. Raphael Clint, late 1820s.
Drawing by George Clint, 'Portrait of His Son Raphael Clint', British Museum, no. 1913,0528.13.

Clint's circumstances, therefore, merit further attention. More broadly, his biography reveals how the depression of the 1840s impacted on an entrepreneurial artist and surveyor who served the colonial real estate industry by transforming 'wasteland' into alluring European visions.

Clint before St Vincent

Born in Hereford, England, in 1797, Raphael Clint was the second son of George Clint, an English artist known for his theatrical paintings, among other genres.[2] Raphael served a five-year apprenticeship (1813–18) with the engraver Thomas Warner on Tottenham Court Road, London, before working as a seal engraver in London and Glasgow. He began exhibiting intaglios at the Royal Academy in London from 1817 and in the 1820s won a Royal Society Gold Medal in engraving as well as one in mechanics involving a nautical invention for a 'balanced or swinging mast'.

Raphael arrived in Western Australia in August 1829 at the age of 32 and was soon employed as a surveyor's clerk. In 1831, as an assistant surveyor, he produced a map of the upper reaches of the Swan River before leading an expedition from King George Sound towards the Porrong-u-rup Hills with four soldiers and two Indigenous guides, recording many local Noongar placenames in his notebooks. In 1832 he was tasked with initiating a plan to lay out the settlement of Frederickstown (later named Albany).[3]

His wife, Mary Ann, arrived from England in 1831 and, after Clint's salary was reduced, the couple moved to Van Diemen's Land, arriving there on 20 August 1832 aboard the sloop *Mary Ann*.[4] A month later, the island's

---

2   George Clint's obituary in the *Art Journal* (1 January 1854, 212–13) describes how he experienced periods as a struggling artist. His wife died a fortnight after giving birth to their ninth child, leading to a period of 'frightful family privations'. He subsequently established the Artists Benevolent and Annuity Fund. The sculpture on a plinth in the background of the portrait of Raphael Clint in Figure 11 bears a resemblance to George Clint (see the self-portrait in London's National Portrait Gallery). See also Bryan, *Bryan's Dictionary*, 303. Clint is holding an engraving instrument.
3   'Swan River', Sheet 8, Woodbridge and Helena River, by Raphael Clint and George Smythe, 1831, State Records Office of Western Australia, AU WA S234-cons3844 012. For a detailed account of the 1831 expedition, see 'Early Records of Exploration', *Inquirer and Commercial News* (Perth), 21 October 1898, 10; *Albany Advertiser*, 22 March 1930, 2; Reynolds, Gillies and Arnold, 'Restoring'. Diary extracts from Clint's expeditions to the Stirling Ranges and Wilson Inlet have been published in Shoobert, *Western Australian*, 292–7. A copy of Clint's Albany map can be found at Government of Western Australia, Heritage Council, 'Detail of Clint's Survey of Albany and Environs', 1834.
4   *Colonist and Van Diemen's Land Commercial and Agricultural Advertiser*, 24 August 1832, 2. Raphael and Mary Ann (nee Chapple) married on 18 December 1825 at St Martin-in-the-Fields, London. In the General Muster Book of January 1830, Clint is listed as 'single'. See Watson, *Historical Records*, series 3, vol. 6, 628.

surveyor-general, George Frankland, proposed to the colonial secretary that Clint be employed as an assistant surveyor to help reorganise the Survey Office's collection of inconsistent cadastral maps. Frankland was inspired by the Great Trigonometrical Survey of India as well as by Thomas Mitchell's survey of New South Wales, and Clint was employed on this trigonometrical project.[5]

By Boxing Day 1833, Clint was sitting in a wet tent at Muddy Plains on the South Arm Peninsula establishing the survey baseline.[6] Many Vandemonians, including Governor Arthur, opposed the project, with the *Colonial Times* complaining of the 'ridiculous trigonometrical survey which has been on hand for the last twelve months, without producing one last line on paper'. Frankland himself grumbled that Clint had accomplished 'little more than select and clear a base'.[7] In August 1833, James Sprent was engaged to lead the survey and the *Austral-Asiatic Review* later reported that Mr Clint had been dismissed from the 'trigonometrical humbug'.[8]

The Survey Department then called Clint to Black Snake to superintend the convict-built Bridgewater Causeway,[9] before he struck out as a private surveyor in May 1834 based in Murray Street, Hobart. Shortly after, he advertised that he was intending 'to spend a portion of time during the winter months' undertaking seal engraving. This was the first time since his emigration from England that he had had the opportunity to pursue his artistic passion for engraving.[10]

---

5   Drown, 'An Apparatus', 185. There is no evidence that Clint ever officially qualified as a surveyor. However, this was not unusual in the first half of the nineteenth century. See Moyal, 'Surveyors'.
6   Wegman, 'Traces', 1; Murphy, 'James Sprent', 6; Roberts-Thomson, 'The Search', 75; Toms and Plunkett, 'Crown Land', 78.
7   Drown, 'An Apparatus', 36, 168, 174; *Colonial Times*, 1 October 1833, 2; Murphy, 'James Sprent', 6.
8   *Austral-Asiatic Review*, 20 August 1834, 2; *True Colonist Van Diemen's Land Political Dispatch and Agricultural and Commercial Advertiser*, 8 April 1836, 112. According to G.H. Stancombe, Sprent 'distinguished himself' on the survey, but 'most of the earlier men would not measure up to present standards'. See Stancombe, 'The Early', 14.
9   At the time, this was the largest civil engineering project undertaken in any Australian colony. Cooper, 'Bridgewater Bridge', v; *Tasmanian*, 23 May 1843, 1; *Colonist and Van Diemen's Land Commercial and Agricultural Advertiser*, 24 June 1834, 1; *Colonial Times*, 19 August 1834, 3. A premature announcement by Clint that the causeway was ready for use had to be revoked. See *Austral-Asiatic Review*, 1 October 1833, 3.
10 *Hobart Town Courier*, 6 June 1834, 3. He listed his prices for seal engraving in the *Tasmanian*, 1 August 1834, 8. Another seal engraver, Mr Barclay, worked on Elizabeth Street.

5. CLINT THE ENGRAVER AND HIS SURVEY OF ST VINCENT

By mid-January 1835, Raphael and Mary Ann had relocated to Sydney,[11] where Raphael announced in the press that he had 'just arrived in the colony' and was seeking patronage for his artistic talents, including seal, copperplate, stone, gem and armorial bookplate engraving.[12] He did not initially advertise his surveying services, suggesting that he hoped he could survive on his preferred engraving skills in the larger Sydney market.

One mischievous Hobart editor did refer to 'friend Raphael, seal engraver, who is now surveying farms in Sydney by astronomy'.[13] However, his only engagement with this field was to advertise later in the year his manuscript on surveying techniques entitled *A Synopsis of the Mathematics Requisite to the Prosecution of Internal Discovery*. No copy of this book exists, apart from a press announcement Clint wrote that purported to describe an expedition to South Australia 'through a hostile and inhospitable country, and to the most ordinary capacity of persons composing such expedition'.[14]

This sketch of a manuscript was itself the plan of a journey. He had written to the South Australian commissioners on 27 March 1835 offering to deliver livestock, horses, sheepdogs and labourers overland to the new colony from NSW, surveying the land he traversed and presenting the authorities with maps and journals. For this he would charge £10,000.[15] The authorities decided not to pursue the offer. He renewed this offer to the South Australian commissioners in 1837 to no avail.[16]

---

11   Initially, the couple was listed as bound for Swan River aboard the *Eagle* on 9 December (*Hobart Town Courier*, 12 December 1834, 3). However, on 10 December, Mrs Clint sailed from Hobart to Sydney aboard the *Eagle*, arriving on 15 December (*Sydney Herald*, 18 December 1834, 2). On 5 January, Mr Clint set sail to join her on the *Elizabeth* from Launceston (*Launceston Advertiser*, 8 January 1835, 2), arriving at Sydney on 15 January. They initially stayed at 34 Castlereigh Street before moving to 19 King Street East. Later in the year they moved to Bridge House, 15 Bridge Street.
12   *Sydney Times*, 20 January 1835, 3; *Sydney Herald*, 23 July 1835, 1.
13   *True Colonist Van Diemen's Land Political Dispatch and Agricultural and Commercial Advertiser*, 8 January 1836, 6.
14   In the *Colonist* (19 and 26 November 1835; 17 December 1835, 8), Clint announced this book was ready for press and would soon be available for 7s. in Sydney, Cape Town and London. Clint would regularly test the market and seek subscriptions for projects yet to be undertaken.
15   The *Sydney Monitor* (22 July 1835, 3) announced that: 'The South Australian Colony will, we understand, be taken possession of immediately. Mr. Clint, the surveyor, of King-street, has received instructions from the secretary, desiring him to proceed thither immediately, for the purpose of meeting the first body of emigrants, who are expected to arrive there very shortly.' There is no evidence that such instructions were ever issued. Clint's offer is mentioned in an early history of South Australia by Edwin Hodder. See Hodder, *A History*, ch. 5.
16   *South Australian Gazette and Colonial Register*, 8 July 1837, 4; *Australian*, 12 September 1837, 6. Clint's letter is reproduced in full, including his demands and conditions.

The venture had its origins in late 1834 when Thomas Bannister and Clint proposed to the Legislative Council of Western Australia a groundbreaking expedition to bring livestock overland from Sydney to Perth.[17] They requested 24 men, land grants and £10,000. The offer was graciously declined. In 1836 Clint renewed his offer to the Western Australian Agricultural Society, who responded that they were 'apprehensive, indeed fearful, that the risk attending his proposed plan renders it impracticable'.[18]

These proposed South Australian overland ventures were possibly a substitute for Clint 'not finding a sufficiency of employment in the elegant and useful Art of seal engraving to which he has confined his practice in New South Wales'. As a result, in May 1836, Clint announced that he intended to move 'homeward' with the 'first genial zephyrs of the spring'. He thanked the 'few choice spirits' who had extended their 'efficient support' and warned the procrastinators to avail themselves of his services before it was too late.[19]

Clint's plans to 'proceed to a better country' were put on hold, and his fortunes turned for the better, after he returned to his surveying experience, engaging in lithography and cadastral mapping. The value of land was increasing and these maps were particularly valuable to real estate agents soliciting interest on the margins of the limits of location.[20] As Ben Huf noted: 'Cadastral maps used by surveyors and auctioneers together with innovations in land conveyancing transformed colonial "frontiers into assets".' Their ordered street grids offered visual and tangible assurance to buyers that 'there' resembled 'here' during a period when much of the available land remained largely terra incognita in the minds of most colonists.[21] Maps became Clint's staple.

---

17 *Perth Gazette and Western Australian Journal*, 27 December 1834, 415. The scheme was described as 'chimerical' by Frederick Chidley Irwin (see Irwin, *The State*). Both Bannister and Clint worked with Western Australian exploration parties in the early 1830s and arrived in Van Diemen's Land around the same time, where Bannister was acting high sheriff until he resigned in 1836. Both men received reduced pay due to their lack of status and qualification (see Elbourne, 'The Bannisters', 63–5).
18 *Perth Gazette and Western Australian Journal*, 8 February 1837, 844–5. An earlier correspondent felt that Clint 'entertains too sanguine a view of this projected scheme, which he considers is merely reviving the old practice of the Arabians, and other people, of migratory, pastoral habits. He makes no allowance for casualties; all with him must be attended with success, because he wills it so.' See *Perth Gazette and Western Australian Journal*, 26 November 1836, 805.
19 *Sydney Gazette and New South Wales Advertiser*, 21 May 1836, 1; *Colonist*, 2 June 1836, 8.
20 When announcing his intention to produce a chart of Port Essington in northern Australia, Clint reminded readers that the 'importance in a commercial view of this Settlement, renders a knowledge of this location interesting to mercantile men' (*Australian*, 10 August 1838, 3). In 1838, he produced an engraving of the chart of the Arafura Sea compiled by G.W. Earl.
21 Huf, 'The Capitalist', 427. See also Alexander, 'Cartography'; Carter, *The Road*, 218.

In 1836 Clint produced one of the first maps of Port Phillip, copies of which he sold at 5s., and later offered a cadastral map of Port Phillip that exhibited sections to be auctioned at Sydney on 12 September 1838. He also engraved and printed a copy of a 'plan of the town of Adelaide, South Australia' in 1837 and one of the Hunter River district in 1838.[22] By 1837, he had established a map shop on George Street opposite the premises of the Bank of Australasia. On this broad basis, his business was thriving in synchrony with the prevailing economic conditions.

'Clint the engraver' became well known in the town.[23] The upwardly mobile also coveted his heraldic designs as a conspicuous mark of their new social status. The Reverend John Dunmore Lang's paper the *Colonist* complained that 'mushroom aristocrats' were sprouting around Sydney, bearing heraldic designs

> whose coats of arms have been 'found' by Mr. Clint, and are to be seen any day and every day emblazoned on ill appointed equipages, driven by convict coachmen, dressed in dirty drab liveries.[24]

In addition, Clint began producing bronze engraved 'logarithmic sun dials for every ten miles of the colony', anticipating that there was a market for such timekeeping devices on remote properties.[25] He was also a principal agitator to establish the Mutual Insurance Company after a fire at his own King Street premises in July 1835 and a series of damaging fires in George Street, including the destruction of the Royal Hotel in 1840.[26]

---

22 In 1838, Clint produced a copperplate engraving of the township of Adelaide for the South Australian colonisation commissioners (*Sydney Monitor*, 20 June 1838, 2). See also *Cornwall Chronicle*, 5 November 1836, 2. He also reputedly produced the first map of Melbourne's streets.
23 In 1838, Clint boasted that 'almost every Gentleman in the Colony' had 'actual experience' of his 'talent and honourable conduct' (*Commercial Journal and Advertiser*, 2 May 1838, 3). He described his circumstances to a client in 1839, who recorded her visit in her diary: 'Went to Clint's—saw him—said he had been 3 years in VDL—was in Survey Office then set up engraving, but had no business & lost money—came here & succeeds well.' See Franklin, *This Errant*, 228–9. In July 1839, to meet demand, Clint employed John Carmichael, 'by whose extra assistance he hopes to be able to bring up the arrears of work, for which gentlemen have waited so patiently' (*Sydney Monitor*, 12 July 1839, 1; see also Eaton, 'John Black Carmichael'; Neville, 'Printmakers', 15). J.B.M. (*Reminiscences*, 41) recalled that Sydney at the time was represented in the fine arts by 'Clint, the talented seal engraver, Carmichael, the engraver and sketcher, Rhodius the crayon portraitist and Read the water-colour artist'.
24 *Colonist*, 16 March 1839, 4; 11 August 1838, 3.
25 *Colonist*, 26 January 1837. Clint also sold a range of novel goods, such as Dobereiner's 'hydro-pneuma platinum lamp' (*Sydney Herald*, 15 February 1838, 1). The curious could view two seals 'bearing the likeness of himself and Mrs Clint' (*Australian*, 2 March 1838, 3).
26 See *Colonist*, 29 April 1840, 2; *Sydney Herald*, 30 March 1840, 2; 6 April 1840, 2. However, by the end of April, Clint was in dispute with the director of the company over procedural issues, in particular over the appointment of an actuary for the company (see *Sydney Gazette and New South Wales Advertiser*, 30 April 1840, 2; *Colonist*, 2 May 1840, 5). The fires on George Street also included a drapery in 1838 and the Theatre Royal (Old Theatre) in 1840. On the fire at Clint's premises, see *Sydney Monitor*, 22 July 1835, 3.

Clint was not immune from controversy. Had he succeeded in his bold scheme to bring stock overland from Sydney to Perth, he would have received a hostile reception from at least two Perth creditors with whom he had failed to settle before leaving for Van Diemen's Land. Through a solicitor, these creditors had sought a court order to seize Clint's property. The solicitor, Mr George F. Stone, had become the sheriff of the colony by the time Clint revived his planned expedition in 1836.[27]

While residing in Van Diemen's Land, Clint feuded with a newspaper over an allegation that he used a government boat and three convicts at Bridgewater for his personal use. Despite strenuously defending his conduct on the grounds of precedence, on 21 September 1833, Clint was fined £26 plus costs for nine breaches of the *Harbouring Act* for 'employing various men at the Bridgewater Chain Gang'.[28]

He left his supervisory position at Bridgewater in late April 1834 in murky circumstances.[29] Press rumours circulated concerning mutual accusations between himself and 'one or two men employed under him'.[30] Without specifying the charge, the press hinted that action would soon be taken in the case, and, on 25 April, it was announced that 'Lieutenant Wrixon, of the 21st is appointed Superintending Magistrate at Bridgewater, Mr. Clint who has had charge of that important work for some time, having "resigned"'.[31]

A few months later, in August 1834, Clint penned a letter to the *Colonial Times* drawing attention to the incompetency of certain colonial administrators.[32] This letter unleashed a cascade of poisonous correspondence. A letter in the *Tasmanian* from 'Scrutator'—a defender of one of the administrators whom Clint had attacked—levelled a range of scurrilous charges associated with Clint's time at Bridgewater, including hints of drunkenness, 'winging' tame

---

27   *Perth Gazette and Western Australian Journal*, 12 January 1833, 5; 13 April 1833, 60; May 1833, 76. Stone eventually became attorney-general.
28   *Colonial Times*, 24 September 1833, 3; 1 October 1833, 2. Clint accused the paper of 'malicious libel', but the paper stood its ground. See *Tasmanian*, 27 September 1833, 6; *Austral-Asiatic Review*, 24 September 1833, 3.
29   Towards the end of his tenure at Bridgewater, Clint had 'pronounced the mud unfathomable and the work unfinishable'. See *Morning Star and Commercial Advertiser*, 26 May 1835, 2.
30   *Colonial Times*, 22 April 1834, 6; *Trumpeter General*, 25 April 1834, 2.
31   *Tasmanian*, 25 April 1834, 7.
32   *Colonial Times*, 26 August 1834, 7. Worms and Baynton-Williams ('Raphael Clint') also speculate that his removal from his government position might have been a result of this letter criticising the administration. However, this August letter came four months after his 'resignation', and by May he was declaring himself 'late of Bridgewater and the Surveying Departments of this and the Sister Colony'. See Clint's advertisement dated 9 May in the *Tasmanian*, 23 May 1843, 1.

pigeons and misusing government funds to build a pew for his personal use that did not fit through the doorway of the local church. Another anecdote involved an attempt by Clint to convince authorities to 'transmogrify' the infamous mudbank at the Bridgewater Causeway into a meadow. Scrutator claimed that this scheme was abandoned because the 'Hippopotamus had not yet been introduced into the Island, the only animal … which could live and thrive upon such a meadow'.[33] Yet another tale involving alcohol seemed to allude to the April incident that led to his 'resignation'.[34] Clint responded with a letter to the editor of the *Colonial Times* that could only be described as oblique.[35]

The *Tasmanian* was the medium used by A. Waterman to question Clint's scientific and engineering credentials. He described an unreliable, directionless horseshoe punt that Clint had built at Kangaroo Point as an example of 'Clintbungloon'. Clint used the *Colonial Times* to respond, pointing to his Royal Society medal for nautical innovation, and lamenting that most people did not appreciate the role played by experimentation in improving the world:

> There is always a difficulty to encounter in every new undertaking, which is to eradicate the opposition of ignorant classes—such as watermen, have always been, and still are—or, indeed, of every class of labourers … and when that is done by experiment, they are the first to say, 'who would have thought it?'[36]

---

33   *Tasmanian*, 5 September 1834, 6.
34   According to Worms and Baynton-Williams ('Raphael Clint'), a scandal erupted in which Clint's wife was alleged to have been selling sly grog to soldiers, and they speculate that this incident resulted in the government terminating his employment. However, this allegation is not sourced. The same unsourced claim is made in Design and Art Australia Online, 'Raphael Clint'. See also Neville, 'Printmakers', 196; Gray, 'Clint, Raphael (1797–1849)'. The accusation that Raphael Clint himself was a sly grog seller re-emerged in a later court case brought by Clint against one of his employees in Sydney. The allegation was furiously objected to by Clint, leading to both parties being warned by the officiating judge to behave themselves (*Sydney Herald*, 14 September 1840, 3). His misuse of the convict gang in October 1833 involved bringing 'a cask of wine and other little commodities' from Hobart to Bridgewater. This could have been the source of the rumour of sly grog selling.
35   *Tasmanian*, 5 September 1834, 6. For Clint's response, see *Colonial Times*, 9 September 1834, 5. 'Scrutator' published another reply (*Tasmanian*, 12 September 1834, 7) accusing Clint of failing to answer his charges and teasing him for his bombast (as well as obliquely noting his 'improvements' in the 'price and distribution of rum and forage').
36   A. Waterman wrote to the *Tasmanian* on 12 September 1834. See *Tasmanian*, 12 September 1834, 4, 7. Clint's response appeared in *Colonial Times*, 30 September 1834, 6. Ironically, contrary to Clint's elitist statement about the labouring classes on 30 September, his original complaint about colonial administration on 26 August expressed a radical call for democratic reform. After Clint left the island, his horseshoe punt was bought by a Mr Murdoch who found that it 'answers very well' (*Hobart Town Courier*, 21 October 1836, 2). Who would have thought it?

However, an editorial in the same issue of the *Tasmanian* as A. Waterman's letter pointed to the admirable progress that had been accomplished at Bridgewater since Clint's departure.[37]

The letters became uglier and more sarcastic. 'Tom Tough' mocked Clint's 'balderdash and hyperbole':

> I love to copy Raphael's euphonious style of his information, and, above all, the classical purity and elegance of his scriptural diction ... Of all egregious geese, who dare to pretend to literary notoriety, commend me to Gander Clint.[38]

'Tripod' was equally cruel, caricaturing Clint's tone and summarising the previous correspondence in overblown praise for:

> Raphael the Saint, Raphael the rum, Raphael the punt-builder ... Friend Raphael F.R.S. of seal cutters, pulpit manufacturer of Bridgewater notoriety, and political economist of Van Diemen's Land ... Does the shoe pinch thee, fell destroyer of tame and timid pigeons.[39]

By this stage, Clint quite sensibly had stopped responding. Small islands can generate a strong sense of community, but, by the end of 1834, Van Diemen's Land must have seemed a very parochial, alienating and oppressive place to Raphael Clint.

In Sydney, Clint's name was often associated with libel and copyright cases. One of the earliest accusations came from his previous abode, where the *Hobart Town Courier* accused 'Mr Clint of Sydney, formerly of this place', of publishing the map of Port Phillip without the 'consent or acquiescence' of the surveyor Mr Wedge.[40] He was also accused by fellow lithographer, E.D. Barlow, of 'disgraceful conduct', deceptive advertising and breaching Barlow's exclusive patent for using zincography printing equipment.[41]

---

37 For a synopsis of the causeway's history, see *Morning Star and Commercial Advertiser*, 26 May 1835, 2. Under Wrixon, it opened in October 1836 (see *Launceston Advertiser*, 27 October 1836, 3).
38 *Tasmanian*, 10 October 1834, 7.
39 *Tasmanian*, 24 October 1834, 7. The contemporary term for such behaviour is 'trolling'.
40 *Hobart Town Courier*, 21 October 1836, 4.
41 *Commercial Journal and Advertiser*, 9 May 1838, 3; 29 September 1838, 1; 3 October 1838, 1. In 1837, Barlow had worked out of Clint's George Street shop, but by 1838 both men claimed to have purchased zincography printing equipment from the lithographer J.G. Austin. See Clint's advertisement in *Commercial Journal and Advertiser*, 2 May 1838, 3. Despite Austin's defence of Clint's right to use the equipment, Barlow warned that 'Raphael Clint cannot work Drawings or writings, not having the means or being acquainted with the Secrets of the said Art; and secondly, HE DARE NOT as the Patent ... belongs exclusively to me'. Clint also warned the public not to negotiate any bills drawn on him by Austin, as they would not be paid 'on very justifiable and legal grounds'. See *Sydney Monitor*, 25 June 1838, 3.

As noted in his Vandemonian period, Clint presented himself as a Renaissance man, a polymath, well versed in science, industry and the arts. His proposed overland South Australian expedition in 1836 was only one of many examples of how he advertised an impressive array of skills beyond most mortals. In March 1839, he ventured opinions on the issue of hydrography that caused a minor stir in the press. The *Colonist* was concerned about the capacity of a tunnel, known as 'Busby's bore', to feed water to Sydney in the midst of the drought.[42] It approached Clint and published his views, which happened to contradict those of Major Barney, who had reassured the public that the bore would be sufficient for the following 12 months. Clint then wrote a furious letter to the editor expressing his 'disgust' at the 'mass of twaddle and falsehood' reported under his name, and hinted at 'some base object' in blackening his name in the eyes of Major Barney. The paper defended its 'editorial authority', leaving the impression that Clint's 'intemperate' response was due to overstepping his limits of expertise.[43]

Clint faced ongoing frustration in finding and retaining assigned or bonded apprentices and regularly reported absconders.[44] In 1837, he penned a letter of complaint to the colonial secretary over the mis-assignment of skilled convict labour, which he felt could be better employed by himself.[45] In the same year, he offered a 'course of gratuitous instruction in the art of drawing to young gentlemen' in Maitland.[46] This effort to produce 'colonial bred surveyors' was prompted by his high labour turnover.

In April 1839, Clint took an employee, John Price, to court, alleging he was 'employing himself for his own benefit while under the said agreement'.[47] The charge was dismissed. Two months later, Clint returned to court, charging

---

42   Also known as 'the tunnel'. See Maclehose, *Picture*, 165–8.

43   *Colonist*, 30 March 1839, 2. For the original article, with Clint's hydrographic insights, see *Colonist*, 27 March 1839, 2.

44   One sour note in a review of Maclehose's book was that the illustrations were 'precious trash'; the reviewer lamented the scarcity of good engravers, noting that 'a most superior engraver' had absconded from the assigned service of Clint. See *Sydney Times*, 27 December 1837, 3. Mary Loungs and Ann Mellors had earlier absconded from Clint's service. See *NSW Government Gazette*, 22 June 1836, 474; 18 January 1837, 56. For an unnamed male found guilty of absenting himself from Clint's services on several occasions, see *Sydney Gazette and New South Wales Advertiser*, 14 July 1838, 2. The man's excuse was that Commissary Hayward used to converse with him in French and treat him to wine and biscuits. Hayward denied knowing him.

45   See Raphael Clint to colonial secretary, 28 July 1837, State Records Authority NSW, Colonial Secretary's Correspondence, 4/2372.4 - 37/6922. In 1836, Clint was assigned two male convicts off the ship *Moffatt*, an engraver and a copperplate printer, and in 1838 one lithographic printer. *NSW Government Gazette*, 26 October 1836, 830; 28 March 1838, 327.

46   *Colonist*, 30 May 1837, 3. This offer was readvertised in Sydney the following year, this time for draftsmen (*Colonist*, 19 May 1838, 3).

47   *Sydney Monitor and Commercial Advertiser*, 8 April 1839, 3. See also Clint's advertisement and reward for evidence leading to a conviction, *Sydney Monitor and Commercial Advertiser*, 29 March 1839, 3.

Henry Milson, a young man in his employment, with absconding. Once again, the case was dismissed when it was revealed that Clint was aware that the boy was not only underage but also a runaway apprentice from London.[48] In September 1840, he unsuccessfully took an employee named Charles Lilly to court over criminal damage.[49] At the end of the same month, Clint accused Price of 'harbouring' Lilly, whom he claimed 'was under engagement to serve him for three years'. The court again dismissed the case when it emerged that Clint had paid Lilly's wages to another person, remarking that he would 'not take Lilly into his employ upon any consideration'.[50]

The 'irascible' Clint[51] was then involved in an another 'pirating' case. On 1 January 1840, coloured versions of a map of Port Phillip were available for £1 3s., produced by a former draftsman from the Surveyor-General's Department, Mr William Henry Wells. It was described as a 'well-executed' map of Melbourne.[52] With more Port Phillip land sales scheduled for 5 February, accurate maps of the new town were a coveted commodity. Clint wrote to the press accusing Wells of 'public robbery' and proclaimed that he would pirate the map as compensation for previous losses.[53] He argued that the previous year he had offered the government's surveying department £1,000 for plans they held, but was refused. Wells subsequently came to Clint's shop offering the materials for 5 guineas, half of which Clint handed over upfront. Instead of supplying the map, Wells contracted with one of Clint's former employees, the aforementioned John Price, to engrave it.[54] Clint therefore

---

48 *Sydney Herald*, 24 May 1839, 3. The 'Court was much amused' by Clint's efforts to prosecute his case himself. Adding salt to the wound, Milson, after running away, entered the services of Mr Barlow. See *Sydney Gazette and New South Wales Advertiser*, 25 and 28 May 1939, 2.
49 *Sydney Gazette and New South Wales Advertiser*, 15 September 1840, 2: *Sydney Herald*, 14 September 1840, 3; *Sydney Monitor and Commercial Advertiser*, 14 September 1840, 2. The case was dismissed. In 1836, a servant in Clint's employ, Catherine Mahon, was also charged with stealing prints from the Clint household in Bridge Street (*Sydney Monitor and NSW Advertiser*, 13 July 1836, 2).
50 *Sydney Monitor and Commercial Advertiser*, 30 September 1840, 2.
51 The assessment is from the art historian, Roger Blackley. See Blackley, *Stray Leaves*, 11.
52 *Sydney Monitor and Commercial Advertiser*, 1 January 1840, 1; *Colonist*, 4 January 1840, 2. The latter paper added: 'We have seen a very complimentary epistle from Mr. Clint to Mr. Wells, threatening to pirate the map as soon as published: we hope Mr. C. would be ashamed of robbing any man of the legitimate profits of his labours.'
53 *Sydney Gazette and New South Wales Advertiser*, 9 January 1840, 2. Indeed, Clint had already advertised his version of the map for 5s. See *Sydney Gazette and New South Wales Advertiser*, 4 January 1840, 1.
54 Clint did not appear either aware or concerned that, in revealing this information, he was complicit in aiding and abetting the 'public robbery'. This incident was brought up in *Dent and Another v. Lyons* (see Chapter 3). W.H. Wells was the surveyor of the infamous Berkley Estate 'near' Gosford. See *Australasian Chronicle*, 11 March 1841, 2; *Omnibus and Sydney Spectator*, 20 November 1841, 62. In the March case of *Lyons v. Reynolds*, the chief justice committed Wells to 14 days in Sydney Jail for conducting himself 'very improperly in the witness box' and as an example to other witnesses to 'conduct themselves properly'.

announced that he had 'a right to pirate these works' and he would exercise this right 'even at a loss'. He acted on the principle that any work produced illegitimately or through dishonourable competition was prey to piracy. In the case of Mr Wells, Clint felt that he himself was 'the aggrieved party' and, therefore, he would 'republish everything he or any other man employs my runaway hired servant John Price to execute'.[55]

Both Wells and Price responded two days later, defending their character and conduct. Wells hinted that professional jealousy was Clint's motive, while Price pointed out that—far from being a runaway servant—a court had determined that Clint had no power over him. He hoped that clients would not be intimidated by Clint's bombast and argued that his own engravings were 'executed in a style of superiority quite unknown to Clint'.[56] Throughout the rest of the month, Wells issued threats to Clint. He accused Clint of publicly and seriously calumniating him, and trusted that 'the public will suspend their judgement of my character until a jury have decided whether I deserve the reproaches cast upon me by Clint'.[57]

These threats closed this public dispute between Clint and Wells, but Clint and Price had one more public round, in September 1840. It began with a letter Clint penned on 14 September (and published on 17 September), which is worth reproducing in full as it provides the clearest insight into how Clint viewed the world in which he dwelt, as well as the elevated social and moral position he felt he occupied:

> Immigration of Mechanics.
>
> To the Editor of The Colonist,
>
> SIR,– I was the first to establish in this Colony, such a business, as I now carry on with success under great public patronage.
>
> Previous to my arrival the Art I practise were carried on, with some exceptions, by a class with which I did not choose to associate.
>
> In consequence of holding myself aloof from this class, a powerful confederacy (if not of moral character) of wealth has endeavoured to crush me in my business.
>
> This confederacy seduces all the workmen I import at any wages.

---

55 *Sydney Gazette and New South Wales Advertiser*, 9 January 1840, 2.
56 *Australian*, 11 and 14 January 1840, 3.
57 See, for instance, *Colonist*, 22 January 1840, 4.

I find that workmen will not come out sufficient for the increasing business of the Colony, except I guarantee for a long period; and when they arrive, after having received an advance at home, to carry them from indigence to affluence, they have not the honesty to ask for a discharge, which I should be most happy to give, on the contrary, under seduction, they commence a series of unmanly annoyances and destruction of my property, with the intent of betraying me over some overt act, under which they may have a claim upon me for damages. When I seek the protection of the law in my own defence, the confederacy employ their worthy and talented organ to defend them, and the uprightness and integrity of my conduct attempted to be maligned and my character traduced. My witnesses are made drunk and the witnesses for the defence remain cautiously sober. The simple ease which requires for other persons only a few minutes to adjudge, is by legal chicanery, made to occupy as many hours, with the hope of tiring the Bench, and I generally come off the vanquished party, not, however, without knowing and feeling that the Bench has done its conscientious duty to the evidence, which this confederacy had the power to suppress, and which I had not, from the drunkenness and intimidation of my witnesses, the power to produce.

Meantime my property is destroyed, and my character maligned, and for what? because I will not submit to be hail-fellow-well-met with a class of persons among whom I cannot associate, and with whom, if I did associate, I should lose the respect of that portion of the public in which it is my desire to be held in the estimation I enjoy.

My principles in engaging workmen are to give them a 'carte blanche' to fill up their wages and the period of services, according to their own estimate of their abilities, and to make them an advance to pay their passage. I always write to tell them to make the period as short as they please; and I always find them wishing to bind me for a long period under their fears of leaving home, and shortly after arrival I find that instead of honourably asking for their discharge, which I publicly profess I should be willing to give, that they commence a series of infamous conduct, at not openly asking for or accepting such discharge, but holding me to my agreements while they openly violated theirs.[58]

---

58   In the Milson case above, Clint agreed 'to find him in board and lodgings for three years, at £20 for the first year, £30 for the second and £40 for the third'. The court found it non-binding because Milson was underage. The court also noted Milson's vulnerable negotiating position, given that Clint was aware that Milson was a runaway from Bath, England (*Sydney Gazette and New South Wales Advertiser*, 25 May 1939, 2). In Clint's mind, three examples of the 'confederacy' that 'seduced' his workmen were Lilly's move to work with Price, Milson moving to Barlow and the absconded worker mentioned in the *Colonist*'s review of Maclehose.

It is this unmanly conduct alone which compels me to resort to legal remedies, when I find 'I have caught a Tartar who will not let me escape from his clutches.'

I have been long enough in the world, and in business to know and to despise the public reports of a case in the press, to which, in this colony in particular, the most abandoned persons can find ready access. I shall not therefore attempt a collision in which the public can feel no interest; but, I will conclude with a direct challenge to any man in New South Wales to produce an instance in which I have done him wrong.

R. CLINT.

Engraver and Lithographer, George-street, Sydney, opposite the Bank of Australasia.[59]

John Price took it upon himself to defend the fraternity of printers and lithographers from Clint's broad charges, as well as presenting a number of instances in which Clint had done employees wrong. Price gave the impression that Clint found it impossible to maintain personal relationships without them sinking into acrimony. This showed him in a far less generous light than he presented himself.[60]

Clint had previously raised showing disrespect towards one's competitors to an advertising principle. Two years before, he had distinguished himself from other engravers by claiming to be

> beyond all competition in any of the SHAM AND QUACKERY SHOPS in town, where the public is victimized by the unblushing effrontery of men, who, heretofore bred to common labour, seek to gull their customers, by pretending to have suddenly—miraculously—and by inspiration—without education—become Engravers.[61]

Despite his acrimonious relations with fellow craftsmen and artists, Clint was able to prosper at a time when demand for land remained strong. By 1840, he had struck a rich vein of employment for his talents in the production of lithographic plans for the sale of allotments.[62]

---

59   *Colonist*, 17 September 1840, 3.
60   *Commercial Journal and Advertiser*, 23 September 1840, 3.
61   *Sydney Monitor*, 30 July 1838, 3; 31 December 1838, 4.
62   Between 1840 and 1843, Clint produced plans, mostly for Thomas Stubbs, but also for other auctioneers featured in these chapters, including Lyons, Blackman, and Foss and Lloyd, as well as Laban White and W.H. Chapman (the city auctioneer until his resignation in 1845). A sizeable number of these plans are held at the NLA.

His familiarity with the inflating land market was heightened through his professional connections with Thomas Stubbs's Auction Mart and his role selling Hughes & Hosking's Melbourne suburban lots. This might have prompted his uncharacteristic foray into landholding, purchasing—along with J.J. Peacock—the 320 acres in late 1840 at Long Beach. They received their land title in February 1841.[63]

It is also possible that, in a heady moment after the satisfying January sales of the township lots at St Vincent, Clint offered to subdivide and draw up plans for Edward Lord's land, using his previous experiences as a surveyor, and then acting as an agent in the sales campaign. Thomas Stubbs's April 1841 advertisement of Lord's allotments suggests that the decision to subdivide the land into 'suburban farms' and an 'extension of the town' was taken after the sales of the Hughes & Hosking/Clint lots 'at the request of purchasers of allotments at St Vincent' (see Chapter 3). The possibility of recouping some of Lord's debts would have appealed to Lord's trustees.

Clint at St Vincent

On 2 February 1841, four days before he received the transfer of the 320-acre title for Long Beach, Clint set sail for Batemans Bay. The *Australasian Chronicle* on 4 February included the following item in its list of departed outward coasters: 'The *Star* for Bateman's Bay, with sundries—passengers, Messrs. Clint, Thomas, Hoape, and Malton.'[64] It is likely that the aim of Clint's voyage was not simply to view his new property, but also to consider a range of other opportunities.

---

63 There is a Western Australian qualification. While in Western Australia in the late 1820s to early 1830s, Clint had been granted a town allotment in Fremantle, but it was resumed by the government in 1839 after the 'requisite improvements had not been effected' (*Perth Gazette and Western Australian Journal*, 3 July 1939, 108). Further, as noted earlier, along with Thomas Bannister, Clint had asked for land grants as part of the deal involving the delivery of livestock overland to Western Australia. He also intermittently acted as a land agent. For instance, he acted as a sales agent for a property at York, Western Australia, citing his surveying past by labelling himself 'late surveyor of the Swan' (*Sydney Times*, 20 August 1836, 3). In 1838 he was an agent for the allotments of Captain Brown's Five Dock Farm (*Sydney Monitor*, 25 April 1838, 4).

64 There is a possibility that 'Malton' was a misspelling for 'Mallon', John Mallon being the person who purchased a publican's licence at St Vincent in June 1841 (see Chapter 3). Thomas was possibly William Thomas, mentioned alongside Mallon in Chapter 3.

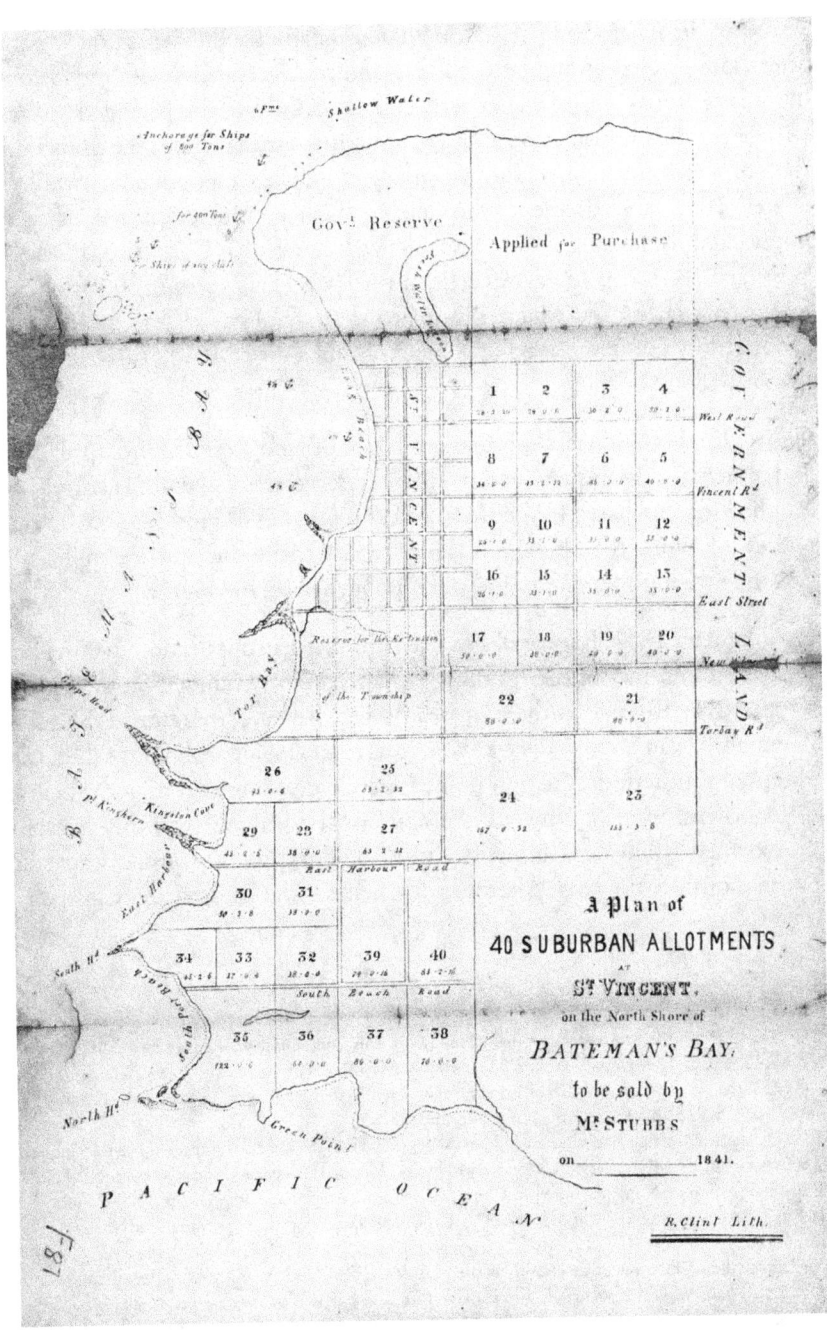

Figure 12. Lithographic map of the township of St Vincent, 1841.
'A Plan of 40 Suburban Allotments at St Vincent [Cartographic Material] on the North Shore of Bateman's Bay ... 1841, R. Clint, Lith.', NLA, digitised item, MAP F 87 copy, catalogue.nla.gov.au/Record/1105999.

As noted in Chapter 3, it is clear that someone subdivided Stubley Park after Lord's failed attempt to sell the land in December 1840 and before Thomas Stubbs's April 1841 advertisements. Someone also provided Stubbs with additional information about the quality of the land and the timber on the property. This makes Clint the likely 'purchaser' mentioned in Stubbs's March 1841 advertisement who 'lately returned from examinations' and 'reported most favourably'.[65] The evidence suggests that Clint used this early February 1841 trip to examine his property and its surrounds, including Lord's property, and that this expedition resulted in the lithograph produced by Clint and used by Thomas Stubbs to sell Lord's suburban lots in April 1841.[66]

Clint's lithographic plan also marks a block of land west of Lord's property and north of the Square Head village reserve on Cullendulla Creek as 'Applied for Purchase'. Given that Lord and Hughes & Hosking were in the process of selling their blocks, it is more likely that Clint was the 'applicant' and this was another reason for, or consequence of, his voyage.[67]

On 9 January 1841, Raphael Clint had submitted an application to purchase 1,280 acres on the southern side of Batemans Bay, 'bounded on the North by the Clyde River—on the East by a Village Reserve' (the future village of Bateman).[68] On a map, the site would have looked appealing to Clint as a potential southern destination point for a Clyde Mountain dray road close to his township of St Vincent. An additional advantage was that Edward Lord owned 1,030 acres immediately north of his property on the other side of the mouth of the river. After his experience at the Bridgewater Causeway,

---

65 The *Star* returned to Sydney from Batemans Bay carrying ballast on 17 February. There was no record of the passengers (*Sydney Herald*, 25 February 1841, 2). According to the *Sydney Herald* (3 March 1841, 2), the *Star* was the only recorded ship that visited Batemans Bay in February 1841, making it likely that Clint left Batemans Bay on the *Star* on January 16.
66 Previous maps that had charted Batemans Bay included Lieutenant Johnston's 1821 sketch and Thomas Florance's 1828 survey. There was also Thomas Mitchell's 1834 map of the 19 counties of NSW and Dixon's map of NSW. As noted in Chapter 2, James Larmer had surveyed the 320-acre property at Long Beach in June 1839 and produced a Crown plan prior to the government advertisement of August 1839.
67 If so, then Clint was unsuccessful, as the block remained Crown land until it was subdivided in the 1880s, parts of which were sold to Honora Ryan and her two youngest sons, Michael and John. Charles Henry Higgins Jr—who married Honora's daughter, Mary Ann Ryan—purchased the northern section of the village reserve in March 1913, after holding it as a special lease since 1898 (Special Lease No. 1918). See *NSW Government Gazette*, 25 March 1899, 2476–7.
68 State Records Authority NSW, Colonial Secretary's Letters, INX-14-17710, item 2/7827, reel no. 1111.

5. CLINT THE ENGRAVER AND HIS SURVEY OF ST VINCENT

Clint would have felt confident he could find a means to convey goods across the river to St Vincent, or build a wharf on the southern side. If the surveyor-general allowed Clint's application, then Clint and Lord together would have monopolised all private land east of Waterfall Creek on the Clyde River to the Pacific Ocean. This would have left the southern shores of Batemans Bay as the only remaining Crown land.

The response from the deputy surveyor-general to Clint's request for the land on the southern side of the bay suggests that, at this time, the government had not given much consideration to Batemans Bay as a port, while keeping its options open for the future:

> I think it advisable to dispose of the land hereabouts in small portions … [T]he area comprized within applicant's description far exceeds 1200—I therefore recommend that the applicant confine the quantity to portions of 100 acres, when of course it will be entertained. I await His Excellency's instructions on the subject. There is a reserve for a town here but it is small. If his Excellency the Governor approves of the sale, the Surveyor could report if the reserve is sufficiently extensive and in the proper plan.
>
> Decision: The land cannot be sold as one block. The suggestions of the Deputy Surveyor Genrl may be acted on.[69]

Clint's application was likely another reason for Clint's visit to Batemans Bay in early February 1841. After visiting the 1,280 acres, he might have been disappointed by the quality of the mangrove-flanked land. Cullendulla Creek might have looked like a more promising option. Yet, although there is no record of Clint reapplying, on 4 May, the governor announced that he had approved an application for a 640-acre portion of land 'near the mouth of the Clyde River, Bateman's Bay' that would, 'after measurement, be put up to sale at an early date'. This portion could have been either a smaller portion of Clint's south-side application or the 'applied-to-purchase' land beside Cullendulla Creek identified on Clint's lithograph. The lack of interest in Lord's auction might have ultimately persuaded Clint not to

---

69 The decision was released on 4 February 1841, after Clint had set sail for Batemans Bay. State Records Authority NSW, Colonial Secretary's Letters, INX-14-17710, item 2/7827, reel no. 1111. The reserve mentioned, east of McLeod's Creek, would be advertised and sold as the 'Village of Bateman' in 1859.

pursue either portion of land. Indeed, the following section of this chapter confirms that Clint's appetite for real estate had disappeared altogether by mid-1841.[70]

Clint's lithograph was the first known map to adopt the name 'Long Beach' for the 2-kilometre crescent of sand east of Cullendulla Creek.[71] Larmer's 1839 Crown plan of the 320 acres does not name any coastal features apart from Batemans Bay. On Clint's map, what is now Maloneys Beach was named Tor Bay, while Quiriga Beach immediately west of Reef Point (called Gipps Head on the map) was named Kingston Cove. Yellow Rock Beach was named East Harbour and North Head Beach was South Port Beach. North Head was given its contemporary name. Between Kingston Cove and East Harbour, the headland was named Point Kinghorn, while the first rocky outcrop on the Pacific Ocean side of North Head (below what is now North Head Lookout) was called Green Point. Clint's map thus honoured the two men who announced in November 1839 that they had found the road to Batemans Bay.[72]

---

70   *Sydney Herald*, 5 May 1841, 3. The portion of land marked on Clint's lithograph as 'applied to purchase' is approximately 640 acres. Alternatively, he could have reapplied for exactly half of his original 1,280 acres on the south side of the mouth of the Clyde River. In January 1842, 640 acres at Batemans Bay (no further details) appears to have been passed in at auction (*Sydney Herald*, 12 January 1842, 4). A 640-acre portion without an owner's name appears at the top of Cullendulla Creek on Baker's map (see Figure 7). However, Clint's request might have been the catalyst for the government decision in December 1841 to auction 10 blocks ranging from 80 to 145 acres on the site corresponding with the dimensions he requested on the southern side of the Clyde River. The auction produced no results. See *Australasian Chronicle*, 11 September 1841, 4; *Sydney Herald*, 17 September 1841, 3. See also Figure 7, this volume, for the small blocks on the southern side of the mouth of the river.
71   If the name 'Long Beach' at Batemans Bay originated with Clint, it was not the first time he printed this name on a lithographic map. On his 'Map of Australia from Moreton Bay to the New Colonies in Australia Felix with the Discoveries of the Recent Expeditions in the Interior, 1835 and 1836', almost the entire southern coast from Cape Howe to Wilsons Promontory was named 'Long Beach', following the map of Australia in T.J. Maslen's *Friend of Australia* (1827). On this map, the Maneroo Plains extend down to this beach. W.H. Wells kept this 'Long Beach' on his map of Australia in his *Geographical Dictionary or Gazetteer of the Australian Colonies* (1848).
72   While there is a Tor Bay on England's Devon coast, Raphael Clint had explored the district around Tor Bay in Western Australia in 1831–32, and this could be the direct origins of the name on his plan. Kinghorne had also requested the government advertise the 320 acres at Long Beach in 1839. Clint specifies that the property was on the 'North Shore' of the bay, unlike Stubbs's more indeterminate press advertisements.

5. CLINT THE ENGRAVER AND HIS SURVEY OF ST VINCENT

In producing his lithographic map, Clint might also have received assistance and advice from Charles E. Langley, a surveyor and civil engineer who specialised in 'laying out and projecting townships'. He shared Clint's offices on George Street during February and March 1841. However, the association was predictably brief.[73]

The plan also indicated that ships up to 800 tons could anchor at the western side of what is now called Square Head at the mouth of Cullendulla Creek (neither Square Head nor Cullendulla Creek is named on the plan). At the end of the headland, vessels of 400 tons could find anchorage, while ships 'of any class' could anchor on the Long Beach side of Square Head. The source of these measurements cannot be verified, although Stubbs's advertisement in April 1841 promised that more detailed surveys would be conducted in the near future.[74]

These soundings within the bay had practical real estate value given the absence of an existing wharf (other than a natural wharf)—a deficit Stubbs's advertisements promised would be remedied by an officer engaged to lay down moorings and improve the 'natural' wharf. While no more was heard of the wharf improvements, it will be revisited in Chapter 9.

Clint used images of anchors in his lithographic plan to indicate where the moorings would be located, along with water depths in fathoms. These recordings can be compared and contrasted with a 1901 map that provided more detailed soundings, produced by Principal Engineer of Harbours and Rivers William T. Keele.[75]

---

73 *Sydney Monitor and Commercial Advertiser*, 12 March 1841, 1. After advertising his services at Clint's office until the first week of April 1841, Langley moved to other shared premises (*Free Press and Commercial Journal*, 7 April 1841, 3). He claimed to have worked 'for some years' laying out towns and other engineering feats in North America. See also *Sydney Gazette and New South Wales Advertiser*, 11 March 1841, 3.
74 There is a reference in Stubbs's January 1841 advertisements to soundings taken by Lieutenant Johnston on his journey up the Bhundoo/Clyde River in the early 1820s, but those do not refer specifically to the northern stretch of Batemans Bay. Lieutenant Robert Johnston should not be dismissed as the source of the soundings, however. He made a rudimentary survey of the Bhundoo/Clyde River and Batemans Bay in early December 1821, and informed the governor in a letter dated 10 December that: 'should it please the Government to establish a Settlement on the Banks of this River, I have no hesitation in saying, that Communication can at all Times be had with such a Settlement, as Boats can land on either Side of the Bay, should the Sea make the Bar impassable.' He presented a sketch of the bay to the governor that might have provided soundings. See *Sydney Gazette and New South Wales Advertiser*, 15 December 1821, 1.
75 William Thomas Keele, 'NSW Harbours–Batemans Bay', 30 June 1901, Sydney, photo-lithographed by W.A. Gallick, Government Printer.

Table 3. Soundings around Long Beach and Cullendulla Creek, 1841 and 1901

	Raphael Clint, 1841	William T. Keele, 1901
Cullendulla Creek Mouth	36 ft (6 fathoms)	9.5–12 ft
Directly off Square Head	36 ft (6 fathoms)	18–25 ft
West Long Beach	18 ft (4.5 fathoms)	26–30 ft
West of Snapper Island	18 ft (4.5 fathoms)	11–14 ft

Sources: 'A Plan of 40 Suburban Allotments at St Vincent [Cartographic Material] on the North Shore of Bateman's Bay ... 1841, R. Clint, Lith.', NLA, digitised item, MAP F 87 copy, catalogue.nla.gov.au/Record/110599; William Thomas Keele, 'NSW Harbours—Batemans Bay', 30 June 1901, Sydney, photo-lithographed by W.A. Gallick, Government Printer.

Clint's soundings appeared to exaggerate the water depth at the west of Cullendulla Creek, directly off Square Head and west of Snapper Island, while underestimating the depth at the west end of Long Beach. Even by his own measurements, the recommended ship tonnages on Clint's map do not correspond to the sea depths.

The comparison suggests that either the seabed of the bay had altered considerably in the intervening 60 years or Clint's soundings were calculated guesses. The possibility of seabed changes at Cullendulla Creek over time should not be dismissed. It has been claimed that when punts brought logs down Cullendulla Creek from the sawmill at the headwaters of the creek during the last decades of the nineteenth century, awaiting ships anchored at the mouth of the creek would jettison ballast of sandstone and brick before loading their cargo.[76]

Apart from the promised wharf, neither Clint's lithograph nor Mr Stubbs's January 1841 advertisements indicates any town amenities or facilities. Nor do they suggest any distinction between residential, commercial or administrative zoning. This was in contrast with the plan for the private town of Brecon in the Hunter Valley, for example—also auctioned in 1841 by Stubbs and mentioned by Marjoribanks—that assigned space for marketplaces, churches, parks for recreation, cemeteries divided for different religious denominations and spaces for municipal institutions such as the police office and pound.[77]

---

[76] NSW National Parks and Wildlife Service, *Cullendulla Creek*, 15.
[77] See NLA, MAP F 788, 1841, Town of Brecon, T. Bird, surveyor, W. Baker, lithographer.

5. CLINT THE ENGRAVER AND HIS SURVEY OF ST VINCENT

Presumably, Clint remained faithful to the original layout of the plan catalogued as 359(A) for the 320-acre private township of St Vincent (see Chapter 3) when he produced the lithograph of Lord's suburban blocks and extension of the township. While visiting Long Beach, however, Clint must have seen the impracticality of the rectilinear-gridded layout of this original plan from a topographical perspective. Some north–south and east–west streets are drawn over sheer cliffs and the presence of gullies and swamps made some allotments unsuitable for building. Purchasers would have been unaware of these obstacles from a two-dimensional lithographic plan without a detailed relief map.

Clint's lithograph of St Vincent illustrates the important role that mapmakers, lithographers and surveyors performed in commodifying the frontier.[78] Surveyors' maps helped familiarise the remote, little-known reaches of the colony. To use a term Amitav Ghosh adapted from science fiction, survey maps and cadastral maps 'terraformed' the landscape in the minds of urban colonials.[79] It presented them with a vision of the 'limits of location' cleared of what Thomas Stubbs called the 'state of nature'. Looking at the map of St Vincent, the colonial gaze apprehended a comforting Euclidean geometry imposed upon the topography, with distances and angles measured out using chains and theodolites, depicting the familiarity of town centres protected by a boundary of suburban farms on the periphery of settlement.

Cadastral maps transformed the land into a cultural terrain that conformed with the habitus of modern urban Europeans. It presented settlers with a 'previsioning of occupation'.[80] J.M. Drown has argued that the 'work of both exploration and surveying worked … to erase Indigenous geographic associations and replace them with European meanings'.[81] Real estate agents such as Stubbs relied on lithographic grid plans to entice potential buyers with a vision of an 'improved' landscape. For authorities, they represented the 'logic of administrative power', but, at the same time, they also 'spoke to' settlers as recognisable and authoritative extensions of 'civilisation'.[82]

---

78 Huf, 'The Capitalist', 427; Alexander, 'Cartography'.
79 Ghosh, *The Nutmeg's Curse*, 54–6, 63: 'Narratives of terraforming draw heavily on rhetoric and imagery of empire, envisaging space as a "frontier" to be "conquered" and "colonized".'
80 Carter, *The Road*, 134 (see also ch. 7, esp. p. 210).
81 Drown, 'An Apparatus', 5.
82 Seddon, 'The Suburban Landscape', 150–2; Carter, *The Road*, 216. As Carter later pointed out, the 'grid survey guaranteed … that what lay beyond resembled precisely what was already familiar' (p. 227).

Thomas Stubbs's reference to Clint in his April 1841 advertisement as the contact for further information about Edward Lord's Stubley Park provides further grounds for assuming Clint's familiarity with the property and its surroundings. In effect, his lithographic map enhanced the appeal of his own newly purchased 320 acres at St Vincent by extending the town limits to the edge of Edward Lord's property, while giving Lord's surrounding property the appearance of proximity to a bustling hub of traffic and commerce.

Clint produced other lithographic plans for auctions in mid-1841, including that for the June 1841 sale of Edward Deas Thomson's allotments at South Huskisson at Jervis Bay (see Chapter 4).[83] Even though this scheme was all but abandoned by the 1850s, 100 years later the township was renamed Vincentia—a name derived from St Vincent.

Clint after St Vincent

In June 1841—while still the owner of the Long Beach property—Clint published an announcement in the Sydney press signalling his intention to focus on finer pursuits than real estate.[84] He admitted that during his seven years in Sydney his chosen profession of seal engraving had afforded only a precarious living and he had been 'compelled to acquire other branches of business, by no means congenial to his taste or in unison with arts'. However, he was now prepared to devote his full attention to seal engraving for customers willing to pay promptly on completion of work.[85]

It is possible that the descending 'badness of the times' along with the lack of progress in selling Lord's suburban lots at St Vincent had made Clint reconsider his involvement in real estate. Yet, a series of frustrations involving

---

83   The NLA holds 11 allotment plans drawn by Clint in 1841.
84   *Sydney Herald*, 19 June 1841, 3; 26 June 1841, 1.
85   Clint signed off with a somewhat misleading claim that, between 1824 and 1826, he obtained three successive gold Isis Medals from the Royal Society of the Arts in London for the best production in his field. There is a faint air of puffing in this claim. In 1824 he was one of three recipients of a Royal Society of the Arts gold Isis Medal in the field of 'Medal Die and Gem Engraving' for 'an original intaglio of a head' (*Transactions of the Society, Instituted at London, for the Encouragement of Arts, Manufactures, and Commerce* 43 [1825]: 366). In his father's 1854 obituary (*Art Journal*, 1 January 1854, 212–13), Raphael is described as a 'gem engraver' who 'possessed considerable talent'. In 1823, in the field of 'Mechanics', he was the recipient of a 'large silver medal, or twenty guineas' for his 'balanced or swinging masts' (*Transactions of the Society, Instituted at London, for the Encouragement of Arts, Manufactures, and Commerce* 42 [1824]: 107–10). This was the same prize to which Clint referred in his self-defence after A. Waterman ridiculed his punt at Kangaroo Point in September 1834. Raphael also exhibited in 1817 and 1828. See Bryan, *Bryan's Dictionary*, 303.

lithography might have also prompted his decision. Four days before the newspaper announcement, Clint had lost another court action 'of *assumpsit* for goods sold and delivered, and work and labour done' involving the production of a lithograph of Melbourne for the *Port Phillip Gazette*. Among other faults, Clint had mistaken buildings for trees in the original sketch.[86]

Around this time, Clint was involved in another controversy over allegations of illegal copying of a lithograph he had produced of Port Nicholson, New Zealand, which the *New Zealand Gazette and Wellington Spectator* described as the work of 'a most unskilful hand'. Having produced early maps of Melbourne, Adelaide and Port Essington, Clint appreciated the public and commercial interest in new settlements. He produced at least 10 lithographs of New Zealand territory during 1840 and 1841, but his foray into trans-Tasman mapping did not enhance his reputation. While containing 'useful information', they have subsequently been considered 'clumsily drawn' and he was accused of failing to 'acknowledge his sources'.[87]

On 5 August 1841, consistent with his June notice, Clint announced that he had sold the lithographic part of his business to the artist and draftsman Mr Forbes Mudie. He also reassured clients that the 'Seal Engraving and other business [would be] conducted as usual'.[88] Yet, Clint did not relinquish the lithographic trade for long.[89] Regardless of 'taste', this part of his business was financially more reliable than seal engraving or gem engraving.

By December 1841, he was again advertising his lithographic services, announcing the recent arrival of artistic materials that 'afforded for the economical conduct of business, of which out of no house out of London but this can offer'. He announced that while he had shut his front shop on George Street in December 1841,[90] he still operated from 'the back building

---

86 *Australian*, 24 June 1841, 3.
87 'Colonial Lithographer as Mapmaker', newzealandresearch.tripod.com/25-col-lithog.htm, accessed 20 January 2023. The *New Zealand Gazette and Wellington Spectator* report was reprinted in the *Sydney Monitor and Commercial Advertiser*, 2 October 1840, 2. It is also quoted in Cottrell, 'Patterns and Impressions', 154–5.
88 *Sydney Herald*, 5 August 1841, 3. If anything, during 1841 Clint appeared to be less discriminating in what he sold, and his offerings included his own nautical and scientific invention 'the thermo-barometer', as well as double-repeating telescopic theodolites and a 'splendid six-year old grey charger'.
89 The NLA possesses a collection of 25 of Clint's lithographs produced for real estate auctions from 1841 onwards. Worms and Baynton-Williams ('Raphael Clint') document a selection of lithographic plans he produced for auction sales, including subdivided land. These real estate plans, including the 1841 Long Beach plan, were produced for landowners and auctioneers between 1840 and 1845.
90 Clint had advertised his counting house, store and shop on George Street for let or for sale of lease in early November. See *Sydney Herald*, 12 November 1841, 3.

of the same premise' accessible from Abercrombie Lane. He justified this move on the grounds that his 'patrons will find greater attention than could be paid in a larger front concern obstructed by the depraved habits of the workmen employed not from choice but of necessity'.[91] More likely, he was trimming his expenses.

Lack of liquidity might also have been the reason Clint sold Long Beach back to Hughes & Hosking in November 1841 for £200, as well as his decision to work for 'prompt payment'. Having purchased Long Beach for £800, he would have made a substantial loss on the speculative venture if buyers at St Vincent reneged on their repayment schedule.

Yet, despite receiving a number of lithographic commissions,[92] in October 1842, he announced that, since the onset of the depression, he had effectively retired. Under the title, 'THE COLONIAL FEVER', Clint claimed that 'during the progress of the existing commercial epidemic, he thought it prudent to retire from the sphere of contagion—that seeing its worst agonies are past the climax, and the period of convalescence arrived, he will resume business in the old way', as an 'engraver in general, a lithographer and a draftsman' from new premises at 36 Hunter Street.[93]

The downturn in his mainstay income encouraged Clint to consider new and innovative projects. For instance, in November 1842, with possibly another hydrographic scheme in mind, he advertised for 'a proper man to sink a well on the North Shore, through rock, as per foot'.[94]

---

91 *Sydney Herald*, 28 December 1841, 3. From late 1841 to early 1842, Thomas Bluett worked briefly for Raphael Clint. Clint possibly became acquainted with Bluett when he was producing maps of New Zealand in 1840–41, as Bluett was the first lithographer in Wellington. See Barton, 'Thomas Bluett'.
92 For example, in February 1842, Clint published sheets of coloured shipping signals and in September 1842 he claimed to be producing cadastral maps of the 19 counties. He also produced a limited number of real estate plans. One of these lithographs was for an 1842 plan for an estate at Crookhaven, near the site where, in 1840, the government advertised land under the name St Vincent (see Chapter 3).
93 *Sydney Morning Herald*, 28 October 1842, 1. Clint signed off with one of his favourite expressions: 'A Rowland for an Oliver.' While Hunter Street was his residential and business address between 1842 and 1845, on the 1843 electoral roll he still claimed to be 'the occupier of a dwelling-house in Abercrombie-place'. See *Sydney Morning Herald*, 6 May 1843, 2.
94 *Sydney Morning Herald*, 30 November 1842, 3. In advertisements in 1840, Clint self-styled himself a 'hydrographer' (*Sydney Gazette and New South Wales Advertiser*, 2 July 1840, 1). Earlier, in 1838, he advertised that he planned to open a hydrographical and a geographical office (*Sydney Monitor*, 22 August 1838, 3). He developed a passion for sailing while living in Glasgow, where he conceived of the idea of 'balanced or swinging masts' for yachts, which won him a Royal Society medal. A Mr Clint engaged his yacht *Ariel* in harbour races in the early 1840s, but this was probably Mr Clint from Little Careening Bay, North Shore.

5. CLINT THE ENGRAVER AND HIS SURVEY OF ST VINCENT

In the same month, Clint announced his return to lithography through the imminent publication of his new plan of the City of Sydney and its suburbs. He mentioned this lithograph a few days later in an uncharitable advertisement clearly designed to undermine William Henry Wells's application for the position of city surveyor by questioning the accuracy of Wells's similar plan of Sydney.[95] Along with Charles E. Langley, Wells was unsuccessful in his pursuit of the government position.[96]

Clint again advertised his lithographic craftsmanship in December 1842, when he tested the market with a book containing a thousand specimens of his previous plans. In this advertisement, he made rather immodest claims concerning the superior quality of his work and characteristically denigrated fellow lithographers. He had been

> specially instructed to state that in properties submitted to public auction where his plans have been used, the clearly defined lines and figures thereon, which no other establishment has, or ever will rival, has given a public confidence, under which all fear of deception having vanished from the public mind, the sales have gone off with equal satisfaction to the proprietors and the purchasers.[97]

His work could be contrasted with those executed by other lithographers,

> where the sales have gone off in a languid half-price feeling, which must ever be the case where bad work and smeared lines, and obscured figures puzzle a bidder at the moment when he is called upon to make rapid mental calculations.[98]

Clint warned that his 'exquisite work' did not come as cheap as the work of his 'inferior' competitors, because his excellence could only be assured by employing the best tradesmen. In Clint's defence, competing lithographers

---

95 Accusations of piracy were common within the lithographic trade at this time. In February 1842, both Clint and Baker simultaneously published sheets of coloured shipping signals (*Teetotaller and General Newspaper*, 19 February 1842, 1) while a book containing cadastral maps of the 19 counties was published by W. Baker in 1843. The Sydney plan published by Wells coincided with Clint's plan. See Clint's opener in *Sydney Morning Herald*, 14 November 1842, 3; Wells's reply in *Sydney Morning Herald*, 15 November 1842, 3. For Clint's announcement of his surveys of each county, see *Sydney Morning Herald*, 27 September 1842, 3. For his announcement of his plan of Sydney, see *Sydney Morning Herald*, 10 November 1842, 2. For the broader context of cartography and map-making, see Alexander, 'Cartography'.

96 Langley came third and Wells fourth in the City Council ballot (*Australasian Chronicle*, 15 July 1843, 2). Wells was offered the position of assistant surveyor in 1849 but resigned the following year before he commenced work. During this period, he was alleged to have organised a fraudulent petition to the council, concocting fake signatures. See *People's Advocate and New South Wales Vindicator*, 17 August 1850, 2.

97 *Sydney Morning Herald*, 7 December 1842, 3.

98 *Sydney Morning Herald*, 7 December 1842, 3.

were not beyond puffing the matchless nature of their skills. Did Clint believe there was a market for a 1,000-specimen manuscript of his work? More likely, he produced this advertisement as an excuse to denigrate his competitors and blow his own trumpet.[99]

During 1843, with encouragement from the newly formed Sydney Salting Company, Clint sought a new avenue of business, inventing an apparatus for curing meats that could 'salt beef thoroughly in three minutes'.[100] No more was heard of the commercialisation of Clint's invention, despite a promised public exhibition of the process and a display of the meat at the offices of the *Sydney Morning Herald*. However, in September 1843 he did exhibit cured mutton hams at the Australian Floral and Horticultural Exhibition.[101]

By December 1843, Clint was again candidly describing his financial difficulties.[102] While continuing to execute his lithographic and engraving orders, 'in a style of elegance not to be excelled by any house in Europe', he pleaded 'monetary distress' as a result of 'having been almost wholly unemployed' during the previous two years. He then repeated the threat that those wishing to avail themselves of his services should do so immediately, as he found it 'requisite to quit the colony at a very early date, in search of that employment which cannot be expected here'. He warned patrons that 'no person will remain in the colony to supply his place'.[103]

It is possible that when Clint complained of 'unemployment', he had in mind his seal engraving services—the art he considered his preferred business. Lithography was merely a means to tidy him over between engagements in his only meaningful employment: practising his chosen art of engraving. Unfortunately, the halcyon days of the late 1830s, when a mixed clientele comprising upwardly mobile emancipists and wealthy elite could be relied upon as patrons of his heraldic designs, were over. During the depression, there was undoubtedly an even smaller clientele for discretionary items requiring engraving. Clint was commissioned in 1844 to produce a seal for the District Council of Parramatta, although he delivered one on a much larger-sized die than the council intended, due to imprecise specifications.[104]

---

99 *Sydney Morning Herald*, 7 December 1842, 3.
100 *Australian*, 13 July 1842, 2; 5 April 1842, 2; *Sun and New South Wales Independent Press*, 1 April 1843, 3; *Sydney Morning Herald*, 1 April 1843, 2.
101 *Australian*, 13 September 1843, 3.
102 *Sydney Morning Herald*, 11 December 1843, 3. However, the NLA possesses eight lithographs produced by Clint for auctioneers during the two years he claimed to be 'almost wholly unemployed'.
103 *Sydney Morning Herald*, 11 December 1843, 3.
104 *Parramatta Chronicle and Cumberland General Advertiser*, 3 February 1844, 2.

The depression had reduced even the clientele demanding lithographed real estate plans. He never again came close to the productivity he maintained before 1841. By 1844, he kept his lithographic business afloat by branching out to satirical designs depicting political issues of the day, including land regulation, squatting and the boiling down of livestock.[105]

Yet, 'Clint the Engraver' remained a well-known public figure. An 1845 poem entitled 'The Mayor's Fancy Ball' contained the stanza:

> At last, when hope began to waver
> The news came out, that Clint the Engraver
> Was labouring secretly, but hard
> In getting up a fancy card.[106]

Around this time, the Clints were rearranging their domestic arrangements, with Mary Ann raising her public profile. While she had held a stock of pret-a-porter items for sale ever since their arrival in Sydney, she now began advertising her craftwork.[107] Freeing time for herself, in August 1844, she had advertised for a cook who would also be 'required to do part of the washing, and to assist in the general work of the house' in Hunter Street.[108] At the beginning of 1845, she informed the public that she had made arrangements with a 'first-class English dressmaker' to solicit 'a share of the patronage of the Ladies of Sydney, trusting her well-known punctuality in matters of business will be appreciated in these trying times'. She also had available affordable ready-to-wear dresses and caps.

In October 1845, Clint again posted his regret that ongoing lack of business would soon force him not only to leave his chosen profession, but also to leave 'the people of these Colonies without any probability of any equal talent supplying his place for many years to come'.[109] Fully aware that his 'elegant arts' were out of step with colonists' capacity to purchase discretionary goods and services, he delivered the following warning:

---

105 Neville, 'Printmakers', 66, 87–8. These 'political sketches' were co-published with E.D. Barlow. See '8 Political Lithographic Cartoons, Mostly by Edward Winstanley, 1844, Raphael Clint & Edward Barlow Publishers', State Library of NSW. Barlow's name is on three, and Clint's name on three. See also *Sydney Morning Herald*, 8 May 1844, 3.
106 *Sydney Morning Herald*, 14 April 1845, 2.
107 *Australian*, 1 January 1845, 1. It was not uncommon for Sydney women to operate businesses during this period. See Bishop, *Minding*. In 1835, a woman named Sarah Whittington was charged and convicted of stealing a muslin cap valued at 4s. from the Clints' shop, then in King Street. In evidence, Clint stated that his wife 'keeps caps and articles of wearing apparel'. The Clints also hired an employee to assist her at that time. See *Sydney Gazette and New South Wales Advertiser*, 25 October 1835, 3; *Sydney Gazette*, 24 October 1835, 3.
108 *Sydney Morning Herald*, 29 August 1844, 6.
109 *Australian*, 2, 4, 7 and 9 October 1845, 2; *Sentinel*, 8, 15 and 22 October 1845, 1.

> It appears to R. C. that as the colonists, are recovering from disaster, they are pushing to the extreme of barbarism by a mistaken economy: for without a taste for Art, Science, and Literature, themselves and their families must become mere savages! Let such as desire to escape this disgrace, patronize the Arts generally, and R. Clint in particular—Mark! No delay![110]

This announcement reinforces the impression that Clint considered seal engraving as his source of 'employment'. Nine days later, he put up for sale three lithographic presses, one large copperplate and several tons of lithographic stones, appended to a notice that lack of business meant he was 'positively proceeding to India this season'. In the meantime, those neglecting to take advantage of the 'matchless style' of his seal engraving 'may thank themselves for the sufferings they will have to endure after his departure'.[111]

It also transpired that in 1845 Clint had written to a stranger he found in London's *Pigot's Directory* requesting that they find him a young stone seal engraver who would emigrate and buy his business. Clint would then retire to England. In this unsolicited letter, he presented a picture of the colony through rose-tinted glasses, claiming that a young man could maintain the same lifestyle in Sydney as London on one-quarter the income. He hoped, rather optimistically, that a 'clever young man' could be encouraged to emigrate 'in a week or a month after the receipt hereof'.[112] He also confessed to this stranger that he had made his fortune in Sydney but lost it all in speculation. It is probable that he was alluding to his reversal of fortune after his St Vincent venture in 1841.

The recipient of the letter forwarded it to an acquaintance in Sydney 'for veracity and authenticity', and this person subsequently published it along with a commentary in the *Citizen* shaming Clint for writing 'a piece of gross imposition' and a 'mendacious fabrication' of the economic conditions facing the colony, given that even a lithographer 'with the most respectable connexions' was 'barely able to exist'. Luring a young person out under such false pretences was an act of 'heartless avarice'.[113]

---

110 *Australian*, 2, 4, 7 and 9 October 1845, 2; *Sentinel*, 8, 15 and 22 October 1845, 1.
111 *Bell's Life in Sydney and Sporting Reviewer*, 11 October 1845, 3.
112 *Citizen*, 6 February 1847, 3.
113 *Citizen*, 6 February 1847, 3. The lithographer mentioned with the 'respectable connexions' was John Allen, a former apprentice of Clint, not Clint himself.

5. CLINT THE ENGRAVER AND HIS SURVEY OF ST VINCENT

Yet, at the same time that he was planning to sail for India, Clint was considering returning to his hydrographic skills for employment. In October 1845, he advertised a public lecture in Maitland entitled 'The Pathology of Rivers of the Whole World, Having a Direct Reference to the Absurdity of the Present Operations on the Hunter', along with an exhibition of 'Plans and Models, &c, in Illustration'.[114] In March 1846, Clint apologised to the people of Maitland for having cancelled the lecture due to 'a flush of business'.[115] However, by then, flushes were rare hands.

This letter of apology to the citizens of Maitland outlined the argument of his lecture in which he opposed the use of a steam-driven river dredge at Maitland and proposed instead a cheaper alternative that would turn mudbanks into meadows. Perhaps embellishing his Bridgewater days a decade before, he recalled

> a wide expanse of nauseous mud converted into the blithesome meadow, and where frogs and curlews uttered their melancholy cry, the careless infant and its jocund lovely nurse sport the live long day, and the lowing herds, &c., &c., &c., make the air resound with the busy joys of human life.[116]

Clint the surveyor was again envisaging the rank 'state of nature' transformed into a 'civilised' idyll. One newspaper respondent suspected that Clint was 'trying it on for a Government berth', which—given his financial predicament—was not beyond the realm of possibility. Otherwise he thought Clint's letter 'lengthy and unintelligible'.[117]

The cancellation of the lecture occurred in the midst of a deterioration in the Clints' domestic affairs. In March 1846, Mary Ann took Raphael to court, suing for maintenance. After lengthy representations from both sides, the bench awarded Mary Ann 12s. 6d. per week, paid monthly.[118] In July, Mary Ann offered her domestic or business services:

---

114 *Maitland Mercury and Hunter River General Advertiser*, 18 October 1845, 3.
115 *Maitland Mercury and Hunter River General Advertiser*, 18 March 1846, 1.
116 *Maitland Mercury and Hunter River General Advertiser*, 18 March 1846, 1.
117 *Maitland Mercury and Hunter River General Advertiser*, 21 March 1846, 3.
118 See *Bell's Life in Sydney and Sporting Reviewer*, 28 March 1846, 3, under the title of 'Matrimonial Comfort'. The maintenance was to be paid to John Wearin, chief inspector of police.

> MRS. CLINT will be happy to render her services in domestic management, or to assist in business; salary would be a secondary consideration, provided the treatment was kind; or to attend a lady to India or England. Painful domestic circumstances compel Mrs. C. to resort to some means of procuring a respectable subsistence.[119]

Straitened times continued to follow Clint, along with more acrimony with other lithographers and map-makers. In April 1846, a series of advertisements and letters were exchanged when Clint accused a surveyor, John Jones, of publishing a 'spurious map of Dr Leichhardt's travels'. Clint informed the public that he was preparing a correct map of the expedition, a claim that was counter argued by Jones and his booksellers. Jones went to the trouble of waiting upon Leichhardt to receive his sanction, which was more—his booksellers pointed out—'than can be said of R. Clint's forthcoming production'. The booksellers, alive to Clint's modus operandi, also warned that they had 'no objection to R. Clint or any one else puffing his goods, but cannot permit it to be done at the expense of the reputation of others'.[120] This was followed by another court appearance, in August 1846, where Clint accused an assistant, William Orr, of stealing two gold seals. The case was dismissed.[121]

On 2 January 1847, Clint joined the 'unhappy band' of insolvents, with with his assets of £69 unable to cover his debts of £101 6s. 2d. The court allowed Clint to keep his 'Wearing Apparel and engraving tools', subject to the payment of a £2 schedule filing charge.[122]

The details of his insolvency schedule give some indication of Clint's personal and professional life at this stage.[123] First, it was clear that he remained estranged from Mary Ann, who was in possession of his household furniture, which accounted for £50 of his £69 assets. There was no report of the bailiffs seizing this furniture, meaning creditors would receive very little in the pound as a dividend.

---

119 *Sydney Morning Herald*, 8 July 1846, 3. The advertisement was signed by 'Mrs Clint' and 'Letters addressed, pre-paid, care of Mr. Smith, Optician, 671, Lower George-street'.
120 For Clint's advertisement, see *Sydney Morning Herald*, 8 April 1846, 1. Jones's response appeared in the *Sydney Morning Herald* (8 April 1846, 3); the booksellers' response appeared on page 1 of the same issue and was repeated on 11 and 13 April. Clint's map can be found in the State Library of NSW.
121 *Bell's Life in Sydney and Sporting Reviewer*, 29 August 1946, 3.
122 The 'unhappy band' was a phrase in a poem by E.H.M. '[w]ritten by the author during the depression in 1843'. See *Port Phillip Gazette and Settler's Journal*, 11 February 1846, 4.
123 Clint's insolvency file is held at State Records Authority NSW, INX-10-5567, item 1601, NRS-13654-1-[2/8805]-1601. See also *NSW Government Gazette*, 19 January 1847, 87; *Sydney Chronicle*, 23 January 1847, 2.

Second, had Clint not been so litigious, the balance of his debt to assets would have been reduced from £32 6s. 2d. to 8s. 8d.—his debt included £31 17s. 6d. in 'judgments' and 'law costs'.[124] Third, had he also been more parsimonious with his advertising in the *Sydney Morning Herald*, another £18 owed to Kemp and Fairfax would had been removed from his debt. However, as this chapter amply illustrates, Raphael Clint's public identity would barely exist without litigation and self-advertisement. Fourth, it is clear that he continued to conduct business with his bitter rival W.H. Wells, whom Clint admitted he owed £2 10s. for 'wages', though Wells swore by his own affidavit that he was owed £4 10s. for 'work and labour done'. Fifth, in his list of assets, Clint claimed that he owned around 'five hundred sheep of which I cannot at present obtain any account not being able to find the parties to whose care they were entrusted—worth £300'. The court ruled this ovine asset inadmissible.[125]

Finally, given the limited value of his allowable assets, it is possible that Clint calculated—quite literally—that he had nothing to lose through taking the path of insolvency. As Chapter 8 will show, critics of the insolvency law felt that many people who filed an insolvency schedule did so more to advantage themselves than those to whom they were indebted.

Soon after, on 29 January, Clint left Sydney, sailing aboard the *Mazeppa* and arriving in Adelaide on 8 February.[126] His intention was unclear, but he soon returned and, in March, announced that he had relinquished his copperplate printing materials—which had not appeared on his insolvency schedule—to the merchant and printer Mr James T. Grocott.[127] He maintained his engraving business and in May was advertising his services from new premises on George Street, claiming 'his business is conducted as usual', though at rates cut by 80 per cent due to 'the still continuing depression'.[128]

---

124 These judgements were for Mr Robertson of Market Wharf (£10), Mrs Waller of Church Hill (£6), Mr Wolfe of George Street (£3 7s. 6d.), two judgements for Mr Burgers and Lochhead (£4), and law costs owed to Mr Stenhouse and Hardy of Elizabeth Street (£7).
125 State Records Authority NSW, INX-10-5567, item 1601, NRS-13654-1-[2/8805]-1601.
126 *South Australian*, 12 February 1847, 4.
127 *Sydney Morning Herald*, 8 March 1847, 1. It is possible that Clint sold this equipment prior to filing his schedule in order to have control over cash to use as he, rather than the court, saw fit. As for his duration in Adelaide, Clint still had unclaimed letters waiting for him on 10 and 13 March, according to the *Sydney Morning Herald*.
128 *Australian*, 22 April 1847, 1; *Sentinel*, 20 May 1847, 3. Clint's office at 478 George Street was also his new residence. In his insolvency schedule, he had claimed his 'working tools' were of 'little or no value—say £1'. This was why the Insolvency Court had allowed him to keep these tools.

By June, 'R Clint, of great professional notoriety', again informed the public that he was 'anxious to return to England for a while'.[129] His prices remained reduced by 80 per cent, but 'procrastination, being the thief of time' meant that Clint could not 'help laughing in his sleeve, at the dejection of persons, who may have delayed their orders (stonily) until his departure'.[130]

Clint's projected return to England was another empty threat to the citizens of Sydney. Two months later he was advertising for a couple of apprentices.[131] By now he was operating out of the engraver H.C. Jervis's premises at 333 Pitt Street.[132] He was granted his discharge from bankruptcy on 25 November 1847.[133]

In March 1848 he produced his last real estate plan for Thomas Stubbs, by now the city auctioneer of Sydney. The commission was for the subdivision of Kellick's Wharf, at the northern end of Sussex Street.[134] He also produced a well-received map of the eastern coast from Port Phillip to Wide Bay, promising to extend his survey to the Torres Strait—another frontier interest that had occupied him since the 1830s. In addition, between June and September 1848, brief advertisements appeared in the *Sydney Daily Advertiser* for his seal engraving, drafting and lithography services.[135]

---

129 *Sydney Morning Herald*, 16 June 1847, 1.
130 *Sydney Morning Herald*, 16 June 1847, 1.
131 *Sydney Morning Herald*, 11 August 1847, 1: 'TO PARENTS AND GUARDIANS. Wanted, two youths about sixteen years of age, with a tolerable education, end of respectable connexion, as Apprentices to the Copper-plate Engraving to Mr Jervis and to the Seal Engraving with Mr. R. Clint. A premium required. 333, Pitt-street.'
132 *Sentinel*, 30 September 1847, 1. Harry Cooper Jervis engraved, printed and published Thomas Stubbs's highly acclaimed 'Lady O'Connell's Waltz' in 1845.
133 The application was recorded in the *NSW Government Gazette* (22 October 1847, 1147) and his certificate confirmation noted in *Sydney Chronicle*, 9 December 1847, 2.
134 For the sale of Kellick's Wharf, see *Australian*, 10 March 1848, 2. The State Library of NSW attributes this plan to Clint. See 'Plan of X Allotments in Margaret Place and Sussex Street, Sydney, Opposite Kellick's Wharf and Hunter River Steam Company's Wharf: To Be Sold by Auction by Mr. Stubbs on March 28th 1848 / R. Clint'. Thomas Stubbs had attained the position of city auctioneer for Sydney in 1845. He resigned from the position in 1850, moving to Melbourne the same year, after clearing a number of debts (see *NSW Government Gazette*, 2 April 1850, 531). Until his retirement in the mid-1860s, he was the city auctioneer for Melbourne.
135 For the eastern coast map, see *Sydney Daily Advertiser*, 28 June 1848, 2. In a June 1848 column, one gossip correspondent for a Melbourne paper reported a notorious Legislative Council electioneering event for the friends of joint candidates William Charles Wentworth and William Bland at the Royal Hotel in which the chair, Edward Flood, was seen 'bandying words' with 'an exuberantly Bacchanalian devotee named Clint'. See *Port Phillip Patriot and Morning Advertiser*, 5 July 1848, 2. Other papers called the event 'stormy' and a 'riot'. As no other paper mentioned Clint, the rumour of his condition remains unverified.

5. CLINT THE ENGRAVER AND HIS SURVEY OF ST VINCENT

However, by the end of 1848 Clint was again in debt for rent and lodgings,[136] and by 1849 he was subletting at Brougham Place, between Pitt and Castlereigh streets. His room was on the Castlereigh Street end of the lane—the street where he and Mary Ann initially lived when they first arrived in Sydney in 1835. He exhibited two works at the second exhibition of the Society for the Promotion of Fine Arts, but the advertisements and letters penned by him that had graced the pages of the Sydney press since 1835 disappeared.[137]

On 13 September 1849, 'after a few days' severe illness', Raphael Clint died at the age of 52 and was buried the following day.[138] While no cause of death was announced, Brougham Place had become increasingly notorious over the previous decade for overcrowding, lack of sanitation and want of potable water. It was a 'gloomy lane' known colloquially as 'Pleurisy Alley'. Less than a year later, a correspondent complained of its 'wretched state', noting the 'several deaths lately occurred'. A few weeks later, another correspondent recommended that the lane required 'water, sewerage and a friendly inspection, ever anon, by that intruding man, Stubbs' (Richard Stubbs, Sydney's inspector of nuisances, and alleged author of Thomas Stubbs's real estate advertisements, mentioned in Chapter 3).[139] Thus, it is possible that the deterioration of Clint's financial circumstances forced him into a living arrangement acknowledged to be 'unfitted for habitation' and that this was responsible for his untimely death.

---

136 See *Sydney Morning Herald*, 5 December 1848, 4: 'NOTICE.—If J. CLINT, Engraver, and T. ARNOLD, late D. C. G., unless they call and pay their debts for Board and Lodging, their things left in my charge will be sold within fourteen days of this date. THOMAS CURTIS. 8345 William-street, Sydney.' Clint might have temporarily moved to Gill's Hotel, Pitt Street, as unclaimed mail was awaiting him there in April 1849.
137 These two items were described as 'classical intaglios of the heads of Lord Byron and von Weber'. See Deutscher and Hackett, 'Important Women Artists', 2021, lot 29, www.deutscherandhackett.com/65-important-women-artists. They were possibly the same pieces exhibited at the Royal Society in the 1820s.
138 *Sydney Morning Herald*, 14 September 1849, 4. When a person died of causes that could not be determined, they were often recorded as a 'visitation from God'.
139 *Pittwater Online News*, 21–27 August 2011, Issue 20; *Sydney Morning Herald*, 20 August 1850, 3; *People's Advocate and New South Wales Vindicator*, 7 September 1850, 6. A lengthy 1851 article from a 'special reporter' on the 'sanitary state of Sydney' featured Brougham Place (*Sydney Morning Herald*, 1 March 1851, 2). The article reflected a growing modern interest in statistically documenting the health and moral status of the poor. A month after Clint's death, a letter was sent to the City Water and Lighting Committee requesting that a water mains pipe be laid from Pitt Street. However, this request was opposed by all bar one of the building owners, whose 26 dwellings housed 102 families (City of Sydney Archives and History Resources, ID A-00434665). An 1854 real estate advertisement for the sale of properties in Brougham Place provides useful detail of two of the similar 26 four-roomed houses in the lane (*Empire*, 15 July 1854, 7). The auctioneers, Rich, Langley and Butchart, included Charles E. Langley, who formerly resided with Clint in 1841. In 1875, the lane was renamed Rowe Street, and subsequently became a gathering place for the bohemian and avant-garde.

A week after her husband's funeral, Mary Ann issued the following plea:

> MRS. CLINT, in returning thanks to those friends who so kindly interred her late husband, begs to solicit a little aid to enable her to obtain her own support, by establishing some business by which her industry might be available; her painful circumstances are well known, and her own partial recovery from a sick bed render her distress greater.[140]

Because Clint died intestate, five months after his death, Mary Ann applied to the Supreme Court, in its Ecclesiastical Jurisdiction, for letters of administration to be granted to her over her husband's estate.[141] In April 1850, she opened her own millinery and dressmaking shop on Lower George Street (see Figure 13).[142]

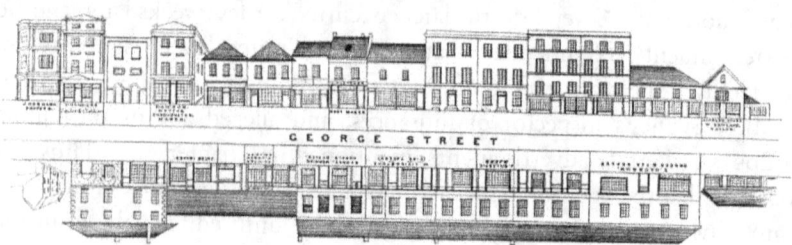

Figure 13. Lower George Street, 1848.
Fowles, *Sydney*, 13. This detail shows the section of George Street where Mary Ann Clint announced she was opening her dressmaking shop in April 1850. Her shop was the fifth from the left on the top row, 'next door to the right of Dawson, the watch and chronometer maker' at no. 146, separated by a small laneway. This was how she identified the location, along with the fact that it was 'nearly opposite' the office of the *Sydney Morning Herald*. On the corner of George Street and Charlotte Lane — far left of drawing — is J. Hordern's Nottingham Warehouse, which opened in 1843 (see Bishop, *Minding*, ch. 2). Samuel Lyons's Auction Mart was on the other side of Charlotte Place. The small street across the road from Mary Ann's shop is Queen's Lane.

---

140 *Sydney Morning Herald*, 21 September 1849, 1. Lists for Mary Ann's subscription could be obtained at the premises of Mr Dixson, tobacconist; Mr Barnett, grocer; Mr Jervis, engraver; Mr Thompson, oil and colourman; Mr Grocott's music saloon; and Mr Illidge's boot and shoe warehouse.
141 *NSW Government Gazette*, 19 February 1850, 278.
142 *Sydney Morning Herald*, 11 April 1850, 1. No further mention of Mary Ann can be found after this notice. Sydney was 'teeming' with women-managed millinery businesses around this period and it is possible that she was among those who 'scraped together a poor living at best, with bankruptcy a constant possibility'. See Bishop, *Minding*, ch. 2.

In the same advertisement in which Mary Ann announced her new establishment, she proposed subletting her premises, suggesting that 'a respectable female engaged abroad during the day, may find a quiet home on reasonable terms'. The genteel, respectable tone of Mary Ann Clint's few advertisements seem wholly inconsistent with a person who allegedly ran a sly grog shop in her Vandemonian days.

Conclusion

Raphael Clint's professional life in New South Wales mirrored the turbulence of the land market, from the highs of the late 1830s to the lows of the 1840s. The same peaks and troughs characterised the lithographic and artistic trades more generally. The period of expansion of the printing trade in the late 1830s was 'certainly the most prolific time for lithographic printmakers', while the 'depression of the early 1840s very effectively squashed that buoyancy; it was never really to recover for the rest of the decade'.[143] The majority of the Sydney lithographers, engravers and surveyors associated with Clint fared badly during the depression and even thereafter (see Table 4).

Table 4. The fortunes of Raphael Clint's professional circle mentioned in Chapter 5

W.H. Wells	Jail/insolvency/jail	1841/1842/1855	NSW Government Gazette, 23 November 1841, 1623
J.G. Austin	Insolvency	1842	Australian, 5 February 1842, 4
John Price	Deceased, aged 40	1844	Sydney Morning Herald, 30 July 1844, 3
E.D. Barlow	Maintenance order	1845	Maitland Mercury, 8 February 1845, 3
T. Bluett	Debt/absconded	1845	Paul Barton, 'Thomas Bluett, Lithographer', Australiana 28, no. 2 (May 2006): 20–6
Forbes Mudie	Deceased, fell from horse, aged 32	1846	Maitland Mercury and Hunter River General Advertiser, 12 August 1846, 3

143 Neville, 'Printmakers', 16.

H.C. Jervis	Insolvency	1847	NSW Government Gazette, 6 October 1846, 1187
W. Baker	Meeting of creditors	1847	Sydney Morning Herald, 23 December 1847, 3
J.T. Grocott	Insolvency/ insolvency/ insolvency/ insolvency	1842/1848/ 1855/1869	Pittwater Online News, 7–13 November 2021, no. 517
C.E. Langley	Insolvency/ insolvency	1855/1860	NSW Government Gazette, 15 May 1855, 1387
John Carmichael	Insolvency	1857	Karen Eaton, 'John Black Carmichael 1803–1857', Australiana 37, no. 4 (November 2015): 6–18

Like so many others involved in the sale of the township of St Vincent, Clint never recovered and eventually succumbed to insolvency, suggesting a causal link between the downturn in his fortunes and his involvement in the St Vincent venture.[144] Not only did the depression reduce the circle of his clientele, but also it appears that his attraction to Batemans Bay was the road to ruin.

It is occasionally possible, 180 years later, to bid for one of Clint's sundials, which can fetch between $4,000 and $6,000, at auction.[145] Alternatively, his work can be accessed at the National Library of Australia, certain state libraries and local museums, such as Port Macquarie. A navigational hazard in the Great Australian Bight was named Clint Rock,[146] while Clint Place in the Canberra suburb of Macquarie is named after Raphael.[147]

---

144 Mary Ann Clint experienced less hardship than the spouses of two other lithographers listed in Table 4. E.D. Barlow was sued by his wife for maintenance in 1845 in a court case that attracted considerable public attention. After losing the case, he left the court 'amidst the jeers of the spectators' (*Sydney Morning Herald*, 12 February 1845, 3). Thomas Bluett left the colony to avoid his financial reality, then abandoned his wife and children in Hong Kong. Locals raised a subscription to send them back to England on the *Tory*. The captain of the ship committed a number of murders and tortured members of the crew, whom the allegedly deranged captain accused of mutiny. The ordeal aboard the *Tory* was described in the *London Illustrated News*, 6 December 1845, 354–5. The trial was described in the *Maitland Mercury and Hunter River General Advertiser*, 25 April and 27 May 1846, 4.
145 For an example of his sundials, see Historic Houses Trust of NSW, *Annual Report*, 59. See also Museums of History NSW, 'Raphael Clint Sundial'; Leski Auctions, *Australian & Historical*, [flipbook] 58.
146 The 10-foot rock 'with birds resting on it' east of Kangaroo Island at latitude 37°S, longitude 139°E was sighted on the Clints' 1832 voyage from King George Sound to Hobart, and named presumably after either Mary Ann or Raphael. See Horsburgh, *The India Directory*, 116–17.
147 The streets in the suburb of Macquarie are named after contemporaries of Lachlan Macquarie's governorship (1810–21). It is not clear why Clint was considered appropriate for this honour given he emigrated in 1829. ACT Government, *Canberra's Suburb*.

5. CLINT THE ENGRAVER AND HIS SURVEY OF ST VINCENT

Raphael Clint deserves acknowledgement for producing an accurate and detailed map of the northern shore of Batemans Bay from Cullendulla Creek to the Pacific Ocean,[148] as well as for being the owner of Long Beach during most of the tumultuous year of 1841. He was also the only principal character in this story to have walked on Long Beach and the surrounding land.

Through enabling the colonial population to imagine the landscape cleared of traces of the previous custodians of the land, surveyors and lithographers such as Clint performed a significant role. There was (and is) a world of difference between Walbanja understandings of Country and settler notions of real estate. As Ghosh notes:

> To remake immense stretches of terrain to suit the lifestyles of another continent inevitably entailed the undermining and elimination of the ways of life of those who had inhabited those lands for many thousands of years.[149]

Colonial surveyors, lithographers and map-makers were complicit in this undertaking, and the plan for St Vincent is testimony to Clint's skill. He was sensitive to public demand for illustrations that extended the limits of colonisation. As he surveyed Cullendulla Creek, and contemplated purchasing the block on its eastern bank, did he—like Joseph Phipps Townsend later—encounter the Walbanja people on their periodic gatherings? If so, did he have the vision to understand how his professional practice might affect their lives? Or did he assume that they would somehow disappear without a trace, erased from his future maps?

---

148 Unlike Plan 359(A) for the township of St Vincent, there is no evidence that Clint's subdivision was catalogued as a land titles plan.
149 Ghosh, *The Nutmeg's Curse*, 55.

6

John Staple and the trials of speculation

It is clear as the day, ev'ry man that's in debt
Is going down hill—if he's not of our set:
A fig for his properties, many or few,
His ships, sheep, or cattle. We'll sue! We will sue!
We know there's no money; we know it full well,
That there is no one to buy, and nothing will sell;
But we won't take securities, real and true –
We musht have our monish. We'll sue! We will sue!
There are some of ourselves, though we have no great hoards,
Yet, to pass on our paper, have friends at the boards,
We would not dislike a snug purchase or two
At a tenth of their cost. We will sue! We will sue![1]

The previous three chapters examined the land sales in and around the township of St Vincent from the sellers' perspective: Chapter 3 examined the auctioneers and the advertising materials, Chapter 4 described the main competitors on the South Coast and Chapter 5 explored how Raphael Clint drew on his lithographic and surveying skills (among countless other talents) to promote the campaign. This chapter turns to the purchasers of the subdivided land at St Vincent. It opens with the published sales figures before identifying buyers. It then examines one buyer in particular, John Staple, whose purchases and subsequent financial difficulties reveal further details about the plan for the proposed township of St Vincent. John Staple not only provides a case study of one of many insolvencies during the

---

1   P.N., 'We Will Sue!', *Sydney Morning Herald*, 17 July 1843, 2.

depression, but also, as his colonial career was linked with the operations of the Office of the Sheriff (that part of the legal system most closely related to the execution of insolvency orders), provides insight into the inner workings of an office that became familiar to most of the dramatis personae in the story of St Vincent once the depression gripped the colony.

Sales and speculators at St Vincent

The sale of the 320-acre block of land at Long Beach to Raphael Clint and J.J. Peacock was the first of 13 private transfers of the property between 1840 and the end of World War II. In each case, it remained undivided. Even when Clint sold the property back to Hughes & Hosking on 1 November 1841, this involved 'an undivided moiety of 320 acres at Bateman's Bay'.[2] There were no exempted subdivided sections.

In 1917, when the then owner of Long Beach, Augustus Edmund Blair, submitted a primary application in preparation for selling the property to Mt Kembla Collieries Ltd, he had to show that there were no outstanding claims on the land. The township of St Vincent was one issue raised. The supervising surveyor's report noted that 'the subject land comprises the private subdivision of the Town of St. Vincent in streets and sections as shown on the plan catalogued 359(A), dated 1841'. Clearly the surveyor sighted Plan 359(A). However, his search did not 'disclose any dealings with the lots in the several sections shewn on such plan and no evidence is available as to the dedication of the streets shewn thereon'. Long-time local resident John Ryan also swore on affidavit that there 'is not now and never was any sign of the formation of any village on or about the said land'.[3]

Yet, as noted in Chapter 3, Stubbs's press announcements from late January to early April 1841 reported sales of the subdivided town lots. In March, advertisements even claimed that purchasers had been 'located' at their property and that 'buildings and improvements' had already taken place. This raises the question of the status of the buyers' claims to and interest in these lots, given that, in November 1841, Clint sold the undivided block back to Hughes & Hosking.

---

2   NSW Land Registry Services, Book Y, no. 314.
3   The papers associated with Augustus Edmund Blair's Primary Application are held at State Records Authority NSW, NRS-17513, item 17513-8-34-PA 20438, vol. 2781, folio 34. Later, Blair owned Chatham, the most celebrated horse in Australia after Phar Lap left for the USA.

Considering the imaginative language that was characteristic of auctioneers' advertisements, the possibility should be entertained that Stubbs's announcement of sales and building at St Vincent involved some strenuous 'puffing'. As Marjoribanks noted, auctioneers' representations of properties were often 'highly coloured and exaggerated'.[4] However, this chapter provides evidence of at least three reported cases that not only confirm the 'important results' from Stubbs's auction at Long Beach but also provide further details of the layout of the proposed town of St Vincent.

On 28 January 1841, Stubbs reported that he had sold three-quarters of the subdivisions in the township of St Vincent the previous day 'at prices averaging from 9d. to 2s. 6d. per foot. Total proceeds £2210 14s. 7d.— Suburban acres at £5 5s. to £1 15s. per acre.'[5] After the second auction in late March, Stubbs announced that he had 'effected the sale of … sixty-seven allotments of the judiciously selected Township of St. Vincent, Bateman's Bay at from 8d. to 2s. 6d. per foot frontage'.[6] Whether these 67 allotments represented all the residual properties left over from the January sales is not stated, but this was the last press mention of the sales from the subdivided Long Beach block.

To sum up, on 30 April 1940, Hughes & Hosking had paid £192 for the 320 acres. With the January 1841 sales netting £2,210—and assuming that all the remaining town lots were sold by the end of March for a similar price—this represented at least a fifteen-fold increase in the value of the 320 acres at Long Beach in less than a year, excluding fees for advertising, agents, artists and surveyors.

Unlike these January and March 1841 township sales for Hughes & Hosking/Clint and Peacock's 320-acre block, there were no subsequent notices of sale figures from the April and May 1841 auctions of Edward Lord's subdivisions at Stubley Park. However, sales do appear to have been made for Lord's estate in April, as suggested by the following announcement in August:

> MR. STUBBS is instructed to make known 'That Purchasers of Land at Bateman's Bay, on the 28th April last, will take notice that the surveyor will be on the spot, to point out the Boundaries on the 1st of September next'.[7]

---

4   Such scepticism is warranted according to Dyster, 'Inventing the Suburbs'; Dyster, 'The 1840s Depression Revisited', 604–5.
5   'Theatricals', *Australian*, 28 January 1841.
6   *Australian*, 3 April 1841, 2; see modified version in *Sydney Herald*, 5 April 1841, 3.
7   *Sydney Herald*, 10 August 1841, 1 (also 11 August).

The *Waterwitch* left Sydney for Batemans Bay on 31 August and would have arrived 'on the spot' by 1 September.[8] However, there is no indication how many people disembarked at Lord's Stubley Park to witness the marking of their boundaries. Regardless, as Chapter 3 pointed out, by June 1842 all the original blocks on Edward Lord's estate were again up for sale, meaning that no sales from April and May 1841 were settled.

Three months earlier, one purchaser had chosen to sell their recently acquired St Vincent township lots. In mid-May 1841, 'at the risque of the former purchaser, Mr George Dent', Stubbs put up for auction, without reserve:

> ALL those FIVE SECTIONS, numbered 5, 6, and 7, containing ten lots each, and situated in the TOWNSHIP of ST VINCENT, Bateman's Bay: and which were sold at public auction on Monday, the 25th day of January, at the auction mart, King-street.[9]

George Dent was a Circular Quay ship carpenter/joiner who lived in and worked out of the wreck of the ship *Macclesfield*. During 1840 he had continued to build a portfolio of allotments in the buoyant market, including the notorious land at Berkley Estate (see Chapter 3).[10] Yet, by 1842, Dent and his partner faced insolvency. The St Vincent sales reflected the onset of his liquidity crisis.[11]

A month later, Raphael Clint was looking to secure the sales from January and March. The auctioneer Stubbs was holding the 20 per cent deposits from these sales, but Clint must have been concerned over his buyers' capacity to maintain their payment schedules amid rumours of monetary stringency. On 18 June 1841, Clint announced to 'purchasers of Allotments in the township of St Vincent' that the 'Proprietor is now prepared to complete Titles, and purchasers are requested to notify whether they adopt the long credit, or make arrangements otherwise'.[12]

---

8   *Sydney Herald*, 28 August 1841, 1. The sequence of events here followed those at Hughes & Hosking's Shoalhaven sales (Chapters 3 and 5): advertisement, auction, sales, followed by subsequent visits by surveyor and purchaser to identify allotments.
9   *Sydney Herald*, 19 May 1841, 4; *Australasian Chronicle*, 18 May 1841, 3.
10 For his properties at Albert Town, see *Australian*, 3 October 1840, 3. See *Sydney Monitor and Commercial Advertiser*, 10 November 1841, 2, for the court case brought by Dent against the auctioneer Samuel Lyons over promissory notes for purchases at Berkley Estate. There was another boatbuilder named George Dent, who was later instrumental in settling Huskisson in the 1860s, but the two were not related.
11 *NSW Government Gazette*, 15 November 1842, 1711.
12 *Sydney Herald*, 21 June 1841, 3.

6. JOHN STAPLE AND THE TRIALS OF SPECULATION

Another example of an overstretched speculator was the person for whom the law stationers H. & W. Newman of Pitt Street was acting as agent. In November 1841, along with properties at Craigend, the New Town Road, East Gosford and Jervis Town, 'extremely liberal' terms were offered on 'various allotments' at Batemans Bay. This would have involved either the Hughes & Hosking/Clint property or Lord's Stubley Park property.[13]

The remainder of this chapter explores another purchaser of allotments at St Vincent whose fate reveals more detail about the map of St Vincent.

John Staple's purchases at St Vincent

Even though the private township of St Vincent was never built, the 1907 and 1917 Benandra parish maps superimposed the same street grid onto the Hughes & Hosking block that appears on Clint's 1841 lithograph, overlaid with the words 'Private Town of St Vincent' (see Figure 14).

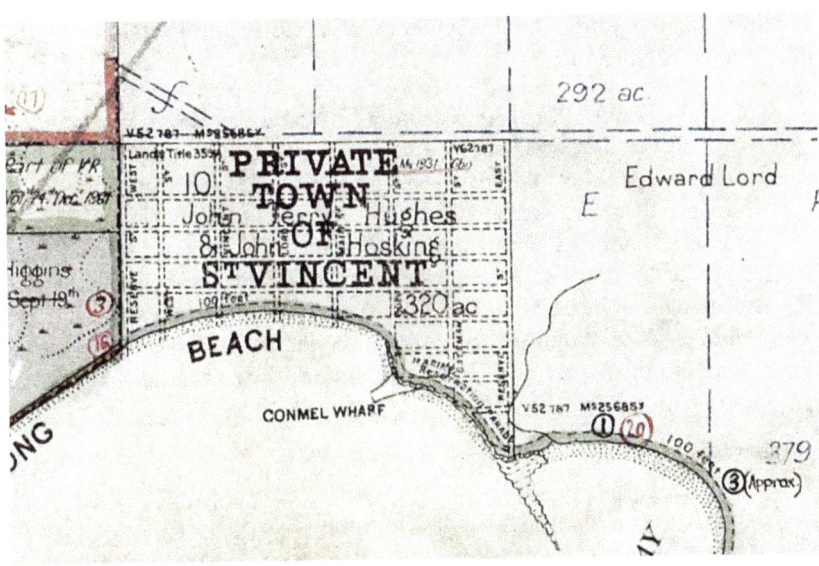

Figure 14. Detail from Benandra Parish Map showing St Vincent street names, 1907.
NSW Land Registry Services, detail from Benandra Historical Parish Map, no. 3, 14 October 1907.

---

13   *Sydney Herald*, 11 November 1841, 1.

Another countywide map of St Vincent, prepared by the NSW Department of Lands in 1931, also shows the town grid, with the name St Vincent superimposed beside it.[14] The name disappeared when the 1964 Department of Lands map was compiled (see Figure 2). By then, postwar houses and roads had imposed a new order on the Long Beach landscape.

The two official parish maps of 1907 and 1917, unlike Clint's 1841 lithographic plan, named all the north–south streets along the beach (see Figure 14). These eight streets, spaced out every 230 metres from west to east (from the beginning of Longbeach Estate to the beginning of Maloneys Beach), were called Reserve Street West, West Street, Vincent Street, Lord Street, Main Street, Quay Street, Bateman Street and Reserve Street East. No streets running west–east are named.

Clues to the origin of these street names can be found in court reports published in the press in late 1841 and early 1842. In January 1842, for example, the Supreme Court's sheriff's office heard a case involving five plaintiffs (Brady, Matthews, Campbell and others, Stokes, and Wade) and a debtor named John Staple. Under Sheriff Cornelius Prout issued the following announcement:

> ON TUESDAY, the 18th instant, at noon, at the Royal Hotel, Sydney, the Sheriff will rouse to be sold all the right, title, interest, and estate, of the above defendant, in and to all those allotments of land situate at Bateman's Bay, being sixteen allotments block P., thirteen allotments block C.; these are bounded by Vincent, High, and Lord streets; also, sixteen allotments in block R., and eighteen allotments in block I., bounded by Quay, High, and Main streets; also, eighteen allotments in block H., bounded by Market-street, opposite the Wharf and Quay-street, unless these executions are previously satisfied.[15]

---

14   NSW Department of Lands, 'Map of the County of St. Vincent: Eastern Division, N.S.W. 1931', [1957], MAP G8971.G46 svar, nla.gov.au/nla.obj-671156524/view.
15   *Sydney Herald*, 18 January 1842 (see also 10 January, 3; 12 January; 15 January). This advertisement had been preceded by a similar announcement in the *Sydney Herald* (18 December 1841), except Wade was not listed as a plaintiff, and the following properties were also to be auctioned:
>At the same time and place, will be sold, all the right, title, interest, and estate, of the above defendant, in and to all that piece or parcel of land, situate in the county of Cumberland, parish of Alexandria, at little Coogee, and containing about five acres, bounded on the west by Holmes's, on the south by the waters of the bay, being Lot 24 of Government Sale of 10th November, 1839. Unless these executions be previously satisfied. CORNELIUS PROUT, Under-Sheriff.

See also sales of allotments at Batemans Bay by the sheriff, in *Australasian Chronicle*, 23 December 1841, 3 (at the London Tavern), and *Sydney Herald*, 18 January 1842, 3 (at the Royal Hotel).

All the streets named (except for High and Market streets) are consistent with the street names on the 1907 and 1917 parish maps of St Vincent. This January 1842 court report confirms that the odonymy of these street names begins with the land-sale campaign of 1841, given that Staple's court case used these same names to identify the allotments sold in January and March 1841. From the court description above, the two streets that do not appear on later parish maps, High and Market streets, are logically consistent with west–east streets.[16] Further, in Figure 14, on the left corner of the superimposed township, the words 'Lands Title 359A' is clearly visible. There is, therefore, a strong likelihood that the original 1841 plan catalogued as 359(A)—which showed the streets and sections of the private subdivision of the town of St Vincent—was superimposed onto the Benandra parish maps of 1907 and 1917.

John Staple can, therefore, be identified as another of the purchasers of allotments at the St Vincent auction in late January and/or late March 1841. Later in 1842, in his insolvency schedule, Staple recounted his assets and debts.[17] In so doing, he provided a long list of property purchases at Seaham, Violet Creek, Morphett, Coogee Bay, Muswellbrook, Cooks River as well as Batemans Bay. The last referred to his purchase of 81 allotments at St Vincent. He told the court: 'I paid £85 on the five sections at Bateman's Bay, and still owe £340.' This is consistent with the terms of sale at Thomas Stubbs's January 1841 auction, where buyers paid down 20 per cent on the hammer. There is no evidence that Staple honoured any subsequent payment schedule.

This means that Staple paid £425 for 81 allotments. It has already been established from Stubbs's announcement in February 1841 that the total sales from the January 1841 auction (representing 75 per cent of the township) was £2,210. Staple, therefore, was responsible for 14.4 per cent of the value of all sales at St Vincent (£2,947). Given Dent also purchased five sections, and assuming Dent's and Staple's sections were of equal size

---

16 Raphael Clint's 1841 lithograph does name north–south running streets outside of, but as a continuation of, streets running from the Hughes & Hosking block. Vincent Street and West Street are consistent with the names on the later maps, while East Street on Clint's 1841 lithograph is later called Reserve Street East. The fact that Lord Street appears on the Hughes & Hosking property provides some support for the contention that Edward Lord and Hughes & Hosking/Clint and Peacock collaborated to some extent in their advertising campaigns.
17 Staple's insolvency file is held at State Records Authority NSW, INX-10-29249, item no. 182, NRS-13654-1-[2/8676]-182. See also *Sydney Herald*, 4 July 1842, 2.

and value, this means 28.8 per cent of purchases at St Vincent have been positively identified. This does not include H. & W. Newman's client nor another possible purchaser named James Lasham.[18]

John Staple is one the few persons, along with George Dent (and possibly H. & W. Newman's client and John Lasham), identifiable as purchasers of allotments at St Vincent in 1841. These auction sales were not found, or not mentioned, by the supervising surveyor in Blair's 1917 primary application. Yet, these transactions, which have been uncovered incidentally from press reports rather than official documents, are enough to suggest that there was more to Thomas Stubbs's claims of 'important results' in the township of St Vincent than over-fertilised hyperbole.[19]

Dent's sections might have been sold on or passed in at his May 1841 auction, but what happened to Staple's claim? This issue is addressed in the following section.

John Staple and the Office of the Sheriff

This incidental detail about John Staple from a Supreme Court sheriff's office report remains one of the few pieces of positive evidence substantiating that land sales were transacted at Long Beach, St Vincent, by Thomas Stubbs in January to March 1841. John Staple's story is worth recounting, not simply because his documented indebtedness corroborated the original layout of the township of St Vincent, but also because his rise and fall provide insight into the type of 'speculatist' who was caught in the

---

18   In late 1842, in the insolvent estate of John Lasham, cabinet-maker, Pitt Street, the following properties were auctioned:
   St Vincent, all that piece or parcel of land, situate lying, and being in the Township of St. Vincent, and being lots 6, 7, 8, 9, bounded on the west by the Sydney Road 264 feet; on the north by lot No. 10, being a line east 379 feet 6 inches; on the east by lots No. 21, 22, 23, and 24, being a line south 264 feet and on the south: by lot No. 5, being a line west 379 feet to the commencing point. (*NSW Government Gazette*, 18 November 1842, 1727)
Lasham was, therefore, potentially another identifiable buyer, although the reference to 'the Sydney Road' is not consistent with any known road at Batemans Bay, unless it was identified as a future road on Plan 359(A). Stubbs had mentioned the road gang working south from Cook's River.
19   One of Raphael Clint's 1841 lithographic maps of Edward Deas Thomson's South Huskisson for Samuel Lyons provides valuable information of the land sales at the auction. On the left-hand side of Map F57, held in the NLA, there is a table with the section numbers, allotment numbers and names of purchasers. See R. Clint, 'Sketch of the Township of South Huskisson', 1841, Lithog., Ferguson Collection, map 57. This evidence shows that by June 1841, when the land was sold at South Huskisson, there was still demand for town land in such proposed private towns.

6. JOHN STAPLE AND THE TRIALS OF SPECULATION

depression of the early 1840s. His story also provides a window onto the workings of the NSW sheriff's office, an institution that so many insolvents encountered during this period of depression.

John Staple and his wife left London on 21 July 1839 aboard the *Orient* and arrived at Sydney on 8 December. Staple presented himself as a 'Gentleman Attorney of Her Majesty's Court of Queen's Bench, Westminster'. On arrival, the Staples resided at 9 Castlereagh Street South and advertised for a cottage of not less than six rooms within 3 miles of Sydney, 'for a term of years'. They found a place on Pitt Street South.[20]

On 7 August 1840, the governor appointed Staple under sheriff in the Office of Sheriff at the Supreme Court.[21] His name first appeared as under sheriff in a 23 July Supreme Court case. The responsibility of the office involved supervising bailiffs and executing Supreme Court judgements.

Staple provided notice of his intention to be admitted as an attorney to the Supreme Court on 19 July 1840[22] and was admitted on 31 October. Eight other candidates were also proposed and admitted as attorneys that day. The fifth candidate was Mr John Staple, proposed by Justice William à Beckett. His admission was ordered without debate.[23]

Within a week, Staple had set himself up as a conveyancer on the corner of King and Phillip streets. His engagements included preparing legal documents for property leases and later for the sale of government land in the recently laid out New Zealand town of Auckland.[24] During this period, he purchased the St Vincent allotments at auction. In his new status as a conveyancer, he must have calculated that the real estate market would remain a profitable proposition for the foreseeable future. In July 1841,

---

20   *Sydney Gazette and New South Wales Advertiser*, 10 December 1839, 2. *Australian*, 14 January 1840, 3; *Sydney Herald*, 21 September 1840, 4.
21   *Sydney Monitor and Commercial Advertiser*, 19 August 1840, 3: 'Notice is hereby Given, that Mr. John Staple has been appointed Under-Sheriff by His Excellency the Governor in the room of Mr. Robert Blake, late Under Sheriff.—J. Macquoid, Sheriff.—Sheriff's Office, Sydney, August 7, 1840.' See also *Sydney Herald*, 24 July 1840, 3, and then regularly after that date.
22   State Records Authority NSW, NRS-13672-2-[9/5190]-[192].
23   *Sydney Herald*, 2 November 1840. See also *Australian*, 3 November 1840; *Colonist*, 3 November 1840, 3; *Commercial Journal and Advertiser*, 4 November 1840, 3. William à Beckett became solicitor-general in March 1841. In this role he expressed his 'disgust' at the 'sound' of Berkley Estate, the real estate case mentioned in Chapter 3. He later presided over the case of two miners arrested at the Eureka Stockade. He also published literary criticism.
24   *Sydney Herald*, 5 November 1840, 3; 27 January 1841; 20 March 1841.

he prepared abstracts of land titles for purchasers at Jervis Town, auctioned by Thomas Stubbs (see Chapter 4). Staple would have encountered Stubbs at the St Vincent auctions in January/March.

Even if he had the inclination, Staple's work schedule did not permit him the time to join the passengers who left Sydney for Batemans Bay aboard the *Star* on 2 February 1841 to view his new property (see Chapter 5). Apart from his conveyancing business, he had retained his position as under sheriff, supplementing his conveyancing income with a salary of £200 per annum, plus fees for various services associated with his duties.[25]

In mid-March 1841, Staple entered into a legal partnership with Mr John S. Clarke at Hunter Street under the business name 'Clarke and Staple' and he resigned as under sheriff. The latter position was resumed by Cornelius Prout, who had held the role in the late 1820s and early 1830s.[26]

In his short period of public service, Staple appeared to have gained a reputation for honesty and diligence. On his new partnership, the *Free Press and Commercial Journal* had 'not the slightest doubt but they will enjoy that success in business which their abilities and perseverance deserve'.[27] Staple continued to operate his conveyancing business as a separate entity, while arranging private land-sale contracts with Clarke.

---

25   *Sydney Herald*, 5 February 1841, 3; 12 February 1841, 4. For the NSW budget, including the under sheriff's salary, see *Australian*, 1 July 1841, 2. The under sheriff drew one-fifth of the sheriff's salary of £1,000. A free labourer in the late 1830s received £36 per annum. See McMichael, 'Crisis in Pastoral', 32.
26   A notice from the Office of the Sheriff dated 17 March stated: 'Notice is hereby given, that Mr. Cornelius Prout has been appointed under sheriff, vice Mr. John Staple, resigned. T. Macquoid, Sheriff.' See *Australasian Chronicle*, 30 March 1841, 4. During 1839–40, Cornelius Prout had been building a bridge over Cook's River on his Canterbury property, 'Belle Ombre', as part of the construction of Canterbury Road. Prout's Bridge is still in use today. Prout was still under sheriff in 1853 when he was involved in a local controversy over the toll he demanded for the use of the bridge. The State Library of NSW holds a lithograph by Raphael Clint for an auction conducted by Thomas Stubbs on 31 May 1843 of the village of Canterbury that shows Prout's Bridge.
27   *Free Press and Commercial Journal*, 27 March 1841, 3. The *Australasian Chronicle* (20 March 1841, 2) predicted that Staple 'will meet that success amongst those who have become acquainted with him that his conduct deserves'. Staple announced the partnership in the *Australasian Chronicle*, 23 March 1841, 3. They had been working together prior to the partnership. See *Sydney Herald*, 5 March 1841, 3.

It is not clear why Staple resigned as under sheriff; however, it is possible that he decided that the salary was inadequate compensation for the stress of the position.[28] Sheriff Macquoid was persistently troubled by high turnover in the 'unenviable and not overpaid position' of under sheriff.[29] The workload of the office included organising the colony's court circuit, supervising bailiffs, the assignment of prisoners, administering the jails, carrying out of death sentences, coronial duties and executing other orders of the courts.

The Office of the Sheriff came under growing pressure as insolvencies rose. Once an insolvent's estate was sequestered, the court would request that the sheriff's office seize and make an inventory of the insolvent's monies, securities for monies, estate and effects. At this stage, the court could also order an insolvent to be held in custody, adding to the sheriff's responsibilities. The under sheriff was also often nominated as an assignee when an insolvent was ordered to surrender their assets.

---

28   As early as 1832, the sheriff had petitioned that 'the salary of £200 now paid to the Under Sheriff is inadequate as a remuneration for the duties and responsibilities of that office' and that it be raised to £500. This was rejected by the Legislative Council by six votes to five (*Sydney Herald*, 18 October 1832; *Australian*, 28 June 1833; *Sydney Gazette and New South Wales Advertiser*, 2 July 1833). Robert Blake was still complaining publicly about the 'poor salary' in 1839 (*Colonist*, 4 September 1839, 3). He had tendered his resignation in April 1839, but continued in the office while the sheriff was given leave of absence to visit Britain (*Colonist*, 3 April 1939, 2). The *Sydney Morning Herald* (23 July 1847, 2) published communication between the colonial secretary and the Office of the Sheriff between 1840 and 1845 concerning the salary of the under sheriff. In 1840, Macquoid argued that supplementary fees for services rendered by the deputy were necessary to attract a 'competent' person. It emerged that these fees had been based on 'custom'. This led to a July 1845 proposal to *reduce* the under sheriff's salary due to these extra fees received by the office. The colonial secretary also noted that the office of under sheriff had never been recognised by law.
29   Letter from Under Sheriff Robert Blake in *Australian*, 18 September 1838, 2. Cornelius Prout was first appointed to the position of under sheriff in 1829 and resigned in October 1832 to become governor of the Sydney Jail (*Sydney Herald*, 18 October 1832, 2). By the end of the year, however, it was reported that he had 'commenced business as an Auctioneer and Land Agent' (*Sydney Monitor*, 29 December 1832, 3). Walter Rogers was appointed the new under sheriff in October 1832, but died the following March, aged 22. The next incumbent, David Chambers, was forced out of the position as it was deemed 'highly improper for an practicing attorney to act as Under Sheriff'. He was followed in quick succession by Robert Stewart (who left to head Campbell Town's police magistracy) and John Brown (who entered the 'mercantile world'), then Edward Pogson, who held the position for year. Pogson was following by Samuel Smart, whom Macquoid was forced to release after nine months when he challenged another public servant to a duel. Edmund Rogers then held the position for a year, before Staple's predecessor, Robert Blake, took over. Blake engaged in a heated exchange in March 1838 with the *Sydney Times*, which accused him of hiring illiterate ruffians as bailiffs, and questioned whether his soldiering past made him fit for such a legal position. Blake resigned in 1840 shortly after his wife died, and he returned to Ireland in 1841. The *Sydney Morning Herald* (1 July 1847, 2) weighed into the debate over the proposed reduction of the under sheriff's salary (see fn 28, this chapter) by stating: 'Not only is the High Sheriff improperly paid a thousand a year for doing nothing, but the Under Sheriff receives the munificent sum of £100 a year for doing the work!!'

Figure 15. John Staple's superior, Sheriff Thomas Hyacinth Macquoid, 1836.
'No.4 Sketches from the Bar/Sheriff Macquoid', in Fernyhough, *Album of Portraits*, collection.sl.nsw.gov.au/digital/g3zVK7m28EkWv.

One of the conditions of the position of sheriff was that the holder was personally liable for any negligence of the office, including actions of the under sheriff and bailiffs. Organising indemnity was the sheriff's own responsibility. During 1841, Sheriff Thomas Hyacinth Macquoid (see Figure 15) was regularly a defendant against plaintiffs seeking costs and damages against him resulting from insolvency cases.[30] For instance, in one case, a plaintiff sought to recover from Macquoid the amount of a jailed insolvent's writ after he had escaped from the debtors' prison.[31]

---

30   At least five court cases were reported in the press during 1841, including *Kettle v. Macquoid* (*Australian*, 8 June 1841, 2), *Wentworth v. Macquoid* (*Sydney Chronicle*, 14 August 1841, 2), *Gore v. Macquoid* (*Australasian Chronicle*, 27 May 1841, 2), *Humphreys v. Macquoid* (*Sydney Herald*, 16 March 1841, 2) and *Barnes v. Macquoid* (*Sydney Monitor and Commercial Advertiser*, 18 October 1841, 2).
31   *Kettle v. Macquoid*, *Australian*, 8 June 1841, 2; *Sydney Herald*, 8 June 1841.

6. JOHN STAPLE AND THE TRIALS OF SPECULATION

John Staple was mentioned in two such cases against the sheriff, and in a case in which two cheques in Macquoid's care were lost. It is clear from these cases that Staple was regularly out of the Sydney office (presumably on work duties) and also had occasion to assume some of Macquoid's authority. Pressure resulting from the rising atmosphere of litigation against the office would have been an added incentive for Staple to leave the position.[32]

The year 1841 was a chaotic one in the overworked sheriff's office. Macquoid, who had been appointed to the position of sheriff in June 1828 —and who had, therefore, witnessed John Staple's appointment as under sheriff in August 1840—had long been in dispute with the governor and the Colonial Office over the status of his role (his 'precedency'), which he felt was undervalued in terms of political and administrative stature as well as recompense.[33]

Macquoid's personal financial position was becoming increasingly perilous. As the drought persisted and livestock prices fell, he placed his Limestone Plains 'Waniassa' property—managed by his son—on the market.[34] On 12 October 1841, the day after Macquoid was ordered by Justice Stephen to pay a plaintiff over £600, he committed suicide at his residence on Woolloomooloo Hill while in a 'fit of temporary insanity'.[35] When the 'deeply affected' Justice Burton swore in the acting sheriff, Mr Hustler, a week later, his speech was sympathetic to Macquoid's earlier demands for the reform of the office. Burton warned Hustler of his heavy responsibility and hoped that 'as it now stands you may not hold it long: for the duties of the office are too arduous, they are too onerous for one mind however

---

32 In *Humphreys v. Macquoid*, the plaintiff's lawyer argued that 'although Mr Staples residence was described as being in Sydney for anything that appeared to the contrary they might have been under sheriffs of some other colony or even of some part in England' (*Sydney Herald*, 16 March 1841, 2). For the extent of Staple's authority, see *Wentworth v. Macquoid* (*Sydney Chronicle*, 14 August 1841, 2).
33 See T. Macquoid to Sir George Gipps, 15 March 1838, and Gipps's dispatch to Lord Glenelg, 28 August 1838, in Watson, *Historical Records*, series 1, vol. 19, 339–41. After receiving no satisfaction from London, Macquoid again wrote to Lord Glenelg through Gipps, on 30 March 1839, and received the same 'conclusive' rejection from Lord Russell on 25 October 1839. See Watson, *Historical Records*, series 1, vol. 20, 87–9 and 373.
34 *Sydney Gazette and New South Wales Advertiser*, 14 November 1840, 1; *Sydney Herald*, 5 March 1841, 1; *Sydney Free Press*, 19 August 1841, 3. Macquoid had previously been posted at Wanyasa, Java. He had first been assigned to Java in 1812 as superintendent of coffee production by his friend Sir Stamford Raffles. For a biography of Macquoid, see Lamb, *Macquoid*.
35 'Melancholy Suicide of the Late High Sheriff of New South Wales', *Sydney Monitor and Commercial Advertiser*, 18 October 1841, 2. The report of how he 'put a period to his existence' is more graphic than would be expected from a similar contemporary account. Charles Edward Langley, the surveyor and civil engineer who had shared Raphael Clint's George Street office earlier in the year, was empanelled as a member of the jury for the inquest into Macquoid's death.

vigorous'. Burton believed that Sydney needed a dedicated sheriff and he hoped 'that the Legislative Council will not separate at its next meeting without making adequate provision for the proper and safe discharge of the duties of your office'.[36]

At the end of October, Governor Gipps sent a dispatch to the secretary of state for war and the colonies, Lord Russell, in which he mentioned 'pecuniary embarrassments' as the reason for the commission of Macquoid's 'rash act'. An amount of £2,400 levied in pursuance of writs ordered by judges was, at the time, held by Macquoid in his responsibility as sheriff. Gipps feared the monies would not reach their rightful suitors. A meeting was called at the Royal Hotel for 21 October 1841 for anyone having claims on Macquoid 'arising from his public duties, or from private transactions', and, on 20 November 1841, justices Dowling, Burton and Stephen rewrote the rules surrounding 'Writs in the Hands of the Sheriff'. During October and November, rumours abounded in the colony that during the previous 11 years the authority of the sheriff had been illegally constituted and all verdicts handed down were invalid.[37] Macquoid's circumstances prompted a review of the office and a subsequent *Act for Regulating the Appointment and Duties of Sheriff in New South Wales* became law in December 1843.[38]

John Staple's departure from the overtaxing environment of the Office of the Sheriff did not improve either his own health or his wellbeing. On 11 October 1841, he announced that: 'Mr. John Staple, Solicitor, &c., begs to inform his friends that, in consequence of ill health, he has removed

---

36   See *Australian*, 14 October 1841, 2; *Sydney Herald*, 15 October 1841, 2. Justice Burton wrote to Lord Glenelg supporting Macquoid's precedency. See Watson, *Historical Records*, series 1, vol. 20, 89.
37   An exchange of official letters associated with the case was printed in the *Australian*, 28 August 1843, 4. *Sydney Herald*, 20 October 1841, 1. See also *Australasian Chronicle*, 25 November 1841, 2; 'The Late Sheriff No Sheriff at All!', *Colonial Observer*, 11 November 1841, 4. Lost and dishonoured cheques had plagued the Office of Sheriff.
38   See Bennett, 'The Office of Sheriff'. See also 'New South Wales Sheriff History', www.bailiff.com.au/nsw/TheSheriffOfNSW.htm, accessed 20 January 2023. Raphael Clint had an awkward court encounter with Thomas Macquoid in 1837—one that provides some support for Justice Burton's concerns about the taxing role of the office. Clint was on jury duty in a case of cattle stealing. After three hours of evidence, Clint stood up and asked Judge Dowling whether the court was legally constituted, given neither the sheriff nor his deputies were present. Dowling told Clint that it was his business to see it was legally constituted and that perhaps the sheriff was elsewhere in the building on other duties. At this moment, Sheriff Macquoid walked into the room, and Dowling explained the pause in court proceedings. The attorney-general said to Macquoid: 'You had had better answer for yourself, Mr. Sheriff: here is a Juror complaining of you for being absent from your post.' The sheriff simply smiled, and the attorney-general turned to Dowling: 'I hope your Honor, the mind of the juror has not been disturbed from his duty.' 'His Honor told the juror to sit down' and the case continued (*Sydney Monitor*, 15 February 1837, 2). As noted in the previous chapter, Clint prided himself on his legal sharpness.

6. JOHN STAPLE AND THE TRIALS OF SPECULATION

from Sydney to Singleton, Patrick's Plains.' Despite this, his office on the corner of King and Phillip streets remained open for business under the care of his managing clerk, Joseph Hill Ward.[39] Staple's friend, the solicitor William Goddard, acted as his agent while he was out of Sydney.

This notice had been preceded six days earlier by a press announcement that Mr Blackman would auction on 7 October at Mr Staple's residence on Pitt Street South ('previous to his removal') a full range of household furniture, including couches, a dining table, a feather bed, a chest of drawers, curtains, chimney ornaments, kitchen utensils and laundry.[40]

The sale of Staple's household effects and his departure from Sydney was followed in December 1841 and January 1842 by the earlier-cited Supreme Court announcement from the under sheriff Cornelius Prout that John Staple was the defendant in a case to be heard on 18 January involving five plaintiffs, and that his St Vincent allotments at Batemans Bay would be offered at auction.[41] Over the previous year, Staple himself had been become adept at writing such court notices in his role as under sheriff.

On 17 January 1842, Justice Burton called Staple into court regarding an affidavit submitted by Mr George Evans, a rectifier, who claimed that Staple's clerk, Ward, had accepted £18 10s. 6d. under writ of the court for Evans, and that the money had gone missing. A similar claim was made for a larger sum by a legal clerk, Mr Barnard Macdermott. When called to account for himself, Staple pleaded ignorance, as he was ill at the time and out of town. Justice Burton ordered that money owing and costs be paid within four days. More seriously, Barton suggested to Staples that he had been employing a person to conduct his legal business who was not competent to undertake the task. He was referring to Mr Ward. Staple acknowledged that this had been the case, and promised to take care that it did not occur again.[42]

---

39 *Sydney Herald*, 11 October 1841, 1. Singleton was another private town, laid out on Benjamin Singleton's Hunter Valley land, which he purchased in 1836. Singleton faced bankruptcy in 1842. For Ward, see *Sydney Herald*, 27 October 1841, 3. As early as 2 October, Ward was appearing in court for Staple's office (*Sydney Herald*, 5 October 1841, 2).
40 *Sydney Herald*, 5 October 1841, 1.
41 In 1813, a colonial Act made land available to creditors for the enforcement of the money owed by debtors. See Kercher, *An Unruly Child*, ch. 6.
42 *Sydney Free Press*, 20 January 1842, 3; *Australasian Chronicle*, 18 January 1842, 2. In July 1842, Evans himself would be acquitted on a charge of possessing an illegal still. The case revolved around the distinction between distilling and rectifying spirits. See *Sydney Morning Herald*, 24 July 1842, 2.

On 31 March 1842, when it became clear that his assets could not resolve his debts, Staple filed for insolvency and his estate was placed under sequestration. A meeting of debtors was organised for 18 April, along with another meeting to arrange trustees to his estate.[43] Staple had debts of £1,042 2s. and held assets or 'credits' of £1,028 10s. Like many who had engaged in land speculation, these credits included 'bad and doubtful debts'.[44] On 24 May, an accountant, Joseph McKenna, was appointed provisional trustee and further meetings of debtors arranged before examinations of Staple proceeded on 1 July 1842.[45]

At this insolvency meeting in July, Staple revealed more details of his assets and debts. His assets included the deposit for the land at St Vincent (see section above). The fact that the St Vincent deposit still appeared in Staple's insolvency schedule meant that he must have satisfied the plaintiffs who were seeking their money at or before the 18 January meeting at the sheriff's office. None of these five plaintiffs was a claimant in Staple's insolvency schedule. Evans and Macdermott, however, remained unsatisfied.

The other issue raised at the July meeting was the conduct of Staple's affairs while he had been absent through illness at the end of 1841. Staple's clerk, Joseph Ward, admitted that in November or December 1841 Staple had placed in his possession a gold watch and asked him to get it fixed. Instead, Ward had presented the watch to the bailiff of the Court of Requests, Robert Purcell, as an inducement (or 'sort of bonus') to stay the executions of insolvency against Staple and himself.[46] Ward admitted that he was acting on his own discretion rather than on the authority of Staple. Around this time, Ward had also brought an action for George Evans against a Mr Messee and, after the court found in Evans's favour, the sheriff presented Ward with a cheque to be passed to his client. Instead, Ward gave part of the money to

---

43 Staple's insolvency file, State Records Authority NSW, INX-10-29649, item no. 182, NRS-13654-1-[2/8676]-182. *NSW Government Gazette*, 5 April 1842, 525.
44 *Sydney Herald*, 5 April 1842, 3. See also *Sydney Gazette and New South Wales Advertiser*, 23 April 1842, 2, for a subsequent meeting of creditors on 18 April. Like Staple, when the merchant and neighbour of Macquoid, A.B. Spark, became insolvent in 1843, his assets were calculated at almost £61,000, just short of his debts. The following year, £56,000 of these assets were reappraised as 'hopeless'. See Broadbent, 'Aspects of Domestic Architecture', 526.
45 See *NSW Government Gazette*, 17 May 1842, 729; *Sydney Herald*, 4 July 1842, 2.
46 Ward's estate was placed under sequestration on 22 March 1841. *NSW Government Gazette*, 25 March 1841, 471.

Staple and used the remainder to pay for office expenses. He then presented Evans with another cheque that was dishonoured. This was the basis of Evans's original grievance.[47]

Three months earlier, the court had heard that, while Staple was absent from his office in November 1841, Ward had drawn up a warrant of attorney that became the subject of a fraudulent insolvency case involving the grocer Edward Jones. This misdemeanour or irregularity on Ward's part reinforced the seriousness of Justice Barton's earlier concerns in January 1842.[48]

In December 1842, Staple's Coogee and Violet Creek properties were put up for auction by Thomas Stubbs. However, there was no further mention of the St Vincent lots. By now, the 320 acres had been mortgaged to the Bank of Australia by Hughes & Hosking. Staple would not have had the means to maintain his scheduled payments on these lots while insolvent.

On 4 January 1843, Staple was back before the court over Evans's claim. William Henry Goddard represented Staple, who did not appear in person. Goddard, motivated by his friendship with Staple and concern over the perilous state of Staple's business, offered to pay the debt to Evans.[49] He warned that Staple's woes would only worsen 'if the strong manner in which His Honor expressed himself on the subject was unmodified'.[50] Justice Burton responded by threatening to make an example of Staple for failing to conduct his legal business in a proper manner through employing a 'disreputable person' as his managing clerk. Burton felt that

> it would hold out a useful lesson to the gentlemen of the profession to bring the matter before the Court, by a rule being issued calling on Mr Staple to show cause why he should not be struck off the roll for having received money on behalf of his client under the writ of the Court, he not having paid over the same.[51]

---

47 *Sydney Herald*, 4 July 1842, 2.
48 *Australasian Chronicle*, 9 April 1842, 2.
49 *Sydney Morning Herald*, 5 January 1843, 2.
50 When Hughes & Hosking auctioned its Mossy Point, Broulee, property in October 1840, along with Long Beach, it was sold to William Goddard and Henry Osborne. See Magee, *All Broulee*, 143. Goddard's estate was placed under sequestration on 18 July 1843 (*NSW Government Gazette*, 21 July 1843, 941), and he applied for his certificate of discharge on 11 April the following year.
51 *Sydney Morning Herald*, 5 January 1843, 2.

Insolvency paled in comparison with this threat of professional debarring.

On 20 January 1843, the attorney-general moved that the ruling, or rule nisi, obtained on the previous occasion—namely that John Staple be struck off the roll of the court—be made absolute. In the ensuing debate, Staple was defended by Sheriff Macquoid's former acting successor, William Hustler,[52] who repeated Goddard's argument that Staple had had no knowledge of what had transpired in his office due to ill health, that he was now prepared to pay his debt of £18 10s. to his former client Evans, and that he would have done so earlier had he not taken legal advice against doing so, 'lest the Court imagine it was done for fear of the consequences of his application'.[53]

In 'addressing themselves to the subject', the learned judges acknowledged that no moral turpitude could be attributed to Staple in the case. However,

> to uphold the honour of the profession, and to prevent the public from losing that confidence which had hitherto been reposed in the profession, they felt bound to visit the case with severe reprehension, and to order that Mr Staple be struck off the rolls of the Court.[54]

On 17 November 1843, the trustee Joseph McKenna informed the chief commissioner of insolvent estates that Staple, late of Singleton, 'can render by his presence in this Colony no service to the interests of the Creditors of his Estate'. On the same day, Commissioner Kerr confirmed that Staple was 'at liberty to leave the Colony having complied with the provisions of

---

52 Lord Russell appointed Adolphus William Young to the permanent position of sheriff of NSW in October 1842. Young had worked for the law firm Carr and Rogers between 1838 and 1840 before returning to England. In 1839 he had resigned from his role as director in the Australian Gas Light Company after acting 'indiscreetly' by purchasing land adjoining that of the company (see *Sydney Monitor and Commercial Advertiser*, 25 October 1839). He accepted the position of sheriff on the understanding that the role of the office would be reformed. William Hustler was one of the Supreme Court judges who ordered Staple's admission as an attorney of the Supreme Court in October 1840. In 1843 Hustler was an unsuccessful candidate in the Legislative Council Election. His campaign was notable for the long poems he penned in the press outlining his policies.
53 *Sydney Morning Herald*, 21 January 1843, 2.
54 *Sydney Morning Herald*, 21 January 1843, 2. The *Austral-Asiatic Review, Tasmanian and Australian Advertiser*, 10 February 1843, 3, adds the information that Evans's money found its way into Staple's list of assets.

the act'.⁵⁵ On 30 December 1843, four years after Staples arrived in Sydney, the *Dispatch* reported in its 'Shipping News' that the *Ratcliff* was departing from Sydney for Hong Kong with Mr and Mrs Staple on board.⁵⁶

Conclusion

There was a marked increase in announcements of insolvency in the *NSW Government Gazette* and the Sydney press from 1841. In this context, John Staple, along with George Dent, exemplified the small-scale 'speculatist' who fell victim by buying land at the bend of the market before stumbling into the depression.

The 18 January 1842 Supreme Court 'rousing' of John Staple's right, title, interest and estate at St Vincent either produced no results or did not proceed. The plaintiffs did not appear as creditors in Staple's later insolvency schedule. It is also possible that the Bank of Australia requested the cancellation of the January 1842 auction of Staple's Batemans Bay allotments, given that Hughes & Hosking had purchased the entire property in November 1841 and had mortgaged it to the bank on 1 January 1842. The deposit was still listed on Staple's insolvency schedule and mentioned during his July 1842 Insolvency Court hearings as an asset. At this stage, it was not clear whether he retained any right to or interest in the title. The deposit could have been returned and surrendered for the benefit of Staple's creditors. Alternatively,

---

55   State Records Authority NSW, INX-10-29249, item no. 182, NRS-13654-1-[2/8676]-182.
56   John Staple had been residing at Patrick's Plains, Singleton, since his illness and financial troubles. In May 1842, a memorial for the appointment of a Court of Requests in Singleton lay for signature at John Staple's, Solicitor &c., John Street, Singleton (*Hunter River Gazette; and Journal of Agriculture, Commerce, Politics, and News*, 14 May 1842). He appears to have continued his law practice while at Singleton, preparing a will for a client in Falbrook (*Sydney Morning Herald*, 29 March 1844, 3). 'Solicitor Staple' also receives a mention in the *Sydney Morning Herald* (9 November 1842, 2) concerning a public meeting at the Singleton Court House called to discuss an anonymous correspondent in the press who allegedly denigrated Patrick's Plains. The paper reported that 'Solicitor Staple' denounced the notice as 'false and scandalous libel upon the district and its inhabitants', and called for a resolution 'expressive of the contempt and indignation it had excited in the minds of the inhabitants generally'. The anonymous correspondent replied in the same paper on 13 December 1842 criticising Staple as a member of a local 'clique' and 'junta' with 'secret designs'. Staple's defence of the local constabulary was considered hypocritical, given he had recently made a public complaint over their negligence after his wife's workbox was stolen from an unsecured window (*Sydney Morning Herald*, 5 January 1843). After leaving the colony, it is possible the couple headed back to Britain. Later in the decade, the *Monmouthshire Merlin* (15 July 1848) reported on a court case involving a land dispute in which the New South Wales Railway Company was represented by 'Mr Staple, solicitor, with whom was Mr Lloyd, barrister-in-law'.

it could have been forfeited on the compelling logic that there was no point throwing good money after bad. There is a chance that the land he bought was now worth less than the £85 deposit he handed over to Thomas Stubbs in early 1841. Many others who purchased lots at St Vincent from Stubbs might have made the same judgement.

This spreading fever of insolvency overburdened the sheriff's office as the depression deepened in 1841. To compound matters, the principal authority of the office was preoccupied with his own financial difficulties. Minutes before he died, Thomas Hyacinth Macquoid—John Staple's former superior—wrote a last note to his wife. It was found in his study on top of his official document box, 'spotted with blood'. Among other issues, he 'alluded to the affairs of the colony'. The 'temporarily insane' sheriff predicted that 'there would be a universal bankruptcy within twelve months'.[57]

Despite his fear of universal monetary collapse, and despite his own financial problems, the sheriff (like his former under sheriff John Staple) was unable to resist joining in the speculative hunt for a great southern port. Macquoid was one of the larger woolgrowers on the Limestone Plains who subscribed £30 towards the development of the Wool Road in 1841. His name also appears as a purchaser of four allotments in Raphael Clint's handwriting on the left-hand side of the lithographic 'Sketch of the Township of South Huskisson', Jervis Bay, produced by Clint for the auctioneer Samuel Lyons in June 1841 (see Chapter 4).[58]

The 'fever' of insolvency and indebtedness within the colony infected the very office whose task it was to act on insolvency decisions handed down by the court. The following two chapters explore other widespread consequences of insolvency. Chapter 7 describes how political decision-makers dealt with the massive problem of the surplus of property surrendered by insolvents in a depressed market, including the former township of St Vincent. Chapter 8 considers the 1841 *Insolvency Act* and the conflicting responses it provoked: some insolvents felt that it made them a scapegoat for the depression,

---

57 *Sydney Monitor and Commercial Advertiser*, 18 October 1841, 2.
58 See the table on the left of R. Clint, 'Sketch of the Township of South Huskisson', 1841, Lithog., Ferguson Collection, map 57, nla.gov.au/nla.obj-229901982. Macquoid's allotments faced Elizabeth Street (Section 47, Allotment Numbers 5, 6, 7 and 8). In contemporary Vincentia, these allotments are situated on Elizabeth Drive, on the second block to the east of Violet Clark Reserve. For Macquoid and the Wool Road, see Chapter 4; *Sydney Herald*, 19 June 1841, 3. Further, Macquoid and Edward Deas Thomson (the colonial secretary and the owner of South Huskisson) were near neighbours at Woolloomooloo. Both were also members of the exclusive Australian Club, whose founding president was the former colonial secretary Alexander Macleay.

while others felt insolvency helped debtors avoid their responsibilities to their creditors. John Terry Hughes's and John Hosking's fortunes were also about to turn dramatically for the worse as the 'colonial fever' of insolvency spread. These two mercantile gentlemen take centrestage in the following two chapters.

7

Long Beach and Australia's first lottery

Where'er we go, from North to South,
In City, Town, or Squattery,
The Talk in everybody's mouth
Is all about the Lottery!
But much I fear that many rue
The cash they chanced abortively,
And wish they'd found aught else to do
With the tin they've lost thus sportively!
Bow wow wow—bow wow wow fol,
Lol de riddy iddy—bow wow wow![1]

Many individuals, such as John Staple, Raphael Clint, Edward Lord, George Dent and William Henry Wells, who became insolvent during the 1840s depression experienced this as a personal misfortune or tragedy. However, the collapse of large companies had wider repercussions that reverberated through the social structure. This chapter explores the cascading events that Golder has called 'one of Sydney's biggest scandals',[2] namely, the collapse of the Bank of Australia, followed by the firm of Hughes & Hosking. In the fallout of the scandal—which had been aggravated by land speculation—another form of gambling was initiated: a government-sanctioned lottery. The fate of Hughes & Hosking's 320 acres at Long Beach was linked to these events.

---

1   Anon., 'The Lottery. A New Comic Song', *Bell's Life in Sydney and Sporting Reviewer*, 27 January 1849, 3.
2   Golder, *Politics*, 6. Brian Fitzpatrick (*The British Empire*, 73) described this scandal as a feature in 'the dire disasters of 1842–43'.

The collapse of the Bank of Australia and of Hughes & Hosking

After the March 1841 Albion Wharf fire at Darling Harbour, Hughes & Hosking continued to trade, moving initially to Dickson's Old Mills further along Sussex Street. They sustained further stock losses soon after in the May floods, followed by the collapse of a recently erected building they owned near the Cattle Market.[3] Like many other merchants, they buckled as economic conditions worsened.[4] Their various misfortunes weakened their capacity to trade and their extensive real estate holdings continued to decline in value.[5]

To compound matters, their financial backer, the Bank of Australia, collapsed on 2 March 1843. By 26 September 1843, Hughes & Hosking was also placed under sequestration with debts of over £327,000, of which £143,497 was owed to the Bank of Australia.[6] As security, the Bank of Australia had valued the assets of Hughes & Hosking, along with Hughes's personal property, at £600,000. This valuation was made before the 'fearful, unprecedented, and extraordinary depreciation, resembling a pestilential breath, devastating, and drying up, blasting, every description of property'.[7] When debts were called in, the company—like many individuals such as Edward Lord and John Staple—could not find the ready cash.

---

3   *Sydney Herald*, 4 March 1841, 3; *Sydney Gazette and New South Wales Advertiser*, 7 September 1841, 2.
4   See Morrissey, 'The Pastoral Economy', 86–91. The *Australian*, 4 March 1841, 2, predicted that the calamity of Hughes & Hosking would reverberate throughout the colony: 'In the present state of the mercantile world, the ruin of the firm would involve the ruin of two-thirds of the merchants of Sydney.'
5   In particular, interest in their East Balmain subdivision later in March 1841 was disappointing. This 5-acre block bordering Johnson, Darling and Union streets was purchased in 1836, and the surveyor John Armstrong was commissioned to subdivide the property (see Hamey, 'John Hosking', 3). However, contrary to Hughes & Hosking's expectations, sales were sluggish, with only 13 of the 29 lots sold, despite Thomas Stubbs wielding the auctioneer's hammer. See Reynolds, 'From Johnson', 23–6. Hosking Street still runs within the subdivision between Johnson and Union streets.
6   *NSW Government Gazette*, 29 September 1843, 1251. See also Sykes, *Two Centuries*, ch. 2; Butlin, *Foundations*, 345–55.
7   The valuation and the phrase are found in a letter written by John Terry Hughes to the *Sydney Morning Herald*, 27 June 1846, 1. See also letter written by Hughes to the *Commercial Journal and General Advertiser*, 7 June 1845, 3. Hughes borrowed the phrase from Chief Justice Stephen's decision to accept John Hosking's appeal to grant him his certificate of insolvency. See *Sydney Morning Herald*, 28 April 1845, 4.

In the midst of this financial turmoil, which enveloped entities previously considered the pillars of the commercial community, the Legislative Council established a Select Committee on Monetary Confusion in September 1843. One banking witness expressed a widespread view that the source of the colony's current 'monetary embarrassment' was the result of

> over-speculation of every description, particularly in land purchases —that the Banks by their liberality in advancing money materially aided these speculations there can be no doubt, and unfortunately the large Government deposits which at one time were about £40,000 in each Bank, besides Commissariat balances to nearly an equal extent, afforded them the means.[8]

However, at the end of 1840 and the beginning of 1841, the government withdrew its money from the banks, which then 'had to call up their advances and press the public'.[9]

Thomas Stubbs was called as a witness before the committee. He presented 18 theses on the source of 'the great fall in the selling price of property', most of which came down to the want of assigned labour after the end of transportation, the want of credit and the want of confidence.[10] Stubbs's own profession was blamed for the state of the New South Wales economy in a pamphlet published in London in 1842. Attacking 'land gambling', the author, pen-named Philo-Palinurus, lamented that

> the natural means of acquiring competence by honest industry is now, alas! a hopeless case, by reason of land not being to be had, except through a gambling-shop, otherwise the auction rooms, the bane of Sydney.[11]

---

8   *Sydney Morning Herald*, 21 November 1843, 4.
9   *Sydney Morning Herald*, 21 November 1843, 4. On the Committee on Monetary Confusion, see Butlin, *Foundations*, 329–32; Braim, *A History*, vol. 2, 11–19; Sidney, *The Three Colonies*, 104, 121–3.
10 *Sydney Morning Herald*, 23 November 1843, 4. Transcripts were reproduced in the press two months after the hearings.
11 Philo-Palinurus, *Land Gambling*, 6. The author was principally targeting the conduct of government land auctions, but also the 'land-jobbers' who frequented them. The *Sydney Morning Herald* (9 April 1843, 2) published a review of Philo-Palinurus's pamphlet, which summarised an earlier review published in the *Colonial Magazine and Commercial-Maritime Journal* (August–December 1842, vol. 1, 490–1). It is possible that one reason the pamphlet received scant attention was that the author offered remedies that grated against recent legislative reforms granting greater popular participation, which the author considered 'inimical to the natural prosperity of the colony' (7). In *Land Gambling*, Philo-Palinurus supported more direct colonial control (11–21) as well as the reintroduction of transportation (21–2). Taking the colony back to the early 1830s, he also advocated an adequate grant of free land to all British migrants (24–5) and the abolition of the sale of Crown land.

The Bank of Australia became the reference point for the banking malpractice associated with 'the monetary embarrassment'. A joint-stock company that had always received mixed press, it was seen by some newspapers as a secretive, opaque and undemocratic agent of the squattocracy. This critical press labelled it the 'pure merino bank' and 'the squatters' bank' run by 'monopolists'. Trevor Sykes refers to its 'extreme exclusiveness'.[12] When Hughes & Hosking mortgaged its Long Beach property to the Bank of Australia on 1 January 1842, the director who acted for the bank was the prominent 'exclusive' Hannibal Hawkins Macarthur, nephew of John Macarthur.[13] Later, after the bank's insolvency, concerns were raised over the lack of due diligence involved in its large loans to Hughes & Hosking, particularly the extent to which it exposed the bank to the fortunes of a single client.[14]

The legal and financial repercussions of the collapse of the Bank of Australia and Hughes & Hosking dragged on throughout the 1840s.[15] The remaining assets of the bank involved an enormous portfolio of land, a portion of which had been mortgaged by Hughes & Hosking as security for loans from the bank, including Long Beach, site of the soon-forgotten town of St Vincent.

Australia's first publicly sanctioned lottery

Rather than liquidate the bank's landholdings at the basement prices prevailing during the depression and then distributing the diminished proceeds to its depositors, in 1844 Member of the Legislative Council William Wentworth introduced a Bill proposing an 'Act to Enable the Bank of Australia to Dispose of Certain Real and Personal Property in the Colony of New South Wales in Certain Shares by Lot'.[16] This Bill for a government-sanctioned lottery was supported by most of the NSW Legislative Council.

---

12   Sykes, *Two Centuries*, ch. 1.
13   See Augustus Blair's 1917 Primary Application for the title at Long Beach, State Records Authority NSW, NRS-17513, item 17513-8-34-PA 20438, vol. 2781, folio 34. Hannibal Macarthur also become insolvent in the wake of the bank's collapse in 1843. See *Morning Chronicle*, 4 December 1844; 8 February 1845, 2.
14   Details concerning the loans were revealed in the Judgement of the Judicial Committee of the Privy Council, 15 February 1848, and reported in full by the *Sydney Morning Herald*, 23 June 1848, 2–3. See also the correspondence in the *Sydney Morning Herald*, 20 July 1844, 2.
15   Dyster, 'The 1840s Depression Revisited', 606.
16   *Sydney Morning Herald*, 5 October 1844, 3; 12 October 1844, 2; 18 October 1844. According to Butlin's (*Foundations*, 345–55) detailed account of the lottery, the scheme originated with the banks. See also Braim, *A History*, vol. 2, 111–14. Wentworth had a significant interest in the Bank of Australia and other banks.

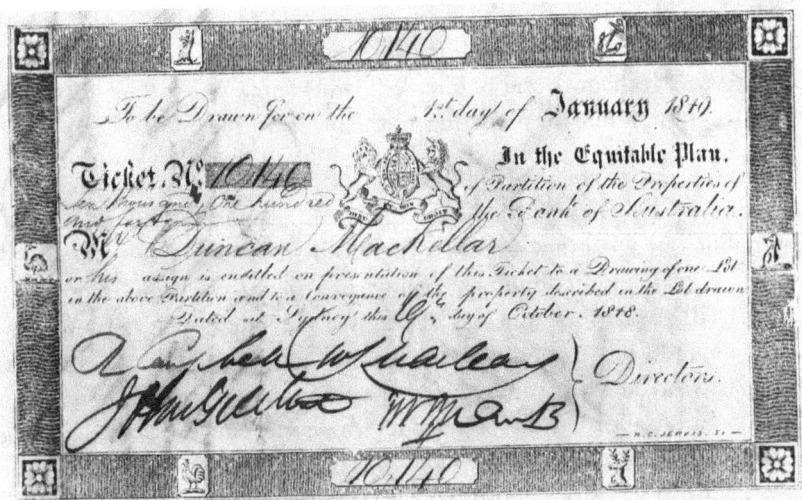

Figure 16. Bank of Australia lottery ticket no. 10,140, 1848.
'Bank of Australia Lottery Ticket Number 10,140 Issued to Duncan Mackellar, Dated 19 October 1848, Drawn on 1 January 1849. Endorsed in Ink on Back for £4', NLA, Ms-1602, nla.gov.au/nla.obj-260007374/view.

However, such a lottery had no precedent, and the Legislative Council sought Royal Assent for their Bill. The attorney-general reluctantly decided that the Bill was 'not such as the Governor of the colony ought to give the Royal Assent to'.[17] The British Government then rejected an appeal to the Crown. Regardless of this advice, the Legislative Council eventually decided that it was their duty to avert the catastrophe of financial ruin that would befall the many shareholders, the community of property owners and the wider colony if the scheme should not go ahead.[18] After all, there was no specific legislation prohibiting such a lottery.

Thus, after much public anticipation, on 19 October 1848, 11,248 lottery tickets worth £4 each were distributed to the bank's depositors according to the size of their deposit (see Figure 16). The lottery was divided into 11,248 lots so that each ticket would win a prize. The catch was that the lots ranged from a very valuable estate worth around £6,000 down to properties considered next to worthless (the latter were known euphemistically as 'Fitz

---

17 *Sydney Morning Herald*, 1 January 1845, 4.
18 The 1841 *Insolvency Act* (see Chapter 8) was criticised for contributing further to the 'frightful depreciation of property' through forcing insolvents' assets onto the already depressed market. There was widespread fear that if the Bank of Australia's trustees forced their large portfolio of properties onto the market, the value of all property in the colony would collapse catastrophically. See 'Dr Nicholson in The Legislative Council, November 21, 1843', in *Sydney Record*, 25 November 1843, 59.

Roys' and 'Hastings' after the two places where the majority of the least valuable lots were located).[19] Should they wish, those holding tickets were allowed to sell them to the public. William Henry Wells, Raphael Clint's rival, was responsible for preparing all the plans for the properties.[20]

The lottery for the bank's landholdings was a three-day extravaganza held at Sydney's City Theatre, Market Street, on 1–3 January 1849. It captured the public's imagination, as tickets had been freely circulating among the populace.[21] Despite its dubious legality, prominent citizens clamoured to be associated with the event, 37 of whom were appointed to superintend the drawing of lots, including the mayor, aldermen and sheriff, as well as Thomas Mort and the joint owner of the *Sydney Morning Herald*, John Fairfax. Fairfax printed the booklet for the event entitled *Schedule of the Lots in the Plan of Partition of the Bank of Australia*.[22] It explained the rules of the lottery draw and listed the names of those superintending the lottery, followed by 32 pages detailing the schedule of the lots with a brief description of each property.[23]

Ticket 3,174, held by a tenant farmer from the Isle of Skye, Angus McDonald, took 'first prize'. Much publicity surrounded McDonald and his prize, which included an 8,320-acre farm on the 'William River' north-west of Dungog named 'Underbank', 3,700 head of cattle and 40 horses, among other real assets. Allegedly McDonald had tried to sell his ticket at a discount prior to the draw. However, his luck ran out a few months later. As he rode home after a meeting to organise the management of his newly acquired cattle, he sustained fatal injuries from falling off his horse. An inquest found that he was 'not a skilful rider' and his stirrups were too long as he descended a depression.[24]

---

19 The *Argus* (23 January 1849, 2) listed the value of the most valuable lots (*Hobart Town Advertiser*, 6 February 1849, 3).
20 *People's Advocate and New South Wales Vindicator*, 17 May 1856, 12–13.
21 J.B.M. (*Reminiscences*, 38) recalled that the lottery 'set the whole colony gambling in tickets'. The *Daily News and Evening Chronicle* (16 November 1848, 2) spoke of 'lottery mania'.
22 *Schedule of the Lots in the Plan of Partition of the Bank of Australia. The Drawing to Commence on Monday January 1st, 1849* (Sydney: Kemp and Fairfax, 1848).
23 An account of the lottery also appears in Sykes, *Two Centuries*, ch. 2.
24 *Maitland Mercury and Hunter River General Advertiser*, 7 April 1849, 2. In 1856, W.H. Wells claimed that he still held in his possession 'all the Original Surveys and Plans; he retains a list of all Tickets with the Prizes'. He also claimed that 'some most valuable Prizes remain, still "unclaimed". Persons, therefore,—holding tickets would do well to communicate with him'. See *People's Advocate and New South Wales Vindicator*, 17 May 1856, 13. See also Chapter 10 for a court case involving Wells and the sale of one of the lottery prizes.

The fate of the Long Beach property

The 11,248 lots on offer at the January 1849 lottery—some consisting of multiple properties—did not constitute the whole of the bank's portfolio. For instance, the 320 acres at Long Beach and Hughes & Hosking's remaining Broulee properties, among others, were not on offer due to a 'difficulty which prevented the Bank from including the properties formerly belong to Messrs Hughes and Hosking in the first Drawing of the Partition' (see Chapter 8).[25]

However, within a month of the lottery, the auctioneer Samuel Lyons announced that this difficulty had been 'removed' and the Bank of Australia would hold a 'second and final drawing' of these properties on 9 April 1849. On the proposed day, Lyons issued another announcement that the 'equitable partition' of these properties had been postponed until 14 May.[26]

The organisers continued to carefully avoid the word 'lottery', due to ongoing concern over the questionable legal status of the January event. The press was also now more circumspect about the social and moral value of another mass gambling event.[27]

Many ticketholders from the January draw were disappointed with their prizes. Indeed, it was reported that over 10,000 lots (88.9 per cent of all lots) had a combined value of only £11,000.[28] The organisers of the lottery had not supplied advice on the value of 10,822 of the 11,248 lots, including the 8,880 lots at the 'townships' of Fitzroy and Hastings. Most of the latter were valued no higher than 10s. Meeting the demand for information, the Clints' friend J.T. Grocott was selling descriptions and valuations of

---

25 *Sydney Morning Herald*, 1 February 1849, 1. These difficulties involved various complications in which Hughes & Hosking's assets were 'encumbered with trusts, mortgages, marriage settlements, etc.'. See Butlin, *Foundations*. Some properties belonging to J.T. Hughes were among the more valuable lots in the lottery. See also Chapter 8 for Hughes's legal battles.
26 *Sydney Morning Herald*, 9 April 1849, 1.
27 The *Sydney Morning Herald* (22 January 1849, 2), getting wind of the new proposal, objected to another lottery, considering the initial one a necessary evil that had had the demoralising consequence of creating a large number of 'Fitz Royals'. *The People's Advocate and New South Wales Vindicator* (27 January 1849, 6) accused the *Herald* of hypocrisy, never having aired its anti-gambling views during the initial lottery mania, with Fairfax even printing the lottery schedule and acting as a lottery superintendent.
28 See *Daily News and Evening Chronicle*, 16 November 1848, 2.

ticketholders' newly acquired property for a shilling, while George Pickering of Pitt Street was offering plans previously prepared by W.H. Wells of every prize 'for a very moderate cash charge'.[29]

Most ticketholders felt 'Fitz Roy-ed' or 'Hasting-ed'.[30] By the end of January, one paper had published a 'new comic song' entitled 'The Lottery' in which the protagonist's friend cursed the day that he'd 'gained a loss' from his £8 gamble, while he himself won two useless lots at Hastings (see chapter epigraph). He also pondered whether the entire show was a 'scheming job' between 'Messieurs Wells and Grocott'. In the concluding verse, he ruefully warned that if 'unlucky dreamers' wished to 'throw their cash away—They'll find no want of schemers now', and that 'any one with land to sell/Will find this plan the dandy, oh!'.[31]

On 21 April, the *Sydney Morning Herald* announced that the attorney-general had determined that the second lottery scheme could not be allowed.[32] It appeared that the government was concerned that the first lottery had set a precedent that might offend the Crown, as it had much of the public.[33] On 29 June, a final notice from Samuel Lyons appeared on the front page of the *Sydney Morning Herald* announcing that the:

> Drawing of the second and Final Partition of the Properties of the Bank of Australia having been prohibited by the Government, all parties acting as agents are authorised to return the sums received by them on account of Tickets.[34]

---

29 For Grocott and Wells, see *Sydney Morning Herald*, 3 January and 8 January 1849, 1. Other disappointing locations included St Peters, Bello Retiro, Tempe, Battersea, Allendale, Ellenborough and unnamed lots at 'five Sydney suburbs' (*Argus*, 23 January 1849, 2; *Hobart Town Advertiser*, 6 February 1849, 3).
30 The copy of the lottery pamphlet held by the NLA has the handwritten names of 17 people who held 30 tickets. Twenty-three of the 30 tickets were properties at either Fitzroy or Hastings. An apocryphal tale involved a cook quitting his secure job and assuming a gentlemanly demeanour now he was a man of property. He left for Sydney to find out more about his allotment at Hastings (*Hobart Town Advertiser*, 18 May 1849, 4). For a satirical letter from the fictitious Betsy Pumpkin, who won 10 allotments at Hastings and Fitzroy, see *Bell's Life in Sydney and Sporting Reviewer*, 24 February 1849, 1. She wrote 'to give an accurate description (of Hastings), it only requires A POLACK or A STUBBS to do them justice'. The auctioneer Abraham Polack and W.H. Wells were jailed in 1854 for property fraud involving a lottery property.
31 See *Bell's Life in Sydney and Sporting Reviewer*, 27 January 1849, 3.
32 *Sydney Morning Herald*, 21 April 1849, 4.
33 William Wentworth, who initiated the lottery Bill in 1844, received a substantial number of properties in the January 1849 draw. He subsequently organised a private lottery to dispose of his land. However, along with the second drawing of the Bank of Australia's Hughes & Hosking properties, the government explicitly forbade Wentworth's private lottery. He was likely the person referred to in 'The Lottery' song 'with land to sell', who would find the scheme 'dandy'.
34 *Sydney Morning Herald*, 29 June 1849, 1.

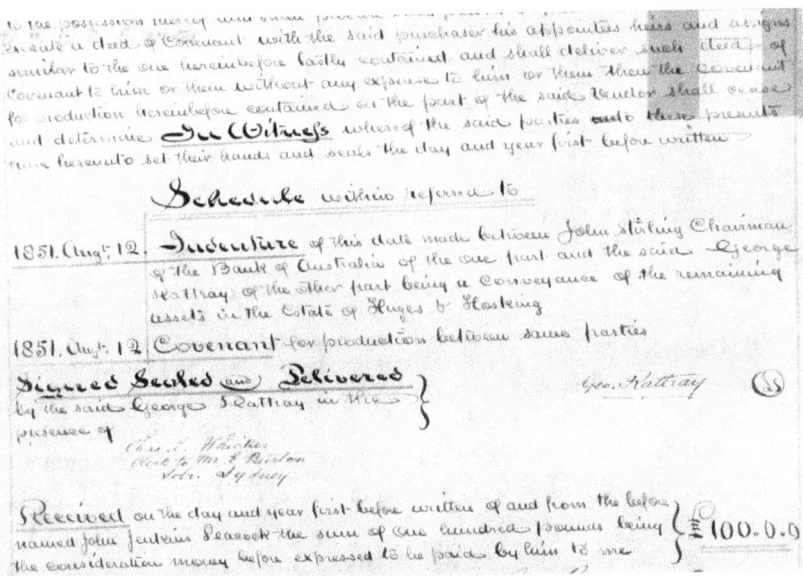

Figure 17. Detail from 1861 indenture showing George Rattray bought Long Beach in 1851.
NSW Land Registry Services, Book 71, no. 804.

The fate of these properties was eventually resolved in January 1851 when auctioneer Lyons was instructed by the chairman of the Bank of Australia to conduct 'an important closing sale of properties of the Bank of Australia'.[35] Among the 85 lots up for auction, 45 were formerly in the possession of Hughes & Hosking (including the remaining Broulee, Queanbeyan and Violet Creek landholdings that the firm had held since 1839–40), or were associated with John Terry Hughes, his wife or his aunt/mother-in-law.

While the Long Beach property does not appear in the schedule of the first 83 individual properties, Lot 84 was described as 'residue of Hughes and Hosking's real and personal assets'. Some of the lots for the January 1851 auction, including Lot 84, were 'unavoidably postponed' until another announcement in the *Sydney Morning Herald* on 6 June 1851 set the date for 9 June 1851. The Long Beach property was part of this 'residue' in Lot 84 and sold to the Sydney magistrate George Rattray. This can be confirmed

---

35 *Sydney Morning Herald*, 21 December 1850, 3; 4 January 1851, 3. The auction for the residue of Hughes & Hosking's property was initially set for 6 January, but was 'unavoidably postponed' until 9 January. See *Sydney Morning Herald*, 6 January 1851, 4. Lot 85 was the final lot, consisting of the residue of John Terry Hughes's personal property.

from an 1861 indenture when Rattray sold the 320 acres at Long Beach back to John Jenkins Peacock for £100.[36] On this later document, there is a reference to a schedule of 12 August 1851 that states:

> Indenture of this date between John Stirling Chairman of the Bank of Australia of the one part and the said George Rattray of the other part being a conveyance of the remaining assets in the Estate of Hughes & Hosking. (See Figure 17)

Conclusion

The fall from grace of Long Beach as the 'Great Southern Township of St Vincent' could not have been more stark. In 1841 it was acclaimed as a future port to rival Sydney; 10 years later it was merely unnamed residue bundled together as part of a lot in the sale of a bankrupt estate. Clint and J.J. Peacock had purchased the land from Hughes & Hosking in February 1841 for £800. Yet, 20 years later, George Rattray disposed of the property to J.J. Peacock for £100 (6s. 3d. an acre) at a time when economic conditions were more buoyant than 1841 due to the gold rushes and mass immigration.

Further, by 1861—when Rattray sold the property to Peacock—the government had already laid out and sold land within the village of Bateman on the southern side of the bay, east of McLeods Creek. The shape of settlement at Batemans Bay was beginning to emerge, but the northern side of the bay was now part of its periphery, and the value of land there had dropped considerably.

More generally, this chapter has considered the responses within the colony to the consequences of excessive land speculation. As noted at the end of Chapter 2 and the beginning of Chapter 3, the price of land had risen to unprecedented levels on the eve of the 1840s depression. Since the introduction of government land auctions in the early 1830s, various

---

36 NSW Land Registry Services, Book 71, no. 804. A notice in the *Sydney Morning Herald*, 12 June 1851, 1, requested that the successful bidders from these last sales come forward to complete the conveyancing of their properties. Evidence from Augustus Edmund Blair's Primary Application for the property in 1917 (held at State Records Authority NSW, NRS-17513, item 17513-8-34-PA 20438, vol. 2781, folio 34) suggests the title-deed transfer of Long Beach occurred on 1 August 1851.

commentators had criticised colonial land speculation, including those speaking on behalf of new immigrants. Yet, as long as prices rose, there was little appetite to change the system.[37]

In the decade after the bubble burst, 'land gambling', 'land mania', 'land-jobbing' or 'land quackery' tended to be framed as an aberration surrounding the early 1840s depression, with particular emphasis being placed on Governor Gipps's policies on land auctions, land pricing and land release.[38] This was an understandable assessment when it is considered that the colonies had only recently experienced their first speculative boom and bust. Later entrepreneurs could not use this excuse.[39]

Land was never far from the centre of colonial discourse and practice, most prominently in the mid-1840s over the terms under which squatters held their land. By the late 1850s, when the Legislative Assembly once again debated 'the land question', arguments in favour of restricting the sale, or lowering the upset price, of Crown land were advanced in the hope of avoiding another bout of land mania and 'national insolvency' similar to the late 1830s and early 1840s. In contrast, those who argued for more Crown land to be released dismissed such fears by proclaiming that 'surely men are made much wiser by the experience of suffering than by legal precautions—"burnt children dread the fire"'. On such rationalist grounds, it was argued, colonists would avoid future bouts of land mania.[40] The debate was framed by comparisons with the late 1830s and early 1840s—whether lessons had been learnt, whether market conditions had changed and whether the quality of remaining Crown land was different.[41] What remained constant in land debates was the failure to adequately address the legal and moral issue of the 'dispersal' of Indigenous people from Country.

---

37   For example, see Mann, *Six Years Residence*. Almost the entire 40-page chapter on NSW land regulation is devoted to a transcript of an 1837 Supreme Court criminal case in which John Terry Hughes colluded with other 'gentry' to suppress government land-sale prices (see Chapter 2). Mann presents two 1838 Port Phillip land-sale tables that illustrate why land reforms were necessary to discourage 'land-jobbing speculatists' and 'land monopolists'. The tables make it clear that Hughes & Hosking was the target of his criticism, as they dominated the land sales. Many of his proposed reforms would later be echoed by Philo-Palinurus (see fn 11, this chapter).
38   For example, see Sidney, *The Three Colonies*, 106, 121–3.
39   Sykes, *Two Centuries*, ch. 2.
40   *Empire*, 2 December 1857, 5.
41   An editorial in the *Maitland Mercury and Hunter River General Advertiser* (6 October 1857, 2) also argued that experience and conditions made it unlikely that land mania would recommence if the upset price was reduced. At a public meeting on the land question at Raymond Terrace on 13 October, a good deal of time was spent debating the similarities and differences between current conditions and the land mania of the late 1830s. See *Maitland Mercury and Hunter River General Advertiser*, 17 November 1857, 4.

Subsequent 'land booms', in particular in 1880s Melbourne, would confirm that the land gambling and land mania of the early 1840s were no aberration.[42] In retrospect, the boom of the late 1830s and the depression of the early 1840s were merely the first manifestation of what Leonie Sandercock later called 'the land racket'. Many historians, sociologists, economists and planners have subsequently treated this 'land racket', along with 'land mania' and 'land gambling', as a long-term structural phenomenon surrounding Australia's property market (what Sandercock also described as a 'national hobby') that is associated with a wide range of pervasive social problems: suboptimal town planning; the diversion of capital away from productive sectors of the economy; corruption and collusion involving land speculators, land developers and politicians; the distortion of population policy; the exclusion of modest-income households from the housing market; and, overall, the promotion of private over public interest.[43]

In this light, there is something both ironic and suggestive in the way the events in this chapter unfolded: the Legislative Council responded to the calamitous social and economic consequences of 'land gambling' by supporting a public lottery of unsaleable properties. As the 1849 song 'The Lottery' predicted: 'They'll find no want of schemers now.'

---

42 See Cannon, *The Land*. The opening pages recall the early 1840s land inflation in Port Phillip. The early 1850s gold rush initiated a bout of 'land-allotment mania' that 'bade fair to surpass what it was previous to the disastrous 1842'. See Hewitt, *Land, Labour*, 17 and ch. 16. Hewitt likened Melbourne's land speculation in 1853 to seventeenth-century Dutch tulip mania and called Melburnians 'the maddest speculators in the world' (193–4). He delayed, in vain, the publication of his book in the hope of dealing fully with the 'land question'. Hewitt sided with those who wanted to throw open more land and 'make it cheap' (196).

43 See Sandercock, *The Land Racket*. Sandercock's argument reinforced the US economist J.K. Galbraith's statement that when 'public services have failed to keep abreast of private consumption' we witness the confluence of 'private oppulence and public squalor'. Galbraith, *The Affluent Society*, ch. 18. See also Egan and Soos, *Bubble Economics*; Sandercock, *Property*.

8

Mercantile chicanery: 'It's a way that they have in Australia'

You may talk of your honour and honest repute,
And for loss of your credit may fret; –
But when you can't pay there's nothing will suit,
But to schedule and get out of debt

...

In the 'grand reservoir of colonial things,'
Where the mean and the mighty are met,—
You may nestle beneath the Commissioner's wings;
And when the set time your certificate brings,
Turn accountant, sport blood horse and diamond rings,
Go snack, and run into debt![1]

The previous chapters have noted that the first three landholders on the north of Batemans Bay each faced insolvency during the depression. In this chapter, a biographical approach affords the opportunity to highlight the different strategies adopted by John Terry Hughes, John Hosking and Edward Lord in attempts to control their fate. Yet, all three shared a similar set of social attributes, buttressed by family trusts, and this afforded them possibilities of maintaining or rebuilding their livelihoods. This chapter also records how an air of popular suspicion hung over those in the mercantile world who volunteered for insolvency in the early 1840s.

---

1   H.P.S., 'Get Out of Debt!', *Melbourne Times*, 1 December 1843, 1.

John Hosking

According to the *Sydney Morning Herald*—the same paper that had opposed his election as mayor in 1842—when John Hosking performed the role of mayor between November 1842 and September 1843, 'he carried out the duties of his office with credit to himself and satisfaction to the citizens'.[2] Once 'the utter hopelessness of the affairs of Hughes and Hosking became apparent to him', he promptly resigned his mayoral position, was fined £50 by the council and was replaced with Alderman Wilshire.[3] Both he and John Terry Hughes had also accumulated personal debts, in Hosking's case totalling £59,066.[4] While his assets almost equalled this amount, he faced the difficulty of liquidating them while the depression persisted, especially as they mainly consisted of depreciating landholdings and stock (or 'bad and doubtful debts').

Hosking was widely considered a popular figure, but never again ascended in public life after relinquishing his mayoral title. He lost a 'severe' contest for his old ward of Bourke in the 1848 City Council elections. A return could have reignited his political ambitions. He had campaigned on the importance of public lighting, the cheap supply of water and 'underground drainage', but his opponent James Simmons responded drolly that he considered the city 'very effectively drained already'. Simmons won the contest by 193 votes to Hosking's 142 votes. In 1859, Hosking declined a nomination for the Yass Plains in the Legislative Assembly elections.[5]

Fortunately for Hosking and many others, the 1841 *Insolvency Act* allowed insolvents to retain control over their property provided the court was satisfied that a plan of distribution would allow all registered creditors to receive an equitable return. One advantage of this Act was that insolvents

---

2 *Sydney Morning Herald*, 22 September 1882, 11.
3 *Australasian Chronicle*, 27 September 1843, 2; *Sydney Morning Herald*, 28 April 1845, 4.
4 Golder, *Politics*, 6.
5 *Sydney Morning Herald*, 28 September 1848, 3; *Bell's Life in Sydney and Sporting Reviewer*, 7 and 21 October 1848, 2. One paper claimed that if Hosking was returned 'it is supposed that something like the Mayoralty will follow' (*Sydney Daily Advertiser*, 25 September 1848, 2). For the Yass Plains, see *Yass Courier*, 14 May 1859, 2. Raphael Clint maintained good relations with Hosking in the wake of their dealings at Long Beach. He was one of 144 citizens pledging support for him at the 1842 Sydney Council elections (*Sydney Morning Herald*, 28 October 1842, 1).

could resume business quickly after receiving their certificates of insolvency, subject to the court hearing objections from creditors. It allowed many among the wealthy, like Hosking, to avoid immediate financial distress.[6]

In the parlance of the day, a declaration of insolvency was called 'taking Burton's purge to Whitewash Hall' (after the legislation's framer, Justice William Burton) or 'joining Colonel Kerr's regiment' (after Chief Commissioner of Insolvent Estates William H. Kerr). The Act came into effect on 2 February 1842, and, of the 1,881 insolvencies up to June 1849, 1,168 were registered in 1842–43. This provoked moral outrage that some insolvents could 'get out of debt' through 'fraudulent insolvency' simply through 'filing their schedule'.[7] In Legislative Council debates in late 1843 over reforming the Act, critics alleged widespread fraud, while others emphasised the widespread hardship associated with trading conditions.[8]

Hosking's February 1845 application for his certificate of insolvency tested the chief commissioner's powers of deliberation in this regard: did Hosking act recklessly in 1843? The chief commissioner concluded that if Hosking had sequestered his estate earlier, he might have paid 'a respectable dividend to his creditors':

---

6 See Kercher, *An Unruly Child*, ch. 6. The objective of the Act was revealed in its opening sentence: An Act for giving relief to Insolvent Persons and providing for the due Collection Administration and Distribution of Insolvent Estates within the Colony of New South Wales and for the prevention of Frauds affecting the person same [29th December, 1841].
Debt and insolvency law reform was an ongoing subject of discussion in Australia and Britain concerning the competing rights of debtors and creditors. However, the specific case that prompted Burton's reform was discussed in *Sydney Herald*, 11 September 1841, 2.
7 One contemporary observer described the consequences of 'Burton's purge' as follows:
Many availed themselves of the opportunity to clear accounts with their creditors by going through the Insolvency Court, who had no occasion to adopt any such course. The restraints that had bound society to honour and plain dealing broken down, men turned upon their creditors at pleasure … Those who would not pay, often could have paid. (McCombie, *Arabin*, 23)
See also Brodribb, *Recollections*, 126. Morrissey ('The Pastoral Economy', 88) also notes that the Bill 'was extremely generous to the debtor'. Another contemporary, Thomas Braim (*A History*, vol. 1, 292) took an opposing stance to McCombie:
The wisdom of the measure has been disputed; but there can be but one opinion as to the amount of relief it has afforded during an unprecedented pecuniary struggle, and it is something in favour of the measure, that the objections against it have generally proceeded from the grasping and disappointed usurer.
For a general assessment of Sydney merchants between the late 1830s and early 1840s, denouncing those 'thorough-paced swindlers' who 'took advantage of the Colonial Insolvent Act', see Balfour, *A Sketch*, 82–5. These two positions represent the conflicting ends of the reform debate discussed in Kercher (*An Unruly Child*) in the attempt to balance the rights of creditors and debtors.
8 *Weekly Register of Politics, Facts and General Literature*, 25 November 1843, 268–9; Butlin, *Foundations*, ch. 10; Decker, 'Monetary Recovery'.

Having therefore, reference to the conduct of the insolvent, in so recklessly contracting debts previous to his insolvency—at the time he was sued and pressed on all sides in carrying on business, and living in the style of a man of fortune, when he knew that his affairs were deranged, and common prudence should have shown him that he was in an insolvent state.[9]

The chief commissioner suspended Hosking's certificate for a further 12 months.

At the hearing, a number of creditors and trustees had opposed the granting of the certificate, but all opposition was eventually withdrawn.[10] While the chief commissioner could not determine why the objections were withdrawn, he also could not rule out the possibility that Hosking had come to some accommodation with the complainants that could be prejudicial to a future equitable plan of distribution of Hosking's estate among all creditors.

Figure 18. John Hosking, c. 1860.
'John Hosking 1806–1882', City of Sydney Archives, SRC18683.

The chief commissioner's decision left the impression that Hosking had engaged in 'misconduct'. Hosking's defence team mounted an appeal in mid-April 1845 before Chief Justice Stephen and Justice à Beckett. His team argued that until September 1843, Hosking believed he was solvent and therefore capable of discharging his debts. Further, he could not have anticipated that his assets would depreciate so alarmingly. Finally, there was no evidence that Hosking had colluded to persuade parties to withdraw their objection to his certificate.

The defence also accused the chief commissioner of bias, claiming that Hosking was being treated differently from other insolvents,

---

9   *Sydney Morning Herald*, 28 April 1845, 2–4.
10 Thomas Stubbs was one of the objectors, and his ornamental furniture featured in the case.

considering that no appellant's affairs had ever been scrutinised as thoroughly as Hosking's. The defence put it to the chief commissioner that he had been influenced by popular sentiment in a time of collective trauma:

> In a crisis such as that through which they had been and were passing, men's minds, heated and distracted, looked round for some one who should bear all their sins as well as his own, always at such periods there was a desire for a victim or a scape-goat—a sacrifice, and who a fitter victim than Mr. Hosking? … [I]n every national calamity some one would be laid hold of to offer up on the altar of popular vengeance … [T]he tendency of man;—as old as their earliest records—to make a scape-goat, to lay hold of some one to bear all our sins, is still liable to bias the minds even of the highest … [The chief commissioner] must have had the thought—'Here is Mr. Hosking—the Hosking—the man—one of that firm whose speculations have been so prominent amongst all the speculators of this dreadful crisis;—what will be thought if I allow him to pass?'[11]

The chief justice allowed Hosking his certificate on 23 April 1845. When his bankrupt estate was finally distributed in 1851, only 1.25 per cent of his debt could be recovered, leaving creditors with a dividend of threepence to the pound.[12]

Hosking retained sufficient capital to move from his Pitt Street home and his Macquarie Fields estate (both held in his wife's name) to an Italianate mansion named 'Carrara' that he purchased and completed at Vaucluse in 1855.[13] However, later he fell upon harder times, including further bankruptcy proceedings in 1866–67.[14] Despite this second bankruptcy, he maintained his residency at Vaucluse until 1876. He and his wife also spent decades contesting his father-in-law Samuel Terry's will.[15]

---

11   *Sydney Morning Herald*, 28 April 1845, 4. For a critique of the certificate system, see *Parramatta Chronicle and Cumberland General Advertiser*, 13 April 1844, 1.
12   Dyster, 'The 1840s Depression Revisited', 606. In the late 1840s, the Bank of Australia took control over some of Hosking's unsold land at East Balmain but after it did not feature in the lottery it was returned to Hosking (see Reynolds, 'From Johnson', 26–7).
13   Hosking and Martha lived in Vaucluse House while the mansion was being built. They named their new home 'Carrara', where the Italian marble for the house originated. It is now known as Strickland House and Estate. The portrait of Hosking in Figure 18 is possibly at Carrara with Rose Bay in the background.
14   In 1867, the chief commissioner directed the assignee to allow Hosking to keep his 'wearing apparel' and 'realise his other assets' (*Sydney Morning Herald*, 9 February 1867, 5).
15   See 'An Act to Authorize the Sale and Exchange of Property Held in Trust for Mrs. Martha Foxlowe Hosking and Her Issue', [9th May, 1861], legislation.nsw.gov.au/view/pdf/asmade/act-1861-hta. There is mention in this 1861 document (known as 'Hosking's Trust Act') of various well-publicised court cases prior to 1861 associated with Samuel Terry's will, as well as mention of Hosking's intention to sell Foxlow Estate on the Molonglo River due south of Bungendore.

Hosking died at his Mount Pleasant residence in Penrith in September 1882.[16] An obituary in the *Sydney Morning Herald* gave the impression that his later years of life were conducted in the shadow of his fame up to the early 1840s:

> He had a commanding personal appearance, and was always noted for his genial kindly nature and hospitality. For the last few years of his life he suffered much from ill health, which resulted in paralysis, under which he ultimately sank. At the public sale at Sydney of allotments in the 'town of Melbourne,' Hughes and Hosking were the largest purchasers, nearly one-half of several main streets having been bought by them at about upset prices. If these properties were now put into figures at their present value they would represent millions of pounds sterling, and yet the subject of our sketch died a poor man.[17]

John Terry Hughes

John Terry Hughes maintained a higher public profile than Hosking, regularly featuring in press court reports during the next decade in a variety of cases. As early as mid-1841, relations between John Hosking and John Terry Hughes appear to have deteriorated, when Hosking and his wife, Martha, first took Hughes to the Supreme Court over Samuel Terry's will.[18]

Despite accolades from some sections of the press, John Terry Hughes had also been associated with the notorious 'land conspiracy case' in 1837, in which he was found guilty of colluding with others to pervert the conduct of a government land auction and defraud the Treasury.[19] In 1838, he was a defendant in an action in which William Bland sought to recover payment for medical services for Hughes's late father-in-law Samuel Terry. The attorney-general commented during the trial that John Terry Hughes 'was not fond of parting with money' and 'was fond of trying the chances of law'.[20]

---

16 The death notice appeared in the *Sydney Morning Herald*, 14 September 1882, 1.
17 The obituary appeared in the *Sydney Morning Herald*, 22 September 1882, 11. The obituary for Hosking was preceded by one for Lieutenant Johnston, who had been cited in Thomas Stubbs's January 1841 advertisement as the surveyor of the Bhundoo/Clyde River in 1822.
18 *Sydney Monitor and Commercial Advertiser*, 2 August 1841, 2.
19 See Mann, *Six Years Residence*, 163–203. See also Chapter 2, this volume.
20 *Sydney Gazette and New South Wales Advertiser*, 18 October 1838, 2.

8. MERCANTILE CHICANERY

At the distribution of his personal estate in 1846, only 2.5 per cent of Hughes's unsecured debt was recovered.[21] His parsimonious nature was raised again in the wake of Hughes & Hosking's misfortunes in 1841. After the Albion Wharf blaze, he was criticised for opposing a building act designed to reduce the spread of fire. Later in the year, after one of his buildings collapsed, the editor of the *Sydney Gazette and New South Wales Advertiser* suggested that his woes were self-inflicted:

> Mr. J.T.H. would doubtless find it more to his interest to abstain from building by cheap contract. We do not see the buildings of Mr. Lyons, Mr. Grose, or Messrs. Cooper & Chapman fall down almost before they are put up.[22]

Joseph Fowles was also critical of the building standards used to remodel the Hughes-built Royal Hotel, the first five-storey structure in the town. Recalling the fire that destroyed the original Royal Hotel, he considered it reckless to rebuild the frontage of the upper storeys in wood. Further, many of the 100 apartments received no natural light and remained unused. Architecturally, Fowles was equally scathing: no comparatives 'that we can command, are adequate to a faithful description of this "Curiosity of Colonial Architecture"' and he condemned 'this wilderness of stone and wood' as a salutary lesson to any apprentice builder wishing to avoid 'the "Hughesionian" style of architecture':

> With Mr. Hughes's system of building we are not acquainted, but we presume that he never could have placed upon paper, a plan of the huge mass of cumbersomeness which he has piled in George-street?[23]

John Terry Hughes's fondness of legal remedy also continued to test the patience of the public and the authorities. He was involved in cases of deceased estates (1841–51), the theft of cattle and fraudulent insolvency

---

21 The plan of distribution calculated 'sixpence two-ninths in the pound' (*Sydney Morning Herald*, 2 April 1846, 2; Dyster, 'The 1840s Depression Revisited', 606). At the first meeting of Hughes's creditors, Raphael Clint had a claim for £20 2s. rejected because he did not appear to defend his claim (*Sydney Morning Herald*, 12 October 1943, 2).

22 *Sydney Gazette and New South Wales Advertiser*, 7 September 1841, 2. On the Building Act, see *Sydney Herald*, 22 March 1841, 2. Prior to the Albion Wharf fire, the *Australian* (1 December 1840, 2) had attacked government building regulations and supported Hughes.

23 Fowles, *Sydney*, 53. The hotel was subject to a number of breaches of the *Building Act* (see *Australasian Chronicle*, 14 January 1841, 3). The building had its admirers, such as the Reverend Thomas Braim (*A History*, vol. 1, 283), who thought it would be 'an ornament to any city in the world'. The *Sydney Gazette and New South Wales Advertiser* (7 April 1840, 2; 20 November 1841, 2) also commended the 'spirited townsman John Terry Hughes esq.' for building a New York–style establishment. See also Marjoribanks, *Travels*, 21. Marjoribanks calls the hotel one of the world's largest outside the USA, and described Hughes as 'enterprizing'.

(1845–51), libel (1847), dishonoured cheques (1847), stealing (1849), malicious libel (1849),[24] non-payment of wages (1850) and perjury (1851),[25] on top of ongoing claims involving the estate of Hughes & Hosking, his late father-in-law's will and repeated requests for his certificate of insolvency.[26] He also challenged the legality of offering many of the Bank of Australia–mortgaged properties in the January 1849 lottery (see Chapter 7).[27]

In 1846 Hughes complained that his insolvency was treated by the courts and by the public less sympathetically than that of Hosking.[28] It was incontrovertible that by the mid-1840s sections of the press were portraying Hughes as the personification of the evils, excesses and corporate deceit that had aggravated the depression.[29] He keenly felt this as an injustice. After his certificate of insolvency was again refused by the court in 1846, he complained of 'persecution': 'I am now to be held up to the wondering world as the scape-goat, to bear all the sins of those who have preceded and succeeded me in insolvency.'[30]

---

24 *Sydney Morning Herald*, 9 November 1849.
25 *Moreton Bay Courier*, 26 January 1850; *Courier*, 12 March 1851.
26 In the midst of the court's refusal to issue Hughes his insolvent's certificate, on 24 June 1846, the court requested that he end his persistent appeals:
   In the present case the proceedings had extended over a long period of time, and the defendant, who had had the most able legal assistance, had had full opportunity of bringing forward everything which he deemed necessary to his defence. The whole case had also been considered with the most extreme care by all the Judges, who had repeatedly met in consultation respecting it, and it ought now to be considered at an end. (*Sydney Morning Herald*, 25 June 1846)
This request was to no avail (*Sydney Morning Herald*, 26 October and 9 November 1848). His perjury case was associated with the ongoing fraudulent insolvency case (*Courier*, 12 March 1851, 2).
27 For example, see *Sydney Morning Herald*, 5 December 1848, 4:
   BANK LOTTERY. THE public are hereby apprised that the property in King-street, near the corner of Pitt-street, and destined by the Bank of Australia as a prize in their scheme, was purchased by the late Mr. Samuel Terry many years ago; remained in his possession till his death, when, in terms of his will, it came into the possession of his widow, Mrs. Rosetta Terry, who has ever since retained it, and receives the rents. JOHN TERRY HUGHES, Executor under the Will of the late Mr. Samuel Terry. Albion House, December 4. 1848.
28 *Sydney Morning Herald*, 27 June 1846, 1. However, as noted earlier, Hosking's legal team had also argued that their client was being made a 'scape-goat'. Hughes shared the same defence team as Hosking, namely Windeyer and Foster.
29 For a morality tale, clearly embellished but designed to show the miserliness and depravity of Samuel Terry and John Terry Hughes, see Byrne, *Emigrant's*, 37–9.
30 John Terry Hughes to *Sydney Morning Herald*, 27 June 1846, 1. This letter is Hughes's clearest statement of self-defence. Hughes drew on Hosking's April 1845 appeal as precedent to argue his claim for his certificate to be allowed. Many of his arguments resembled those advanced by Hosking's legal team, Windeyer and Foster, and the decision by Chief Justice Stephen, sometimes quoting verbatim (see previous section).

8. MERCANTILE CHICANERY

An article from the *Sentinel* entitled 'The Celebrated John Terry Hughes', written after the court found Hughes guilty of stealing, illustrates the opprobrium he generated within much of colonial society:

> The terrible evils which the insolvency of this man brought upon many respectable persons, evils which extended to the suspension of the operations of one of the leading banks of the colony, have given such notoriety to his name, as to render his imprisonment for stealing, a matter of more than ordinary interest. An action had already been commenced against him by the chairman of the Bank of Australia, for fraudulent insolvency, his certificate of discharge having been refuted by the Supreme Court; and should the action be maintained, we sincerely trust that the law will cause this unprincipled man to feel the effects of that course of mercantile chicanery which has already elicited the strong indignation of the whole community. The defalcations of men of Hughes' stamp reflect discredit on the Community to which he belongs, and though it may not be often that a single individual, of a single firm, has the power of shaking the public character to such an extent, the occurrence of such nefarious transactions ought to be and in this instance, we hope will be, followed, not only by the condemnation of public opinion, but by the severest punishment which the law allows to be inflicted.[31]

After the Court of Quarter Sessions sentenced Hughes to six months' imprisonment for the 'stealing' offence, Governor FitzRoy issued him a pardon, which was followed by an action for libel from the jurors in the case, whom Hughes had accused of being 'of the lowest grade'.[32]

Hughes was back in court towards the end of 1847 (in the other case referred to in the *Sentinel*) charged with fraud. The case was brought by Mr John Stirling from the Bank of Australia and was associated with allegations

---

31   *Sentinel*, 11 February 1847, 2. The *Sydney Morning Herald* (1 July 1846, 2) had reached a similar verdict on the justice of refusing to grant Hughes his certificate of insolvency. The *Parramatta Messenger* (reprinted in *Port Phillip Patriot and Morning Advertiser*, 31 March 1847, 2) defended Hughes, criticising the 'heavy sentence'.
32   Once the governor announced his pardon, Hughes laid out his version of events leading to the trial in a letter headed 'The Case of John Terry Hughes.—Quarter Sessions, February 5th, 1847; Before a Petit Jury of the Lowest Grade' (*Sydney Morning Herald*, 26 March 1847, 2). One juror responded to this 'infamous' charge, stating he was at a 'loss to know how Mr J.T. Hughes could write me down as a person of the lowest grade, without even having any acquaintance with me'. The editor accepted that Hughes had acted 'unwisely, indiscreetly, and discourteously' (*Sydney Chronicle*, 31 March 1847, 2). A member of the jury, William Willmington (possibly the letter respondent), then sued for libel, but Hughes offered a satisfactory apology (*Sydney Chronicle*, 10 April 1847, 3).

surrounding the September 1843 sequestration of Hughes's estate.³³ The principal complaint involved the removal of cattle from his Albion Park property at Illawarra after his insolvency. Hughes was committed to trial and given bail of £200.³⁴ When he appeared before the Supreme Court on 8 March 1848, he was acquitted, despite a jury finding him guilty.³⁵ The fraudulent insolvency case was still ongoing in February 1851, complicated by a further perjury charge.³⁶

Hughes died on 17 October 1851, aged 48, six months after being finally granted his certificate of insolvency.³⁷ At the time of his death, his wife, Esther, had initiated another suit in his name against John Hosking,³⁸ while his only son, 22-year-old Samuel Terry Hughes, was in the Insolvent Debtors Court. This latter ongoing case had generated much 'unusual interest' among the public since May 1850. It arose from money owed by Samuel while still a minor to the tailor James McEvoy. Restricted in funds by his father, the spendthrift son had accumulated debts of £7,568 4s., including buying 650 waistcoats over a two-year period, which he sold on to dealers. McEvoy took Samuel to court to recover the money, even though John Terry Hughes had warned McEvoy that debts accrued by his son would not be honoured.³⁹

The trade name Albion was often associated with John Terry Hughes. He lived at his Albion House residency, built in 1834 on the corner of Elizabeth Street South and Albion Street in Surry Hills, until his death. Hughes & Hosking's Albion Wharf at Darling Harbour was a magnet for colonial mercantile activity. It was there that the Albion Mill burnt to the ground in March 1841,⁴⁰ along with the wharf and inn. Albion Park in Illawarra was Hughes's station from which he removed the cattle referred to in the fraudulent insolvency case. His Albion Brewery on Elizabeth Street beside Albion House later became the Tooheys Brewery.

---

33   *Maitland Mercury and Hunter River General Advertiser*, 3 November 1847, 4.
34   For John Terry Hughes's earlier denial of the offence, see his long letter in the *Sydney Morning Herald*, 11 December 1846, 3.
35   *Geelong Advertiser*, 24 March, 1848, 4; *Australian*, 9 June 1848, 3; *Sydney Morning Herald*, 14 March 1848, 2.
36   *Sydney Morning Herald*, 11 February 1851, 2.
37   *Shipping Gazette and Sydney General Trade List*, 19 April 1851, 150.
38   *Sydney Morning Herald*, 31 December 1851, 2; 22 November 1851, 2.
39   *Bell's Life in Sydney and Sporting Reviewer*, 2 November 1850, 1; 27 September 1851, 3. In one December 1850 episode that constituted the ongoing drama, the police office was 'crammed to suffocation, and the noise occasioned by persons wishing to force their way in, was so great as to impede the progress of the proceedings'. See also *Sydney Morning Herald*, 23 October 1850; 'A New Catechism', a satirical comment of the McEvoy affair in *Bell's Life in Sydney and Sporting Reviewer*, 5 July 1851, 3.
40   Hughes reopened the Albion Steam Mill without Hosking's involvement in 1846 on his property in Surry Hills. See *Dictionary of Sydney*, 'Albion Mills'.

8. MERCANTILE CHICANERY

Figure 19. John Terry Hughes's Albion House and Albion Brewery with church, c. 1840.
'St. Lawrence Temporary Church, in the residence of J.T. Hughes, Esqre', State Library of NSW, a623016 / PX*D 123, 5c.

In 1838, John Terry Hughes had offered part of his Albion House and Albion Brewery property on Elizabeth Street South to the Anglican Church in the new Parish of St Lawrence. The bishop of Australia, William Broughton, had a temporary church built there while a permanent one was being erected (see Figure 19). The depression prolonged the arrangement, but, in 1845, the congregation moved into its newly consecrated Christ Church, St Lawrence premises at Haymarket.[41]

---

41 In the same year, on 12 March 1845, William Broughton consecrated the St John the Baptist Church on the Limestone Plains on the northern side of the Molonglo River (Robinson, *Canberra's First*, chs 4, 6 and 7. Robinson's history is more a pastoral history of the Limestone Plains in the religious sense, with useful early history of pastoral leases). In 1842, Broughton took out a long-term lease at Goderich House, the residence of the late sheriff Thomas Hyacinth Macquoid, which John Verge had built for him in 1830–32.

Around this time, John Terry Hughes complained that his opponents were attempting to sacrifice him '"on the altar of popular vengeance" amidst the smoke of which the public might lose sight of the peccadilloes of others'.[42] This statement was not groundless. He had always received a mixed press. On the one hand, he was associated with emancipists and undertook 'enterprising' development projects. After his 1847 jail sentence was handed down, the *Parramatta Messenger and Cumberland Express* defended Hughes:

> Deified during a long season of prosperity, as one of the Merchant Princes of Sydney, he, by reason of an accumulation of reverses, becomes the object of fierce animadversion on the part of time-serving sychophants who can no longer swell their fortunes by his means.[43]

Bell's Life in Sydney and Sporting Reviewer also complained that Hughes was being persecuted by the 'verdict of popular opinion'.[44] On the other hand, he flouted the law, was accused of land-jobbing and resented paying debts. Other commentators denounced 'those multifarious proceedings which have invested the name of Terry Hughes with so unenviable a notoriety in every court of justice in Sydney'.[45]

In the midst of the depression, with rising levels of insolvency and the want of confidence in financial institutions, the colony was witnessing a 'moral panic'. Under these conditions, sections of the press had latched upon Hughes as a 'folk devil' who had discredited all that once had seemed so solid, sacred and valuable, especially land.[46]

The 'verdict of popular opinion' was expressed not only in press commentary, but also in contemporary songs.[47] One enduring song to emerge out of the 1840s depression was 'Billy Barlow in Australia', written and first performed

---

42 *Sydney Morning Herald*, 27 June 1846, 1, with a reply from the editors on 1 July 1846, 2. Hughes placed the phrase in inverted commas, perhaps as an acknowledgement that the same phrase had been used by Hosking's legal team, Windeyer and Foster, when appealing Hosking's case in April 1845 (see earlier section).
43 *Parramatta Messenger* (reprinted in *Port Phillip Patriot and Morning Advertiser*, 31 March 1847, 2).
44 *Parramatta Messenger* (reprinted in *Port Phillip Patriot and Morning Advertiser*, 31 March 1847, 2). See also *Bell's Life in Sydney and Sporting Reviewer* (11 March 1848, 2; 4 September 1847, 3) in which a personal vendetta against Hughes by the courts is suggested.
45 *Moreton Bay Courier*, 23 December 1850, 1. See also *Colonial Times*, 26 February 1847, 3; *Sydney Morning Herald*, 1 July 1846, 2. 'Notorious' and 'celebrated' were adjectives often tagged to his name.
46 Cohen, *Folk Devils*. Cohen argued that during times of social turmoil and disruption, the press can target and vilify an individual or a group by defining them as a threat to social values and order. Cohen called such scapegoats 'folk devils' (9–12). In this way, those who have the power to frame and define the source of the breakdown of social norms (or the 'moral panic') manage to divert attention away from the underlying sources of existing social, economic or political problems.
47 Paterson, *Old Bush Songs*. Paterson commented that: 'It is interesting to see how the progress of settlement is reflected in the various songs', (p. xii).

in Maitland in 1843.[48] It was the ballad of a London emigrant seeking to invest the £1,000 inheritance he received from an aunt. A Sydney merchant 'gammon'd the cash out of Billy Barlow' by selling him a squatter station, with stock and supplies on credit. After experiencing the perils of the bush, Billy comes back to 'renew his bill' with the merchant, only to find his debit has been transferred as collateral to a more rapacious merchant (Thomas Burdekin), who fleeces Billy with extortionate interest rates.[49] As his debt rises, Billy is eventually issued with a summons in an action for debt and damages delivered by Burdekin's lawyers (Carr, Rodgers and Co.). The Maitland Bailiff (John Kingsmill) seizes Billy's station, while his sheep are sold for sixpence a head. His assets, however, do not cover the costs and fees of the sheriff's office. So, 'in the lists of insolvents was Billy Barlow'.[50]

Another song from the 1840s depression, 'Don't Go to the Bush of Australia', alludes to bank collapses, insolvencies and 'Burton's purge' as part of the customary practices of colonial finance:

> A thousand or two don't go a long way,
> When every one robs you in open day,
> And the bankers all fail and mizzle away
> From the capital of Australia.
>
> And it's not very easy to keep your cash,
> When once in twelvemonth your agent goes smash,
> And bolts to New Zealand, or gets a whitewash;
> It's a way that they have in Australia.[51]

---

48   The *Maitland Mercury and Hunter River General Advertiser* (3 September 1843, 4) printed the lyrics, which have been attributed to Ben Griffiths Jr of the Maitland Amateur Dramatic Society (Earnshaw, 'A Further Note', 422–3).
49   The merchant Thomas Burdekin would have seemed an apposite choice to a Hunter Valley audience in 1843. In 1842, Burdekin foreclosed on his debtor Benjamin Singleton and, as a consequence, became the owner of most of the land in the private town of Singleton (the town where former under sheriff John Staple resided).
50   Paterson's version of the song changed the names of the merchant Burdekin and the lawyer Carr (see Broadbent, 'Aspects of Domestic Architecture', 523–5). The firm Carr, Rogers and Owen represented the merchant Thomas Burdekin during the early 1840s. This was the same William Carr who purchased Murramarang, north of Batemans Bay, in 1838, and who requested James Larmer survey a town at Kioloa (see Chapter 3; Hamon, *They Came*, 15–22) and employed the future sheriff Adolphus William Young in 1838–40 (see Chapter 6). It was Macquoid's and then Young's responsibility to (re)appoint John Kingsmill—a task often delegated to under sheriffs.
51   Warren Fahey linked this song with 'The beautiful land of Australia' in Paterson, *Old Bush Songs*. The latter is more a simple tale of personal woes, without the financial allusions of 'Don't go to the bush of Australia'. See Fahey, 'Billy Barlow in Australia'.

These songs from the 1840s depression not only drew on the experience of poverty and hardship but also alluded to the circulation of capital and those benefiting from 'mercantile chicanery'. In doing so, they presented a broader and more nuanced analysis of the depression than simply demonising individuals such as John Terry Hughes and John Hosking.

Edward Lord

As noted in Chapter 3, after Edward Lord handed his property and effects over to his trustees in January 1841, 'Stubley Park' was subdivided into 40 suburban lots and 27 township sections before being placed on the market. Next, in May 1841, 452 head of cattle belonging to Lord at Batemans Bay were put up for auction by Mr Blackman.[52] It was not stated on which of his Batemans Bay properties the cattle were grazing but it was clear from the following, later warning that the cattle had belonged to Lord:

> The Public is hereby cautioned not to purchase from J.T. Freer any cattle lately belonging to the Australian Auction Company, running at Bateman's Bay, Buroomer, Maneroo, or at any ether place whatsoever. The above cattle formerly belonged to Mr. Edward Lord.[53]

The warning suggested that Lord was operating a cattle run at Batemans Bay; however, it is possible that the cattle had come down from Lord's relinquished High Country runs. If Lord's cattle were running at Batemans Bay in 1841, then he may have been the person referred to by Stubbs (in the January 1841 advertisement) who 'picked out' the site of St Vincent 'as a squatting station'. In Lord's unsuccessful December 1840 sale, the property was said to be 'admirably adapted' for the establishment of a dairy farm (see Chapter 3).

During the middle of 1841, Lord was briefly detained in custody 'at the suit of Mr Moffit, for the sum of £67 and expenses', but was soon discharged. A second attempt to detain him, on 6 August, was dismissed in the Insolvent Debtors Court on the grounds that, as his 'former discharges had obtained all due publicity, there could be no just reason that any of his creditors should take him again into execution immediately afterwards'.[54]

---

52 *Australasian Chronicle*, 25 May 1841, 4; 1 June 1841, 4.
53 *Sydney Herald*, 26 June 1841, 1. The Australian Auction Company was one of the claimants to Edward Lord's estate.
54 *Sydney Monitor and Commercial Advertiser*, 26 July 1841, 2; 9 August 1841, 2. The defence lawyer in this debt case, Mr Goddard, would make another court appearance in January 1843 when defending John Staple, the purchaser of subdivisions at Long Beach.

On 17 September 1842, after more claims were made against Lord, his estate was placed under sequestration.[55] New trustees were appointed to administer his estate on 5 October.[56] His debts totalled £15,000. At this stage he was living with his family in the Hunter Valley. Eventually, he was discharged from bankruptcy after applying for his certificate on 18 July 1844.[57]

Despite their financial plight, from 1841, the Lords had been acquiring property around Brisbane and the County of Stanley, and, in 1844, Edward moved north with his family, residing at Kangaroo Point on Moreton Bay, on a property bought on trust for his wife, Eliza. Edward acted as a manager for Messrs MacKenzie & Co. In the late 1840s, the family moved to Drayton on the Darling Downs where Edward ran a store he named Lord's Emporium as well as a post office.

One of his notable ventures while at Drayton involved two visits to Germany as an immigration agent in 1854, encouraging and assisting 1,000 migrants to settle in Queensland. He maintained his familiarity with the German culture throughout his life.[58]

The family then moved to Toowoomba where Lord resumed his role as a commission agent, before experiencing further bankruptcies. In the mid-1870s, he received a 160-acre land grant north of Toowoomba at Spring Bluff, which he called 'Calliards' after his grandfather's hereditary woollen mill and farm near Rochdale in Lancashire.[59] He died in 1887, three years after Eliza was laid to rest, and was buried at Beenleigh.[60]

---

55   *NSW Government Gazette*, 20 September 1842, 1403; *Sydney Gazette and New South Wales Advertiser*, 11 October 1842, 3. NSW abolished imprisonment for debt in 1843, after reforms made to the 1841 *Insolvency Act*, and passed on 21 December 1843(2)/83, based on recommendations from the 1843 Committee on the Operation of the Insolvent Act. As Kercher noted: 'No-one was immune from the recession of the 1840s, and that may have been the strongest influence on the reforms of the debt-recovery law.' See Kercher, *An Unruly Child*, ch. 6.
56   *Australasian Chronicle*, 24 September 1842, 3.
57   *Australian*, 13 July 1844, 3. Francis C. Waldron, formerly of Broulee, had received his certificate of discharge two days beforehand (see Chapter 4).
58   Spillman, *Queensland Lords*, 90–103.
59   Spillman, *Queensland Lords*, chs 1 and 2 deal with Edward Lord's ancestors and his time in New South Wales, while the later chapters deal with his life in Queensland and biographies of his descendants. The Lord family in Queensland is also recalled by a granddaughter of Edward and Eliza Lord, Maude White. See Mills, 'The Whites of Bluff Downs', 26–31.
60   *Queenslander*, 5 November 1887, 721.

Figure 20. Edward Lord, n.d.
Photographer: Mathewson & Co. Brisbane, n.d. From the collection: 'Friends and Relatives of the Descendants of Edward Lord', State Library of Queensland.

8. MERCANTILE CHICANERY

Remnants of his Batemans Bay properties remained within his family for decades after he left New South Wales. Like Hughes and Hosking, Lord's family benefited from placing their assets in family trusts. In September 1842, at the time of his insolvency, his largest creditor, Alexander Park, placed advertisements in several papers offering for sale Lord's properties around Batemans Bay.[61] These were offered as five lots: Lot 1 was Lord's 640-acre Cyne Mallowes Creek property north of Nelligen Creek on the Clyde River, Lot 2 was the 1,010-acre property on the western bank of Cullendulla Creek closest to the township of St Vincent, Lot 3 was the 640-acre property further up the Clyde River at Brooman, Lot 4 was 2,560 acres situated near Ulladulla and Lot 5 was the 1,030-acre property adjoining Lot 2 between the waters of Batemans Bay and the Clyde River that Edward Lord had purchased from his brother James. The one notable absence from this list of auctioned properties was Stubley Park surrounding Long Beach.

The sales at the auction were declared 'incomplete' due to a 'misunderstanding' and the auctioneer Mr Blackman subsequently announced that the same five lots would go under the hammer on 13 December 1841.[62] Unlike the initial auction, the second one appears to have generated little interest. Soon after purchasing these properties around 1840, Edward Lord had transferred some of them to a trusteeship under his wife's name, controlled by his brother James. As part of their marriage agreement, Edward could not use the proceeds of his wife Eliza's estate. This legal issue might be what frustrated Alexander Park in his attempt to sell these portions of the estate in late 1842.[63]

In 1863, Alexander Park lodged a primary application for Lord's 1,010- and 1,030-acre land grants at Batemans Bay.[64] He was successful with the 1,030-acre application, which was subsequently subdivided in the early 1880s. The area nearest the bay was bought by William and Michael Peter

---

61   Park was also a Lewinbrook landowner and later a member of the NSW Legislative Council (1853–73). *Sydney Morning Herald*, 15 September 1842, 1, reprinted on 17 September, 1, and 26 September, 4.
62   The announcement of the incomplete sales was placed in the *Sydney Morning Herald*, 3 October 1842, 4. For the notification of the new auction, see *Sydney Morning Herald*, 25 November 1842 and 10 December 1842, 4. See also *Australian*, 25 November 1842, 1; 9 December 1842, 1; 2 and 5 December 1842. Spillman, *Queensland Lords*, 40.
63   See Spillman, *Queensland Lords*, 40–1. Examples are the mortgage for the Burroman property, NSW Land Registry Services, Book S, no. 419 (Lot 3 in the September–December 1842 auction); and the transfer of the 1,030 acres at Batemans Bay from James Lord and his wife to Edward and his wife, NSW Land Registry Services, Book R, no. 854 (Lot 5).
64   *NSW Government Gazette*, 14 August 1863, 1782. This was Lot 5. Alexander Park also seized the 640 acres at Burroman (Lot 3) at Mr Blackman's auction. See NSW Land Registry Services, vol. I, folio 194. See also State Records Authority NSW, NRS-17513-13-36-4-PA 156, vol. 2, folio 204.

Paul Maloney. They further subdivided the land into farm and suburban lots in December 1882—January 1883 as part of the private township of Clyde.[65] A 1901 map entitled 'NSW Harbours—Batemans Bay' also shows an allotment north on this land grant belonging to a 'Joseph Lord'.[66]

The 1,010 acres to the west of Cullendulla Creek was administered by the 'executors of the late Edward Lord' (Lot 5 in the aforementioned 1842 auction) until 1899, when Ada Lord of Taroom, Queensland, the widow of one of Edward Lord's sons, the late John Fletcher Lord, applied for a certificate of indefeasible title over the land.[67] In 1951, 15 years after Ada died, the mangrove-flanked property was declared a Fauna Protection District, although subsequently the western side was developed for residential purposes as the suburb of Surfside.

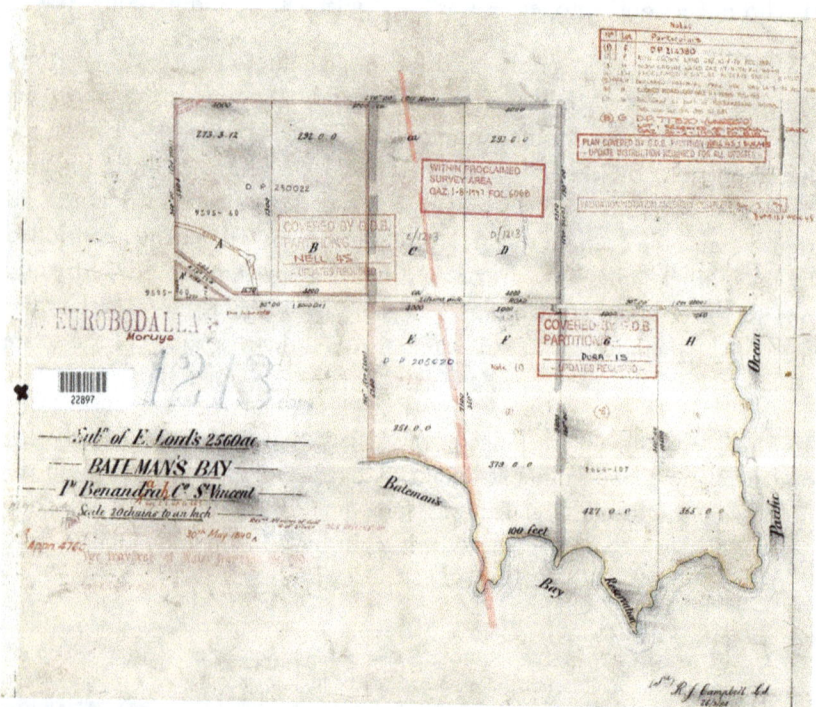

Figure 21. Detail of map showing R.J. Campbell's subdivision of Stubley Park, 1884.
NSW Land Registry Services, DP1213.

65　Biosis, 'Batemans Bay', 21–2. *Sydney Morning Herald*, 2 December 1882, 18; 6 January 1883, 15. The real estate agents were Richardson and Wrench.
66　No Joseph Lord appears in Spillman's comprehensive history. See Spillman, *Queensland Lords*.
67　*Daily Telegraph*, 8 July 1899, 15. Ada Lord featured in Spillman, *Queensland Lords*, ch. 12.

In 1884, the Stubley Park property surrounding Long Beach was surveyed by R.J. Campbell and subdivided into eight lots (see Figure 21). These subdivisions appeared on subsequent Benandra (now Benandarah) parish maps and each has its own history. Lot E, for instance, was purchased by William and Michael Maloney, later becoming the suburb of Maloneys Beach.[68]

Today, a cul-de-sac in North Batemans Bay is named Lord Place. However, Lord Street in the 'Great Southern Township of St Vincent' (see Figure 14) disappeared without trace along with the memory of that speculative 1841–42 venture jointly initiated under Edward Lord's name.

Conclusion

This chapter returned to the three merchant/landowners who initially purchased property on the northern shore of Batemans Bay, John Hosking, John Terry Hughes and Edward Lord. The value of their assets (land, livestock, merchandise) crashed during the depression and all three faced insolvency. For each individual, St Vincent was only a minor cause of their 'financial embarrassment' even though all three men were integral to how the story of St Vincent unfolded. Each of these vertically integrated capitalists found their own way into financial difficulty, and each had access to means of assistance to minimise their losses.

To an important extent, the spouses of these three capitalists shielded their husbands, revealing how a person's financial status could be protected by their spouse's social status. The wives of John Terry Hughes and John Hosking were both daughters of the immensely wealthy emancipist Samuel Terry and they possessed independent means through the way in which their late father's estate was distributed. John Terry Hughes spent much of his life after his insolvency involved in contestations over his father-in-law's will (including court battles with his former partner, John Hosking), and his wife and mother-in-law continued this cause after his death.

---

68 NSW Land Registry Services, DP1213. In 1851, the government had put up for lease three 640-acre blocks immediately to the north of Edward Lord's Stubley Estate at an upset price of 5s. per section (*NSW Government Gazette*, 23 August 1851, 1381). The following year the same blocks were again up for lease, at the upset price of 10s. per section of 640 acres (*Goulburn Herald and County of Argyle Advertiser*, 22 May 1852, 8). There is no record of any lessee taking up the offers and the boundaries of these leases were never marked on later parish maps.

Much of the criticism directed at men such as Hughes and Hosking during the 1840s concerned the manner in which they were able to avoid paying what many considered a just price for their financial failures, while so many others around them experienced hardship or ruin. Creditors only recovered a tiny fraction of Hughes's and Hosking's assets, yet Hughes continued to live at Albion House and Hosking completed his Vaucluse mansion, 'Carrara'.

J.O. Balfour might have had Hughes and Hosking in mind when he deplored the minority of merchants

> who, living in great extravagance previously to 1841, took advantage of the Colonial Insolvent Act and became bankrupt; but, unlike most ruined men, they did not abate one iota of their former extravagance; their houses, carriages, and servants remained the same; their wives, somehow or other, suddenly became heiresses, in their own right; all their kith and kin had legacies left them; while all those who were connected with them in business matters, if honest, were left penniless.[69]

A verse in an 1844 poem 'The Times' by M.F. gave popular expression to the feeling that many among the wealthy did not treat their insolvency with the seriousness that the law expected:

> In the morning, they mount their thoroughbred mare,
> And away to the Law's patent cradle –
> Inform the Commissioner all the affair,
> And ride leisurely back with their schedule.[70]

In the case of Edward Lord, his wife, Eliza, entered their marriage with an agreement to retain her own resources, and this allowed Eliza to claim rights to certain family assets, including some properties at Batemans Bay, when creditors came knocking. This limited the Lords' losses to investments held in Edward's name.[71] On this basis, Lord was able to re-establish a semblance of his former livelihood.

---

69 Balfour, *A Sketch*, 86. See also Mundy, *Our Antipodes*, 41.
70 *Port Phillip Gazette*, 17 April 1844, 4. See also the dialogic poem 'Debtor and Creditor', *Melbourne Times* (28 May 1842, 4) in which the creditor warns: 'I'm sorry that I trusted you, For every body knows you; But if you try the Insolvent Act, By Heaven! I'll oppose you.'
71 Spillman, *Queensland Lords*, 37, 40.

Other main characters in this story—those who acted for such capitalists (the auctioneer Stubbs, the conveyancer Staple and the surveyor/lithographer/engraver Clint)—were not the 'social types' who possessed the status or family wealth on which to fall back. Clint's wife, Mary Ann, was an entrepreneurial craftsperson, yet Clint did not appear to be willing to provide her with the publicity for her business that he lavished on himself. In Chapter 6 it was speculated that even Clint might have taken 'Burton's purge' more for his own than his creditors' benefit.

In the last verse of 'Billy Barlow in Australia', the impoverished and insolvent Billy could only engage in a 'fatuously futile' dream[72] of finding a spouse with an endowment:

> But there's still 'a spec' left may set me on my stumps,
> If a wife I could get with a few of the dumps;
> So if any lass here has 'ten thousand,' or so,
> She can just drop a line addressed 'Mr Barlow.'
> Oh dear, lackaday, oh,
> The dear angel shall be 'Mrs Billy Barlow'.[73]

As a stratum of the capitalist class, merchants tended to possess more resources than the Billy Barlows, but, as the early 1840s depression descended on the colony, there is no doubt that these merchants were caught in the eye of the storm, given their role in articulating a pastoral colonial economy with an imperial industrial centre on the other side of the world. Those committed to the more 'local' practice of land speculation were especially susceptible to what Raphael Clint called 'colonial fever'.

In this chapter, biographical portraits of merchants involved with the township of St Vincent have been employed to assess their ability to ride out the financial pandemic. While this merchant stratum shared many characteristics, care must be taken to avoid using Hughes, Hosking and Lord as typical cases. Merchants adopted different business models and this partly explains their 'fortunes'. Both Hughes's and Hosking's approach to land was to acquire as much as possible wherever it became available in order to resell either wholesale or through subdivision. Lord employed a more strategic—or, to use Stubbs's description, 'judicious'—approach.

---

72 Ward, 'Jemmy Green', 250. A 'dump' was the coin created from the punched-out centre, or plug, of a 'holey dollar'.
73 *Maitland Mercury and Hunter River General Advertiser*, 3 September 1843, 4.

His properties represented 'beads' on a commodity chain from the interior to the coast and then onto the metropolis. His debts were also a fraction of those admitted by Hughes and Hosking.

Another merchant whose approach up to the depression mirrored Hughes's and Hosking's was John Jenkins Peacock, who had jointly purchased Long Beach with Raphael Clint in February 1841. A 'currency lad' like Thomas Stubbs, Peacock initially established himself as a farmer on a grant of land on the Hawkesbury River in the 1820s, before gradually moving into the merchant shipping business. In the mid-1830s, his wharf neighboured Hughes & Hosking's. He later purchased Bettington's Wharf further north in Darling Harbour. Like Hughes & Hosking, he also jointly ran a mill at Darlinghurst and an inn—the Dundee Arms, on Gloucester Street.

Peacock accumulated substantial landholdings, including some of the earliest blocks of land at Balmain, immediately west of Hosking's block. Both subdivided their properties for sale in 1841, and both projects produced the same disappointing results under their agent Thomas Stubbs. In 1842, Peacock was elected the inaugural City of Sydney Council alderman for Gipps Ward, while Hosking won Bourke Ward. In September 1843, Peacock was declared insolvent, three weeks before Hughes and Hosking.

Peacock received his certificate of insolvency in March the following year, through the security of his brother-in-law Michael Gannon, who took over his real estate portfolio, allowing Peacock's creditors to receive 10s. in the pound. However, in 1845, Gannon's own financial 'embarrassments' threw Peacock once more at the mercy of the Insolvency Court. A lengthy court case then ensued with Gannon's and Peacock's creditors, part of which focused on property that had been held in trust for Mrs Gannon.

Peacock's career trajectory diverged from Hughes's and Hosking's through his interest in trading links with New Zealand from the mid-1830s. After his insolvencies, Peacock prospered from merchant shipping on the New Zealand run, into which he had encouraged his son John Thomas Peacock, who later inherited Hughes & Hosking's old property at Long Beach, Batemans Bay, from his father. As noted in Chapter 7, in 1861, Peacock repurchased the 320-acre block at Long Beach from George Rattray for

£100, after having jointly purchased the same block with Raphael Clint in 1841 for £800.[74] The Peacocks became one of the most influential and wealthy families in Christchurch, New Zealand.

Other merchants found new opportunities during the monetary crisis through this trans-Tasman trade. As the market softened, assignments of goods were still arriving from Britain and merchants looked to sell goods at a discount. A poem entitled 'The Lamentations of a Sydney Merchant' spoke of the unsold stocks of luxury goods on consignment:[75]

> For large demands, from foreign lands,
> He now no more rejoices,
> He can't keep pace, for in his face
> Stare large unpaid invoices.[76]

One outlet for these consignments was to sell, or extend lines of credit, to speculators who bartered goods in the Pacific. After the surgeon John Whitehead MacNee emigrated from Glasgow in 1839, he bought land near Nelligen at Cyne Mallowes Creek (which he sold to Edward Lord in 1840; see Figure 7), then opened a line of credit with the merchants Paul & Co. MacNee took the goods across the Tasman Sea to barter for Māori land at Kaipara. In 1842, Paul & Co. attempted to have MacNee's property sequestered and eventually made a claim on his property in New Zealand.[77]

---

74 For a summary of Peacock's life, see Reynolds, 'Peacock', 14–16. See also Lost Christchurch, 'John Peacock'. For Peacock's initial insolvency, see *NSW Government Gazette*, 15 September 1843, 1195–6, and for his subsequent insolvency, see *Sydney Morning Herald*, 17 April 1845, 3. For Gannon's insolvency case, see *Morning Chronicle*, 3 June 1846, 3; *Sydney Morning Herald*, 30 May 1846, 2. Through power of attorney, his son, J.T. Peacock, inherited the 320 acres at Long Beach. The property remained in family hands through J.T. Peacock's brother-in-law Francis Garrick along with John Wetherill in January 1878 (Wetherill, after whom Wetherill Park in Sydney is named, was a draper and land developer, living at Greystanes, Prospect). Wetherill sold Long Beach to J.S. McElveney and C.J. Royle in February 1882 for £133 6s. 8d., still well below its original 1840 price of £192.
75 Sam Slap Esq. in *Sydney Herald*, 30 January 1841, 4.
76 Sam Slap Esq. in *Sydney Herald*, 30 January 1841, 4.
77 Earl (*Enterprise*, 160) later described this circulation of commodities:
    manufactured goods were pouring into the colony from the mother country in quantities far greater than they were required for the consumption of the inhabitants; and as it became necessary to force sales, these were disposed of for bills, at long dates, to speculators who purchased vessels to carry them to all the neighbouring countries that afforded the slightest prospect of a market.
For the agreement between MacNee and Māori chiefs at Kaipara and the goods MacNee bartered, see 'Mihirau Block, Wairoa River, Kaipara District', nzetc.victoria.ac.nz/tm/scholarly/tei-TurOldP-t1-g1-g1-g6-g5-t1.html, accessed 20 January 2023. For MacNee's agreement with Paul & Co., see '(Enclosure in No. 336)', nzetc.victoria.ac.nz/tm/scholarly/tei-TurOldP-t1-g1-g1-g6-g5-t2.html, accessed 20 January 2023.

Other merchants mentioned in this chapter accumulated capital through property during the depression. For example, Alexander Park and Thomas Burdekin lent money as land prices rose, and later acquired an enormous portfolio of land as a result of foreclosing on their debtors, such as Edward Lord, who had purchased property on the crest of the land-mania wave.

The field of literature provides an example of another category of merchant. The one Australian classic novel that focused on the mercantile class during this period, *A House Is Built*, glosses over the experience of the early 1840s depression. First published in 1929, the novel chronicles M. Barnard Eldershaw's[78] family saga, beginning with quartermaster John Hyde's emigration in 1837 when he established his merchant business in Sydney.

The reason the depression remains in the background is not because the author failed to consider it, but because Hyde's business behaviour differed from the many merchants who sunk their profits from the 1830s into property and livestock. Hyde was not a gambler, Eldershaw emphasised. He focused on victualling ships and the 'business of necessities' rather than luxuries from his wharf and store on Windmill Street at The Rocks (the street where J.J. Peacock re-established his merchant shipping business after his insolvency). He also avoided indebtedness, growing only as he earned, and purchased land only for his domestic circumstances. By avoiding the circulation of property capital, Hyde cushioned himself through the depression and the 'Bank of Australia collapse'—unlike Hughes & Hosking, Lord and Peacock. The bank's collapse is broached in financial discussions Hyde conducts with his son William. Other landmark events featured in previous chapters also appear in the novel (such as John Hosking's mayoral ball at the new Royal Hotel in late 1842 and 'Lyons' famous John Verge–designed auction rooms' on George Street).[79]

The comparison between the fictional Hyde and those involved in the real but ephemeral township of St Vincent helps broaden the span of the story of the depression, illustrating the different ways in which individual merchants could respond to the public issues, the financial dangers and

---

78   This was the collaborative pen-name of two authors, Marjorie Barnard and Flora Eldershaw.
79   Eldershaw, *A House*. The hardback cover of the 1972 reissue features a detail from Frederick Garling's painting 'Circular Quay' (c. 1854). In the middle of the detail is 'Grocott's wine store', owned by J.C. Grocott, who purchased Raphael Clint's lithographic press in 1847 and collected subscriptions for his widow, Mary Ann, in 1849.

the pecuniary opportunities that dominated the period. In so doing, this chapter has shown the connection between what C. Wright Mills called 'the personal troubles of milieu' and 'the public issues of social structure'.[80]

Hyde's personal troubles came to a head in another realm. He held an interest in the 'Northern Rivers Packets', while his less scrupulous mercantile rival Franklin dominated the southern shipping line, involving 'Eden, Moruya and Twofold Bay', with his over-insured unseaworthy vessels. That story should not be spoilt by retelling, but the next chapter will return to the story of St Vincent, Batemans Bay, through focusing on the very same southern shipping lane.

---

80   Mills, *The Sociological Imagination*, 12–14.

9

The PS *Clonmel* and the southern shipping lane

So thus you see we're floored at last,
By over speculation;
With discounts, auction companies,
And steamboat navigation.[1]

The January 1841 advertisement for allotments at the township of St Vincent twice referred to the 'magnificent' paddle-steamer *Clonmel*. This chapter shows how the vessel reflected a broader hope that steamships would enhance the competitiveness of ports on the South Coast. It follows the *Clonmel*'s incident-filled month on the southern run, suggesting that the technological optimism of South Coast 'puffers' was misplaced, or mistimed.

The chapter also examines the paddle-steamer's unscheduled visit to Batemans Bay during a mid-December 1840 storm, and trawls through the archival traces that the vessel left in its wake. The *Clonmel* inadvertently helped to establish another southern port, Port Albert, and its history identifies factors that both facilitated and thwarted the establishment of southern ports during this period. Overall, what the chapter suggests is that any 'port hierarchy' along this route would remain unstable during the nineteenth century.

---

1   Anon., 'Hunter River Settler's Song', *Bell's Life in Sydney and Sporting Reviewer*, 1 February 1845, 3.

The celebrity of the *Clonmel*

The *Clonmel* featured in an August 2017 Australia Post stamp series depicting famous Australian shipwrecks. One of the $1 stamps shows the vessel run aground on the morning of 3 January 1841 at Corner Inlet in Bass Strait during its second Australian voyage from Sydney to Port Phillip (see Figure 22).[2] No lives were lost, but the grounding of the ship and its subsequent wreck were widely reported in the press, given that its recent arrival in the southern hemisphere was heralded as symbolising a new era of rapid luxury transport.

Figure 22. The *Clonmel* postage stamp, 2017.
© Australian Postal Corporation 2017. Illustration: Ian Hansen. Shipwrecks stamp issue.

---

2   Australia Post, 'Shipwrecks'. For an account of the wreck of the *Clonmel*, see 'Garryowen', *The Chronicles*, 577–9.

9. THE PS CLONMEL AND THE SOUTHERN SHIPPING LANE

By 1841, Australia had experienced a decade of steam-powered ships, beginning with the locally built *Surprise* and *William the Fourth* along with the British-built *Sophie Jane*.[3] Others followed, both local- and overseas-built, mainly plying their trade between the Hunter River and Sydney or within Sydney Harbour and the Parramatta River.[4]

The establishment of Port Phillip offered more favourable opportunities for southern lines. The fourth steamer brought from Britain, the *James Watt*, began on the Hunter–Sydney route before being redeployed on the Sydney—Port Phillip—Hobart run. It occasionally advertised stops at Batemans Bay and, in 1837, charged £5 for a cabin and £2 10s. on deck for a ticket to Batemans Bay from Sydney.[5] In 1840, Edward Lord became a director of the Hunter River Steam Navigation Company, which, in 1841, plied the northern route with its British-built steamers, *Thistle*, *Shamrock* and *Rose*.

Promoters of southern ports like Lord envisaged the establishment of a similar line that would link South Coast properties with Sydney.[6] When advertising Oldrey's property at Broulee in late 1840, the auctioneer predicted that the arrival of 'steamers' would shortly raise the value of the land 'three or four fold'.[7] The auctioneers of the Goodridge-Leigh estate at Broulee also linked southern prosperity to the emergence of steamships in August 1840:

> It requires no extraordinary stretch of imagination to depict Steam Boats regularly plying between Twofold Bay, Broulee and the Port of Sydney, then it is that the real value of this property will display itself.[8]

When Edward Lord placed Stubley Park at Batemans Bay on the market in December 1840, Samuel Lyons enticed buyers with mention of the emergence of steam vessels running between Sydney and southern

---

3   For a summary of investment in steamships from 1831 to 1842, see Holcomb, 'Opportunities and Risks', 154–9.
4   Up to the arrival of the *Clonmel*, locally built steamers included the *Experiment* (originally operated literally by horsepower), the *Rapid*, the *Comet*, the *Native*, the *Fairy Queen*, *Brothers*, the *Gypsy Queen*, *Waterman*, the *Sovereign*, the *Ceres*, the *Victoria* and the *Maitland*. British-built steamboats included the *King William*, the *Tamar*, the *James Watt*, the *Rose*, the *Thistle* and the *Shamrock* (but no *Leek*).
5   *Sydney Herald*, 24 April 1837, 3.
6   This was one reason why Lord petitioned for a wharf or breakwater at Broulee in 1840 (see Chapter 4). John Hosking was also a director of the Hunter River Steam Navigation Company. See Tegg, *Tegg's*, 199. In 1837, Tegg and Raphael Clint had published *The Australasian and Nautical Almanac for the Meridian of Sydney and Greenwich*. See *Sydney Gazette and New South Wales Advertiser*, 28 February 1839, 1.
7   *Sydney Herald*, 24 November 1840, 4.
8   *Commercial Journal and Advertiser*, 12 August 1840, 4.

settlements.⁹ *Tegg's New South Wales Pocket Almanac and Remembrancer* for 1842 considered steam as the vital missing ingredient in the advancement of the Clyde River. It described Batemans Bay as 'one of the few places in the colony where a considerable population is likely to be collected', combining the attributes of a beautiful river, the facility of communication and central location. Its 'rapid progress of advancement' would be ensured 'once steam navigation is introduced'.¹⁰

While steamships were becoming a familiar sight in the colony, the appearance of the *Clonmel* raised expectations to a new level. The paddle-steamer was built at Birkenhead, England, in 1836 to carry 300 tons of goods and 50 passengers. It spent 15 months working the British coast before sailing to Sydney, arriving on 5 October 1840. Given that it could carry only five days of fuel on board, it came out under sail before being refitted for steam at Girard's Wharf at Darling Harbour. It had been purchased by Edye Manning & Partners for £30,000 to serve the Sydney—Port Phillip—Launceston route.¹¹ Considered Australia's first luxury paddle-steamer, the *Clonmel* was expected to shorten the trip to and from southern ports considerably. It was hailed as a 'valuable acquisition to the Colony' and an 'annihilator of space—a condenser of time'.¹² It was the harbinger of a new epoch.

In the two months after its arrival, the vessel received celebrity coverage in the Sydney press, which monitored its every refit and move.¹³ It then made its maiden voyage on 1 December 1840 under Lieutenant John S. Tollervey RN, who had also captained the ship from Liverpool to Sydney. The voyage to Port Phillip cost passengers £12 12s. for a cabin and £6 for a deck passage.¹⁴ It was announced that the 'Clonmel positively sails for Port Phillip at four o'clock this afternoon, calling at Bateman's Bay to land passengers'.¹⁵

---

9   *Sydney Herald*, 4 December 1840 – 21 December 1840, various pages.
10 Tegg, *Tegg's*, 260.
11 'Wreck of the Clonmel Steam Ship', *Launceston Courier*, 18 January 1841, 2. The *Australian* (6 October 1840, 2) gave its cost as £24,000.
12 *Sydney Monitor and Commercial Advertiser*, 6 October 1841, 3; *Sydney Herald*, 20 January 1841, 2. The *Commercial Journal and Advertiser* (7 October 1840, 2) described it as 'the finest vessel of that description which has ever visited the Colony'.
13 The *Sydney Herald* (31 October 1840, 2) sought to divert readers' attention from daily business—'money matters … immigration, steam navigation, the price of oil, the value of wool'—by drawing attention to a 'neat unpretending little volume of poems' by Mrs Fidelia T. Hill. The volume, 'Poems and Recollections of the Past', could be obtained at Mr R. Clint's, George Street.
14 *Australian*, 1 December 1840, 1.
15 See *Sydney Monitor and Commercial Advertiser*, 2 December 1840, 3.

The *Clonmel* was 'detained' at Batemans Bay for six hours 'to land passengers and luggage'.[16] There is no record of where the passengers alighted. In 1840, more vessels stopped at Broulee than at Batemans Bay, although newspapers occasionally announced that ships heading south from Sydney would be stopping at Batemans Bay.[17]

The *Clonmel* took 72 hours to run from Sydney to Port Phillip, arriving at William's Town on 5 December 1840, where the *Geelong Advertiser* reported that the town had been 'agog with preparations' for the ship's visit. The expectant crowd paid to view its luxurious accommodation.[18] The historian 'Garryowen' later wrote that the 'most exalted notions were entertained as to what the "Clonmel" would do for Port Phillip'.[19]

On 7 December, the vessel left for Launceston where it was delayed by the colony's shipping regulations before returning to Port Phillip on 14 December. The *Launceston Courier* later stated that the ship was 'by far the most splendid that ever visited our shores'.[20] However, by now the *Clonmel* was well behind schedule, shipping agents having previously advertised that it would depart from Sydney again to Launceston on 19 December. More delays followed, including problems procuring coal in Port Phillip. This was not an issue on the northern shipping lane, where supplies were available in the Hunter region. However, when the *Clonmel* visited Port Phillip, coal had to be brought from Newcastle. The *Sydney Herald* chided that this diseconomy 'ought to have attracted attention two years since'.[21]

---

16   *Sydney Monitor and Commercial Advertiser*, 19 December 1840, 2. One of the passengers was probably John Whitehead MacNee (see Chapter 8). One passenger list out of Sydney on 1 December mentions a 'Mr Mcnee'; however, he is not listed on another. Papers claimed the vessel landed passengers at Batemans Bay but there is no mention of embarking passengers. MacNee is listed as a cabin passenger on the only known list of arrivals at Port Phillip. Despite this confusion over where he embarked and disembarked, it is likely that MacNee's presence was one reason the *Clonmel* stopped at Batemans Bay. See also *Australasian Chronicle*, 3 December 1841, 3.

17   For example, the *Sydney Herald*, 27 November 1840, reported that the schooner *Will Watch* would 'sail on Sunday next for Port Phillip and on her way she will touch at Bateman's Bay to land passengers, therefore this will be an admirable opportunity for any person wishing to proceed to that part of St Vincent'. Coincidentally, the *Will Watch* was one of the boats that came to the assistance of the stricken *Clonmel* after it was grounded in Bass Strait.

18   *Geelong Advertiser*, 12 December 1840, 2.

19   'Garryowen', *The Chronicles*, 570. Garryowen was the pen-name for journalist Edmund Finn.

20   *Launceston Courier*, 18 January 1841, 2.

21   *Sydney Herald*, 13 October 1840, 2.

The *Clonmel*'s unscheduled stop at Batemans Bay

When sailing north back to Sydney after leaving Port Phillip on the 16 December, the *Clonmel* ran into a 'gale of three days duration'.[22] At maximum speed, the ship consumed 610 kilograms of coal per hour and the storm threatened to exhaust the ship's supply. On Saturday 19 December, Captain Tollervey took the precaution of sheltering at Batemans Bay. This also allowed him to find safe anchorage, land, gather firewood and replenish his water supply in order to complete his journey. The *Clonmel* was delayed at Batemans Bay for two days 'to procure wood' before limping back to Sydney on 22 December.[23]

Despite these misadventures, the Sydney press announced the return of the *Clonmel* in celebratory terms. One paper reported that as the ship came through Sydney Heads at 5.52pm 'the inhabitants of Sydney on Tuesday last displayed an enthusiasm … which we did not think them capable of'.[24] Other reports included letters from two groups of passengers praising the ship and absolving the captain and his vessel of any responsibility for the delays. One letter addressed to the captain stated that:

> Regarding our situation at Bateman's Bay, we are fully satisfied no blame is to be attached either to yourself or the vessel, but was solely owing to the arrangements at Melbourne being incomplete for the supply of coals.[25]

The *Clonmel*'s unscheduled stay at Batemans Bay remains obscure for want of further information. However, it can be surmised that Captain Tollervey chose Batemans Bay either out of necessity or because it was one of the few bays he was acquainted with, having stopped there on the outward voyage earlier in December.

---

22 *Australian*, 24 December 1840, 2.
23 *Australasian Chronicle*, 24 December 1840, 3.
24 *Sydney Gazette and New South Wales Advertiser*, 24 December 1840, 2.
25 *Sydney Herald*, 23 December 1840, 2; *Australian*, 24 December 1840, 2; *Australasian Chronicle*, 24 December 1840, 2.

Unfortunately, because there is no logbook for the voyage, it is difficult to determine the exact position on the bay where the *Clonmel* sheltered. However, as the ship was struggling against a north-easterly gale,[26] it can be speculated that the captain would have preferred anchoring under the cliffs on the northern side of the bay to maximise shelter and minimise the possibility of being beached.

Another clue points towards the northern shore as the point of egress. The first of Thomas Stubbs's advertisements for allotments within the township of St Vincent was published only 13 days after the *Clonmel*'s return to Sydney and took advantage of the vessel's extended celebrity. Indeed, the *Clonmel* received top billing in Stubbs's 4 January advertisement, which opened with the sentence:

> Most important unreserved Sale of the Township of St. Vincent, situated at the mouth of, and adjoining the Government Village Reserve, at Bateman's Bay, and the navigable River Clyde, and where the Magnificent Steamer CLONMEL landed her passengers and took Wood and Water.[27]

The advertisement later made a more precise claim about the whereabouts of the *Clonmel*'s anchorage:

> The proprietor having resolved to spare no expense by which art can be made to improve the natural Wharf which the plan exhibits, (and at which the *Clonmel* landed her passengers) has already at a great expense purchased and contracted with an eminent ship owner for the laying down of moorings opposite the Township.[28]

It is, therefore, possible that the wharf that Stubbs mentioned was exhibited on the catalogued 1841 Plan 359(A). No wharf was indicated on either Raphael Clint's April 1841 lithographic plan of St Vincent or the 1896 Benandra parish map. However, the parish maps of 1907 and 1917 did acknowledge Plan 359(A). Further, they not only superimposed the streets of the private township of St Vincent, but also included a wharf at the rocks on the eastern end of Long Beach immediately west of Quay Street.

---

26 According to the *Sydney Gazette and New South Wales Advertiser*, 24 December 1840, 2:
  She ran the first three hundred miles with a strong N.E. gale, which was right a-head. On Saturday last she put into Bateman's Bay, where she remained for the space of two days, to obtain firewood, as they were afraid they would run short of fuel.
27 *Sydney Herald*, 4 January 1841, 3.
28 *Sydney Herald*, 4 January 1841, 3 (reprinted in the *Australian*, 9, 14 and 16 January).

On these and subsequent official maps up to 1964 (see Figure 23 and Figure 14),[29] these rocks are named 'Conmel Wharf', which is possibly an orthographic error originating from the *Clonmel*. No rectangular wharf was ever constructed at these rocks, and parish maps from 1984 onwards show the rocks in their natural formation.[30]

Unresolved questions remain: Who provided the information for the 1841 catalogued Plan 359(A) that there was a 'natural wharf' at Long Beach, as announced by Thomas Stubbs in January 1841? Did someone aboard the *Clonmel* provide the intelligence that this was a convenient anchorage and point of disembarkation? What was the provenance of 'Conmel Wharf' and who designed the rectangular shape that the wharf assumes on these maps?

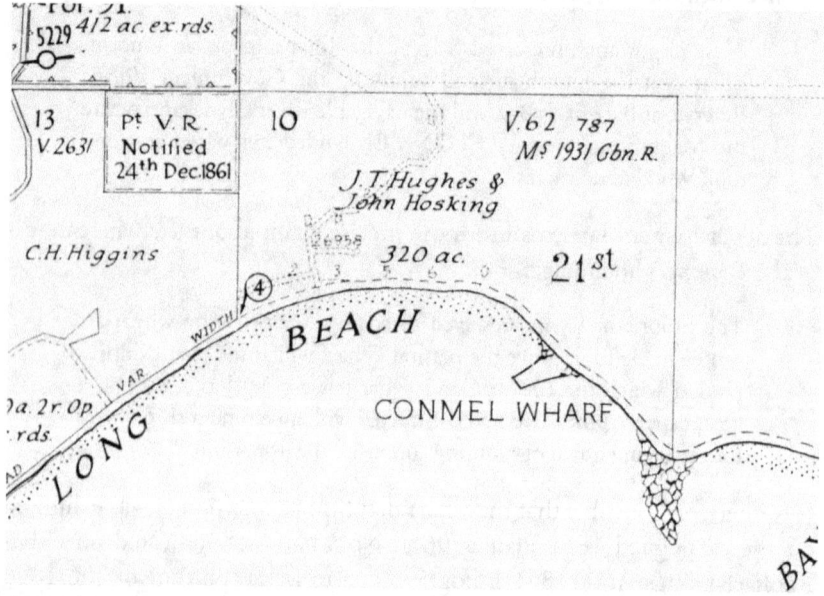

Figure 23. Detail from NSW Department of Lands map showing 'Conmel Wharf', 1964.
Detail from NSW Department of Lands, 'Parish of Benandra, County of St Vincent', 5 March 1964, MAP G8971.G46 svar (Copy 1), nla.gov.au/nla.obj-1351051005/view.

---

29   NSW Department of Lands maps of the County of St Vincent from 1931 to 1964 also show this wharf.
30   NSW Department of Lands, 1979, MAP G8971.G46 svar (Copy 1). Between the 1964 and 1979 maps, the spelling of Benandra was changed to Benandarah.

Allison James's history of Batemans Bay presents an alternative source for the provenance of Conmel Wharf, reporting that when 'the surveyor drew up his plans of the area as early as 1839 there was already a wharf there known as Connell's wharf'.[31] The name Connell had long been associated with the bay area. Michael Connell arrived in the area in the early 1830s, assigned to the settler Francis Flanagan, north of Moruya.[32] Connell's Point at the mouth of the Tomaga River at Mossy Point is situated on land Hughes & Hosking purchased at the 1839 Broulee auctions. Thus, Connell's wharf could be another orthographic variant of 'Conmel wharf'.

While Thomas Stubbs's January 1841 advertisement and the historical parish maps lend weight to the possibility that the rectangular structure named 'Conmel Wharf' was associated with the *Clonmel*, the possibility that it was associated with the name Connell cannot be dismissed. Without further information, the provenance of the wharf depicted on parish maps is currently left floating between the associated words Clonmel, Conmel and Connell.

Glengarry's choice: Caledonia Vincentius or Corner Inlet

The *Clonmel*'s unscheduled stop at Batemans Bay gave rise to an 'alternative history' whereby Long Beach became the antipodean home of a Scottish Highland clan. In Alexander Marjoribanks's 1840s New South Wales travel book, among the vignettes featuring Thomas Stubbs's oratory skills, the final offering involved the township of St Vincent (see Chapter 3):[33]

> In describing the township of St Vincent, he (Thomas Stubbs) states, as one of its qualifications, 'As is generally understood that the highland chief Glengarry, after traversing the Port Phillip district, and arriving here in the Clonmel, selected this locality for the highland home of his clan, it may be reasonably expected that before an other anniversary of the foundation of the colony is celebrated, that the blue bonnets will be over its border, transplanting not only the industry, but the social and moral virtues of their fatherland.'[34]

---

31 James, *Batemans Bay*, 125.
32 See Odgers, *Our Town*, 46–8.
33 Marjoribanks, *Travels*, 29.
34 This is the only printed version of Stubbs's delivery (see the discussion in Chapter 3). It did not appear in any newspaper. However, the prose is classic Stubbs (for instance, the use of passive language—'As it is generally understood'—to suggest a universally known truth).

As noted in Chapter 3, it is not clear how Marjoribanks encountered Stubbs's speech, but it can be verified that Glengarry was aboard the *Clonmel* at Batemans Bay from 19 to 21 December 1840. He appears on passenger lists and was the first signatory on one of two letters to the press on 23 December 1840 that defended the captain and his ship when the *Clonmel* reached Sydney after its lengthy delay. He signed his name 'AE. R. Macdonell (Glengarry)'. It has already been noted how Stubbs exploited the celebrity of the *Clonmel*. What is less clear is how Stubbs gathered this intelligence about Glengarry's intentions.

It is highly plausible that Glengarry walked upon Long Beach between 19 and 21 December 1840. He was an energetic explorer. He was also the most esteemed passenger on board the paddle-steamer and, while it was anchored at Batemans Bay for two days, he would have been curious about his new antipodean surroundings. However, he does not appear to have been active at Stubbs's auction, despite Stubbs's claim that it was 'generally understood' that Glengarry had 'selected this location as the highland home of his clan' and even though he was in the vicinity of Sydney during January 1841.

It was well known, though, that Glengarry was looking for somewhere to replace his lost ancestral land. It was within Stubbs's artistic licence to exercise his audience's imagination by drawing a picture of Glengarry on Long Beach envisaging the remnants of his clan settled at St Vincent and tending their sheep and Highland cattle.

AE. R. (or Aeneas) Macdonell had recently arrived in the colony. He was the sixteenth chief of Clan Macdonell of Glengarry and the son of Alexander Ranaldson Macdonell, on whom Sir Walter Scott modelled Fergus McIvor in his novel *Waverley*.[35] Aeneas, educated at Eton, inherited not only his father's romantic disposition but also his debts. He sold most of his ancestral lands and emigrated to Australia in 1840 on board the *Perfect* with his wife,

---

35 Alexander had led a complex life typical of chieftains whose families had supported the eighteenth-century Jacobite cause to return a Stuart to the throne. He retained those Jacobite sympathies and established 'The Society of True Highlanders'. At the same time, to pay for his stylised image of a Highland chieftain, he was responsible for evicting his clansmen, forcing them into emigration while their ancestral home became sheep runs. For his romantic vision of the Highlander, Alexander was lauded by Sir Walter Scott, but for his treatment of impoverished clansmen he was scorned by Robert Burns. Sir Walter Scott maintained a friendly but turbulent relationship with him. Robert Burns, temperamentally more critical of such chieftains, wrote the poem 'Address to Beelzebub' in sympathy with Glengarry's destitute clansmen who were seeking emigration to the Americas. For Burns, most of Scotland's elite remained 'a parcel of rogues'.

young children and clan entourage, intending to return for the rest of his clan.[36] The 32-year-old chieftain left Glasgow in late June and landed at Port Phillip on 8 November, where locals hoped he would 'fix upon Australia Felix' as the land of his adoption. However, in mid-December he left for Sydney on the *Clonmel*, and—contrary to the passive-voiced Stubbs—the press 'generally understood' he was considering land on the Clarence River.[37]

Rather than heading north from Sydney, in March 1841, Glengarry ventured south with an overland party through the Maneroo and down to Omeo. It was near Corner Inlet in Gippsland that he chose land. Back in Sydney, Glengarry secured a depasturing licence on the land, and sent supplies down to Cornet Inlet on the cutter *Industry*.[38]

Corner Inlet was the vicinity in which the *Clonmel* was stranded in early January 1841 on its second Australian voyage, two weeks after Glengarry had disembarked at Sydney. Meanwhile, encouraging reports of good pasturage from the rescuers of the *Clonmel*'s passengers had prompted an expedition to Corner Inlet from Port Phillip. William Brodribb and other squatters reached an agreement with Lieutenant Governor Charles La Trobe to conduct a special survey of the area. While there, the party took a long boat to visit the recently wrecked *Clonmel* and discovered channels leading into a river. There they found two of the *Clonmel*'s lifeboats and travelled further inland up two rivulets where they found land suitable for a stock station.

Shortly after, in early June, Glengarry's supply boat *Industry* arrived at the party's campsite at Port Albert with instructions from Surveyor-General Mitchell that no land was to be settled until officially surveyed and a village reserve selected. 'Disappointed' and 'lamenting our hard fate', Brodribb's contingent returned to Melbourne before heading north to Brodribb's squatting station where he observed that there 'was a kind of commercial panic in New South Wales as well as Port Phillip'.[39]

---

36 Prebble, *The Highland*, 273–6. The entourage included 'his servants, his piper, clothing, bedding, bolts of tartan, furniture, a comprehensive selection of agricultural tools, and a number of prefabricated timber houses'. The *Fife Herald* (2 July 1840, 2, among many other British papers in a syndicated article) also listed 'a splendid stock of Scottish cattle', shepherds and agriculturalists.
37 Reprinted in the *Colonist*, 17 December 1840, 3.
38 *Port Phillip Patriot and Melbourne Advertiser*, 10 June 1841, 2.
39 Brodribb, *Recollections*, 26–52.

On 26 June 1841, Glengarry, along with his family and entourage, set sail from Sydney to Port Albert aboard the *Brothers*. His depasturing licence was further up the Tarra River, beyond the land earmarked by the surveyor-general. Prior to their arrival, their newly erected hut and stores had been attacked by local Brataualong owners who defended their land to 'good effect', 'throwing spears pointed with glass, about 100 yards'.[40] A similar welcome had greeted a number of boats that anchored at Batemans Bay up until the 1820s from Walbanja people resisting the invasion of their land.[41] Conflict over Gippsland land use continued through the next few years, but by 1848 the Brataualong population had been reduced by 80 per cent due to land invasion, killings (including 'one of the worst massacres in Australia during this period') and diseases caused by loss of land, water, food and community resources.[42]

Glengarry spent much of the next year travelling between his property, Port Phillip and Sydney. By June 1842, he had decided not to renew his lease and to return to his homeland 'for the sake of his family'.[43] On 7 February 1843 they returned to Scotland aboard the *Kinnear*.[44]

The rise and decline of Port Albert

As Glengarry was abandoning his Gippsland station in 1842, Port Albert at Corner Inlet was establishing itself as the southernmost port township between Sydney and the expanding settlement at Port Phillip. It would maintain an important maritime status until the late 1860s, developing its own commercial niche. It did not compete directly with the ports further

---

40   *Free Press and Commercial Journal*, 30 June 1841, 2; *Sydney Gazette and New South Wales Advertiser*, 24 June 1841. According to the Australian Highland Cattle Society, 'The History':
    Chieftain Aeneas Ranaldson MacDonell of Glengarry, Scotland, landed at Port Albert, Victoria, with his clan to set up a system of farming at Greenmount, on the Tarra River, near the present-day town of Yarram. It is claimed that the clan drove its fold of Highland cattle to Greenmount preceded by a piper.
    No welcoming ceremony from the traditional owners is mentioned.
41   Bayley, *Behind Broulee*.
42   Glowrey, *South of the South of the Strzelecki Ranges*, 38–9; Lennon, *Across Bass Strait*, 66–8. Don Watson briefly mentions Glengarry's farewell, but overall highlights the ultimate irony of this episode of colonial 'modernisation' and 'improvement'. Many Scottish Highlanders were evicted from their traditional lands by chiefs such as Glengarry, and the lands were transformed into sheep runs. After a voyage to the other end of the world, these same Highlanders found themselves protecting the sheep stations of settlers such as Glengarry from dispossessed Indigenous owners. (Watson, *Caledonia Australis*, 174–5). Watson's book title inspired the subtitle of this section of the chapter.
43   *Sydney Morning Herald*, 24 August 1842.
44   *Australian*, 8 February 1843, 2.

north, such as Batemans Bay, Jervis Bay and Broulee, yet its rise and decline illustrate how contingent the fortunes of regional ports were on prevailing circumstances as the colonies' political economy shifted.

Port Albert was approximately the same distance from Port Phillip as Batemans Bay was from Sydney. Yet, Port Albert's principal maritime trader was not Port Phillip, but Van Diemen's Land (VDL). The end of transportation to New South Wales in 1840 diverted convict ships to the island. This increased pressure on the VDL Commissariat, which was faced with the task of meeting a demand for meat that surpassed the capacity of local producers. A reliable supply of livestock for slaughterhouses had to be found on the mainland, but the closest market, Port Phillip, was experiencing its own growth and many islanders were relocating themselves and their flocks and herds across Bass Strait to the new settlement. The Imlay brothers at Twofold Bay were filling part of the island's livestock deficit in the late 1830s and early 1840s, but the onset of the depression soon curtailed their activities.[45]

Meanwhile in New South Wales, the search by squatters for new pasture continued unabated. By 1840, grasslands south of the Maneroo (Monaro) and over the Australian Alps had been described in glowing terms, encouraging squatters such as Glengarry to take their flocks overland to Omeo and further south towards Corner Inlet.[46] Apart from Glengarry and other NSW licensees, squatters following Brodribb quickly moved in from Port Phillip. As noted in Chapter 3, Thomas Stubbs used the 'discovery' of Gippsland as grounds for confidence in the colonial economy. Yet, it soon became apparent that Gippsland's overland route to Port Phillip was, at best, seasonal. Port Albert at the mouth of the Albert River improved accessibility to Gippsland, raising its profile as an economic asset.[47]

The Gippsland squatters seized the opportunity to serve VDL's livestock market. Port Albert possessed the geographical advantage of being the closest link with the island—an important consideration for minimising stock loss on the journey over Bass Strait and maximising the chances of landing the

---

45 See Lennon, *Across Bass Strait*, 1–2, 11–13, 25–8; Caldow, 'The Early Livestock Trade', 27; Caldow, 'Gippsland and Van Diemen's Land Livestock Trade', 20–1; Glowrey, *South of the Strzelecki Ranges*, 34. During the 1830s, southern harbours such as Batemans Bay had attracted unwanted attention for their role in the illicit cattle trade with Van Diemen's Land.
46 See 'Discovery of Gipps Land', *Australasian Chronicle*, 7 July 1840, 2; Caldow, 'The Early Livestock Trade', 27; Lennon, *Across Bass Strait*, 47–55.
47 Lennon, *Across Bass Strait*, 74; Clement and Richmond, 'Port Albert', 130–1. See also H.B. Morris, 'A Trip to Gipps' Land', *Courier*, 23 June 1843, 4.

animals in a healthy condition. For the first few years the squatters chartered vessels to ship livestock over to Hobart's auction market on a speculative basis. There was no wharf or jetty until a private one was built in 1846, forcing cattle to swim from the shore, before being hoisted by sling into their awaiting vessel.[48]

This trade in both cattle and sheep proved so profitable that Vandemonian producers demanded protection from the cheaper 'foreign' livestock—a call heeded by the VDL Legislative Council's *Sheep and Cattle Importation Prevention Act* in February 1844. However, as the number of convicts increased by 50 per cent between 1843 and 1847, this did nothing to satisfy demand for fresh meat.

To compensate, local Hobart buyers, merchants and butchers restructured the Bass Strait trade, directly negotiating with Gippsland producers and freight agents to purchase livestock, then contracting ships to deliver their consignments from Port Albert. This transformed the trade from a speculative buyer's market to a seller's market.[49] By 1846, Port Albert was supplying almost three-quarters of the island's livestock imports; from 1842 to 1851, between 62 and 88 per cent of vessels cleared from Port Albert headed for Van Diemen's Land.

Although the port was dependent upon the Bass Strait livestock trade, it benefited as long as convict transportation continued. Subsidiary trade in tallow and hide along with local shipbuilding also developed in the wake of the livestock trade.[50] Vandemonian transportation came to an end in 1853. However, while the VDL Commissariat contracts declined in importance and the Tasmanian market suffered as people left for the goldfields, Port Albert continued to dominate the island's meat supply.

During the 1850s and 1860s, Port Albert attempted to find new markets to balance the volatility of the Tasmanian trade. The rapid population growth in Victoria during the 1850s induced by the gold rushes offered one avenue. Gradually, inland roads to Melbourne were improved, facilitating

---

48   Caldow, 'The Early Livestock Trade', 28; Caldow, 'Gippsland and Van Diemen's Land', 21–2; Lennon, *Across Bass Strait*, 34–5, 79–83.
49   Caldow, 'The Early Livestock Trade', 36; Clement and Richmond, 'Port Albert', 132. Caldow claims this demand lasted until the early 1860s, and Clement and Richmond call the 1850s and 1860s the port's 'halcyon years'. Lennon is more circumspect, providing evidence that the market was more turbulent, including lack of adequate vessels and crews during the Californian gold rush at the end of the 1840s, but from a broader historical perspective, Clement and Richmond's assessment is valid.
50   Lennon, *Across Bass Strait*, 38, 70, 105, 107, 126.

the movement of livestock westward towards Melbourne and the goldfields. However, this path took trade away from the port. Counteracting this, periodic discoveries of gold in Gippsland between 1853 and 1870 ensured trade and passengers moved through the port. Yet, gold could also prove to be a 'resource curse', as populations disappeared from established markets, ships were redirected for passenger traffic and other draught animals redeployed.[51]

Increased demand for timber also resulted in the establishment of steam-powered timber mills around Port Albert in the 1850s, and shipping was the only means of hauling timber over long distances. (This industry would later nourish Batemans Bay after the establishment of the government-surveyed town in 1859.) Local fishermen also used the port to serve the Melbourne market. Further, vessels opportunistically tested the New Zealand market and there was a brief spike in 1863 when 50 per cent of livestock exports went to the New Zealand Commissariat during a period when Gippsland was uniquely free of pleuropneumonia.[52]

However, once the bar opened in front of Gippsland Lakes in 1864, Port Albert lost its port monopoly. The lakes were closer to Sale, which was emerging as an important commercial town in the Gippsland region. Partisan local newspapers vied to highlight the deficiencies of their competitor's port. There was sufficient copy to satisfy rival editors, with the coastline developing a notorious reputation as a graveyard for ships wrecked on its sandbars, narrow, shallow channels and coastline.[53] This was the same problem that had resulted in the loss of the *Clonmel* in 1841 and ultimately the port lost favour by the early 1870s. This decline was reinforced by an inland railway connecting Sale with Melbourne in 1878. Gippsland producers were now less reliant than ever on Port Albert. By 1882, it had 'withered away into a local fishing port'.[54]

---

51 Lennon, *Across Bass Strait*, 78, 154; Glowrey, *SSouth of the Strzelecki Ranges*, 45, 54; Clement and Richmond, 'Port Albert', 132.
52 Glowrey, *South of the Strzelecki Ranges*, 46; Lennon, *Across Bass Strait*, 107, 114–16, 152; Clement and Richmond, 'Port Albert', 133. For the reliance of the timber industry on coastal shipping at Murramarang, see Hamon, *They Came*.
53 Clement and Richmond, 'Port Albert', 134–8; Lennon, *Across Bass Strait*, 79, 85–6, 136; Caldow, 'Gippsland and Van Diemen's Land', 24.
54 Lennon, *Across Bass Strait*, 136, 163.

The rise and decline of Port Albert demonstrate that fleeting opportunities to establish southern ports existed around 1840, and also emphasise the vagaries, volatility and vulnerabilities associated with the rapid changes that the Australian colonies were experiencing. These eventually undermined the economic sustainability of the port.

In 1892, the Great Southern Railway line was built linking Dandenong in Port Phillip with Alberton, 5 miles up the Albert River from Port Albert. In anticipation, a nearby projected city of Liverpool was laid out and most of its allotments were sold at auction. However, the depression took hold even before the railway opened. Like St Vincent during the first great depression, 'the expansionist vision of developers and the township never eventuated'.[55] Steam-driven transport, terrestrial or maritime, could not guarantee the realisation of speculators' dreams.

Port Albert emerged as a dynamic southern port that possessed contrasting features with the NSW ventures explored in this book. There was no mountain barrier separating the port from the producers it served, meaning that livestock could be driven quickly to the stockyards at Port Albert. There was no costly and treacherous dray road to build and maintain. Further, the land route to Melbourne was unreliable, meaning that the sea route through Port Albert was, for many years, the most reliable access to Melbourne, giving it a transportation monopoly.[56] Port Albert was also economically less reliant on Melbourne than Batemans Bay, Jervis Bay and Broulee were on Sydney, given its link to the Vandemonian market. Finally, while those proponents of South Coast ventures believed the horizon was filled with steamboats, sailing ships continued to carry the Port Albert livestock trade.

Even though St Vincent and Port Albert were conceived in the same year, 1841, they symbolised different eras of land-settlement policies. St Vincent sought to take advantage of its position on the southern reaches of the 'limits of location'—a policy the government had maintained up to the mid-1830s. Squatter pressure and the opening of Port Phillip began to erode the government's commitment to this policy. Port Albert reflected a new 'reality' based on the unrestricted 'land rush' by squatters beyond the limits of location (and occasioning a new stage of frontier conflict and Indigenous dispossession). Many of the flocks on the Maneroo, whose wool was expected to come through the projected southern ports of Batemans

---

55 Lennon, *Across Bass Strait*, 68.
56 Glowrey, *South of the Strzelecki Ranges*, 44.

Bay and Broulee, were instead directed south through the High Country to Gippsland. While they were not direct competitors, Port Albert lured part of St Vincent's projected market: the overlanding squatters, such as Glengarry.

The end of the road

The 4 January 1841 advertisement for St Vincent took advantage of the *Clonmel*'s celebrity to sell its allotments. However, by mid-January news of the wreck of the *Clonmel* at Corner Inlet reached Sydney, where the *Sydney Herald* lamented in funereal tones:

> To convey to a stranger in words, the sensation created in our community by the melancholy tidings of her loss would be a difficult task. Indeed it seemed as if some grievous national calamity had befallen us.[57]

The loss of the vessel received more column space in the paper than the announcement of the death of His Majesty William IV in October 1837.[58]

After January 1841, references to the *Clonmel* were dropped by Thomas Stubbs. It is possible that, by then, the auctioneer did not want to associate St Vincent with the ship's misfortune, nor to suggest an analogy between the fate of the *Clonmel* and a sinking land market with stranded assets.

The wreck of the *Clonmel* was auctioned by Samuel Lyons in early March and purchased by the merchant and steamship owner Joseph Grose for £110.[59] In May 1841, Captain Tollervey was given the command of an emigrant sailing ship carrying colonial produce back to London. The ship's name was *St Vincent*.

More broadly, steamships were used by supporters of the projected townships of Batemans Bay, Broulee and Jervis Bay as a symbol of future commercial possibilities, with their advantages of speed, tonnage and manoeuvrability. However, the wreck of the *Clonmel* and Benjamin Boyd's faltering ventures based at Boyd Town, Twofold Bay, suggested that reliance on steamships was premature. When Boyd's steamship *Sea Horse* arrived at Hobart from

---

57   *Sydney Herald*, 20 January 1841, 2. The paper devoted over two columns to this obituary for the *Clonmel*.
58   *Sydney Herald*, 12 October 1837, 2 (with a stop press on 9 October 1837, 2). The monarch had died on 20 June 1837.
59   *Sydney Gazette and New South Wales Advertiser*, 11 March 1841, 2.

Britain in April 1841, it was considered 'an astonishing acquisition to these Colonies, and particularly so, after the loss of the *Clonmel*'. It was also seen as 'a sure sign of the advance in civilization and prosperity'. Even before its arrival, in February 1841, a lithographed drawing of the *Sea Horse* could be viewed at Raphael Clint's map shop.[60] Beginning in 1841, it was introduced onto the southern coastal line, along with two other large Boyd-owned steamships, the *Juno* and the *Cornubia*.

Boyd eventually found the southern route unprofitable. Appropriate fuel was difficult to source, passenger demand was not as consistent as hoped and the *Sea Horse* sustained significant damage in 1843 on the Tamar River, resulting in a prolonged and controversial insurance case that Boyd lost.[61] Joseph Hickey Grose, who had introduced and expanded the steamship business in Australia, joined 'the unhappy band' of new insolvents in September 1843, and, in July 1844, Edye Manning suffered the same fate. R.V. Jackson noted the 'slowness with which the steamship asserted its superiority' and questioned the significance of its contribution to Australia's colonial export trade. Steamboats would find their niche in shorter, local runs along the South Coast.[62]

In the early 1840s, the claims of Broulee, Batemans Bay and Jervis Bay, as well as Twofold Bay, for southern pre-eminence rested not only on a dray road over the mountain range but also on the premise that shipping (especially the advances in steamships) would facilitate the transportation of commodities from the interior to Sydney. These arguments were disrupted by the anticipation and emergence of the steam-powered railway.[63]

As cited in Chapter 4, one Broulee real estate agent in December 1840 had asserted that 'good seaports, of easy access from the interior' would remain important 'until railroads can be established'. In March 1841, the

---

60 *Sydney Gazette and New South Wales Advertiser*, 1 May 1841, 2; *Sydney Monitor and Commercial Advertiser*, 2 June 1841, 3; *Sydney Herald*, 8 February 1841, 2.
61 See Diamond, *Ben Boyd*, 93–8. Diamond also adds that poor management hampered the venture. By the late 1840s, the *Juno* had more success on the southern route, while the *Cornubia* ran the line from Sydney to Moreton Bay (*Geelong Advertiser*, 10 March 1848, 4). Boyd might have been Eldershaw's model for the merchant Franklin in *A House Is Built*. Both Boyd and Franklin engaged in over-insurance and under-maintenance of their vessels.
62 For Grose's insolvency, see *NSW Government Gazette*, 26 September 1843, 1239–40. Jackson, *Australian Economic Development*, 80–2. Jackson acknowledges that 'the greater use of the steamship occurred quite early in the coastal trade'. For a similar assessment, see Blainey, *Tyranny*, 221. Blainey devotes a chapter to steamships, but has little to say about the pre-1850 period.
63 However, steam was not universally popular. Poems published in the press during the late 1830s and early 1840s were divided between celebrating and criticising both marine and terrestrial steam transport.

9. THE PS *CLONMEL* AND THE SOUTHERN SHIPPING LANE

Sydney Gazette and New South Wales Advertiser asserted that railways could halve remote woolgrowers' freight costs. One press correspondent in 1846 foresaw the competitive advantage railways would give to Sydney over proposed southern ports:

> By their successful introduction, Sydney would command the great portion of the commerce of the interior; whereas if the residents are not alive to their interests in this respect, a great proportion of that commerce will be diverted to other harbours on the coast, such as Jervis and Bateman's Bay, Broulee, Twofold Bay, and other harbours.[64]

In the late 1840s, politicians, merchants, pastoralists and auctioneers were predicting that the railway, not the steamship, would become the transport innovation to solve the problems faced by southern pastoralists and settlers.

The *Sydney Railway Company Incorporation Act 1849* stated that the initial rail line would begin at Sydney, pass through Cumberland and Camden before proceeding to Goulburn.[65] Over the next two decades, with each extension of this southern rail line, the inland perception of time shrank and space imploded.[66]

In the meantime, during the post-depression early 1850s, the government began surveying a road from Braidwood to Broulee, before choosing to concentrate on a road to Batemans Bay. Reporting on this road-preference debate, one local press correspondent claimed that while a dray road to Batemans Bay was preferred over one to Broulee, what locals desired was a 'railway from Sydney', or at least a trunk line from Goulburn.[67] The Clyde Road was still considered the best existing route to Sydney on grounds of time and cost savings, but progress was slow, mainly due to the shortage of labour (see Chapter 4). These labour shortages were exacerbated by gold mania as well as demand for labour from the construction of the southern rail line that would eventually thwart the hopes for the road to Batemans Bay.[68]

---

64 *Sydney Morning Herald*, 1 June 1846, 3.
65 'An Act to Incorporate a Company to be Called "The Sydney Railway Company"', [10 October 1849]. See also Mossman and Banister, *Australia Visited*, ch. 14; Sidney, *The Three Colonies*, 275.
66 For a summary history of the southern line, see *Goulburn Herald and Chronicle*, 29 May 1869, 1–4. The southern line moved progressively through Parramatta (1855), Liverpool (1856), Campbelltown (1858), Picton (1863), Mittagong (1867), Marulan (1868) and Goulburn (1869) before moving further south. See Davison, *The Unforgiving Minute*.
67 *Maitland Mercury and Hunter River General Advertiser*, 12 June 1852, 4.
68 *Sydney Morning Herald*, 25 May 1854, 3.

The Clyde Road finally opened in January 1858, marked by the arrival of nine loaded bullock teams along the 32-mile route. It cost £12,000, but this was equivalent to a quarter mile of the Sydney–Parramatta rail line. As one correspondent noted,

> seeing that Braidwood is by any other passable road nearly 200 miles from Sydney—that hitherto every article of slops, every ounce of tea, and every pound of tobacco had to be dragged to this the capital city of the Southern diggings by the horror-laden, dead bullock producing Southern roads of the last few wet seasons, it is almost impossible to realise the enormous importance of this event in Braidwood history.[69]

This historical milestone would allow this correspondent, as a Yass landowner, to make the trouble-free, 80-mile journey to Braidwood, 'then step into a steamer at the Clyde, thirty two miles further only, instead of dragging my weary way 180 miles of trouble and vexation'. He acclaimed that 'nothing but a railway' would prevent southern settlers from taking leave of the Clyde Road.[70]

However, in February 1860, in what became a recurrent problem, heavy rains washed away all the bridges between Braidwood and Nelligen, and landslips on Sugarloaf Mountain made the route impassable. Stores at Nelligen flooded, with heavy loss of stock, while the steamer *Hunter* dragged its anchor and drifted 2 miles up the Clyde River. Braidwood storekeepers and woolgrowers were forced to resort to the old internal road to Sydney.[71]

Despite these problems, now that the Clyde Road existed, Braidwood promoters sought to make hay while the sun shone, and supported the construction of a road connecting the town to Queanbeyan through Little Bombay. Conversely, Goulburn advocates opposed this use of public funds, foreseeing the 'ultimate abandonment of the route' once the railway reached Goulburn. 'The spirit of localism' remained alive, as Queanbeyan's paper, the *Golden Age*, noted in an editorial that considered this debate over 'the diversion of the traffic of the Queanbeyan and Monaro districts from the old overland route to the new line of road to the port of Nelligen'. Taking

---

69   *Sydney Morning Herald*, 21 January 1858, 2.
70   *Sydney Morning Herald*, 21 January 1858, 2. For other celebrations of the road and its compression of space and time, see *Illawarra Mercury*, 4 March 1858, 2; *Empire*, 27 January 1858, 5.
71   *Empire*, 20 February 1860, 3. There were critics and counter-critics of the road, echoing the debates of the early 1840s when supporters of different ports engaged in 'evil' reporting. See Chapter 4. See also *Illawarra Mercury*, 7 June 1858, 2; 22 July 1858, 3; 23 December 1858, 2; 27 December 1858, 4.

a nuanced stance, it was wary of the poor condition of the Clyde Road and the treatment of cargo at the Nelligen wharf, but conceded that the idea of the coastal road as the 'natural outlet' for traffic to Sydney had 'taken too deep a hold on the minds of the Monaro and Queanbeyan people'.[72]

Over the next few years, as the railway crept south past Picton towards Goulburn, this hold on southern minds loosened and the inland rail route to Sydney gradually consolidated its advantage over the coastal route.[73] Jackson contrasted 'the heavily laden bullock dray struggling through a handful of miles a day in dry weather … and the steam train travelling as far in an hour'.[74] On the Limestone Plains, this meant that 'the month-long journey to Sydney with bullock drays passed with the advent of the railway'.[75] In Gippsland, too, the railway between Melbourne and Sale would reduce the interlinking function of Port Albert. The grand vision for southern district ports was eventually undermined by the railway, which annihilated space and condensed time far more effectively than steamships. The railway opened different paths for development, but these paths bypassed the great southern harbours of NSW.

There was nothing deterministic in the relationship between the laying of these rails and the marginalisation of the southern coast. In 1851, the surveyor James Ralphe argued that if the Sydney line did terminate at Goulburn, then the next government project should involve a trunk line from Goulburn to Jervis Bay, noting that this task would be no more difficult than the line from Campbelltown to Goulburn. This proposal would not have undermined the commercial dominance of Sydney, but it would have at least presented greater opportunities for regional trade.[76] This vision of regionalisation had been articulated by the Jervis Bay Wool Road consortium (see Chapter 4).

---

72   *Golden Age*, 25 September 1862, 2.
73   See letter in *Golden Age*, 16 October 1862, 2.
74   Jackson, *Australian Economic Development*, 88.
75   Jackson, *Australian Economic Development*, 88; Robinson, *Canberra's First*, 36. A photograph of bales of wool being unloaded from a horse dray at Queanbeyan Railway Station in the late nineteenth century in Brown (*A History*, 27) illustrates the eventual victor in the competition between the coastal and inland routes to Sydney. Geography was an important determinant in the fate of different means of transporting wool. Even after the emergence of railways, in settlements such as Echuca, ships and barges dominated due to its location on the Murray River and (unlike Batemans Bay) the ease of access that wool drays had in reaching the town from shearing stations.
76   *Sydney Morning Herald*, 3 May 1851, 6.

Henry Lawson's 1889 poem 'The Roaring Days' ends with the lines: 'The mighty bush with iron rails / Is tethered to the world.' However, the route that the railways eventually followed untethered the southern coastal towns from the commerce of the mighty interior. The future of these harbours would now appear to rest more specifically on their own parochial littoral resources. The township of Ulladulla had long recognised this future.

When allotments were auctioned by the government at Batemans Bay and Nelligen in 1859, the villages eventually found a niche by exploiting their local timber resources to support the wider urban, industrial, mining and railroad expansion of the colony and by developing a local oyster industry. These activities did not rely as heavily on a road to Batemans Bay.

10

Conclusion

I started this research process firm in the conviction that I was writing a 'local history'. Having produced a short historical overview of Long Beach for the Long Beach Community Association, I intended to complement it by producing a series of 'historical vignettes' that focused on different episodes from the past.

I felt no compulsion to undertake the task chronologically because the 'origin' of Long Beach is open to interpretation, even though, as Mark McKenna notes, every 'community needs a creation *story*' (my emphasis).[1] Therefore, I chose to start with the material artefact that most diverted my attention, namely the 1841 lithographic plan of the township of St Vincent along the Long Beach shoreline, produced by Raphael Clint for the auctioneer Thomas Stubbs (see Chapter 5).

Locally, the northern suburbs of Batemans Bay have long been considered 'the other side of the bay'. After the village of Bateman had been established in 1859 on the southern side of the bay at the mouth of the Clyde River, the town gradually expanded eastward and southward. The dense spotted-gum forests north of Long Beach could not sustain more than small, ephemeral timber mill communities and limited pastoral activity. Access to the town of Batemans Bay from the northern beaches was restricted until the Princes Highway bridge was built in 1956, after which more holiday cottages began to appear along Long Beach.

---

1 McKenna, *Looking*, 65.

Yet, the 1841 lithographic plan suggested that an earlier, private venture had envisaged a town settlement on this northern shore 18 years prior to the land sales on the southern 'village reserve' at Batemans Bay. I was intrigued that the northern 'periphery' had a real estate history that preceded what became the town 'centre'.

This provoked a number of questions that I felt could constitute a cluster of historical vignettes: Who were the actors behind the scheme to develop the township of St Vincent? What rationale did the creators offer for the establishment of the township? Did anyone associated with the venture visit Long Beach? If so, why did the street grid plan defy local topography? Was it a real estate scam? How were subdivisions sold? How much interest did the campaign generate? Were there any purchasers and, if so, what happened to their claim on the land? Why was the scheme abandoned and what happened to the land in its aftermath? And what was occurring elsewhere in the immediate vicinity during 1841?

Gradually, the research and findings associated with these initial questions coalesced into this book. As the story emerged, it moved beyond the confines of Batemans Bay, confronting the economic conditions prevailing in the colony, in particular the onset of the 1840s depression; attending to Sydney's world of auctioneering and the speculative property market; delving into the laws of insolvency and the Office of the Sheriff that executed the court's decisions; tracing the colonial practices of surveying, mapping, engraving and printing; trawling over the southern shipping lane; and pondering the logistical problem of how southern settlers and squatters brought their produce to market. All these inquiries branched out from what began as a local history.

The arc of this story radiated from a small 320-acre parcel of land at Long Beach to some of the major events of 1841. In April and May 1848, when the *Cornwall Chronicle* spent the month charting annual 'remarkable events' since the arrival of the First Fleet in a series called 'A Knowledge of Our Adopted Country',[2] the first item for 1841 was 'The "Clonmell" Steam Packet Totally Wrecked at Corner Inlet'. Mentions of the arrivals of the *Sea Horse* and the *Shamrock* from England further emphasised the hope invested in steam during the period. Also listed among the most significant

---

2   *Cornwall Chronicle*, 29 April 1848; 3, 6, 10, 13, 17, 20, 27, 29 and 31 May 1848, 4. The paper acknowledged that the outline had been 'extracted from a valuable Almanac and Directory published in Sydney the past year'.

events of the year were the fire at Hughes & Hosking's Albion Wharf, as well as Sheriff Macquoid's act of 'temporary insanity'—all episodes recounted in this book.

These significant maritime, mercantile and legal occurrences in 1841 emerged from milieux that had their own dynamics and timelines. However, their intersection in the depression of the early 1840s contributed to making the year 1841 extraordinary and calamitous for so many (and, for some, worse was in store). Without this structure of events that made up the lifeworld of colonial NSW, the story of St Vincent would not be intelligible. It is within these wider milieux that the intentions of those involved at St Vincent were shaped.

The significance of this wider historical context for understanding land development was noted by Peter Reynolds in his research on 1840s Balmain:

> In writing local history, factors other than family history, land-use and the study of buildings can be significant in the picture of cause and effect. One important factor is the economic history of New South Wales. Economic changes can yield vital information to help determine why a suburban precinct developed as it did. The rise and fall in the fortunes of landowners will naturally be reflected in all the property that they own whether they actually lived on a particular property or not.[3]

The approach Reynolds advocated was multidisciplinary, inclusive and expansive. It was consistent with the direction I was following in my own research on Long Beach. It was also sensitive to the 'fuzzy' boundaries between history and sociology.[4] It fitted comfortably with Hancock's idea of 'span' and C. Wright Mills's definition of 'the sociological imagination':

> No social study that does not come back to the problems of biography, of history and of their intersections within a society has completed its intellectual journey … Perhaps the most fruitful distinction with which the sociological imagination works is between 'the personal troubles of milieu' and 'the public issues of social structure'.[5]

Yet, while I was comfortable drawing pragmatically on whatever archival, statistical, biographical, literary and secondary material I could gather in search of answers to my questions, I became less certain whether the genre

---

3   Reynolds, 'From Johnson', 23.
4   Burke, *Sociology*.
5   Mills, *The Sociological Imagination*, 12–14.

I was producing could be labelled 'local history'? Social history? Historical sociology? Biographical portraits? Three questions arose and remained during the course of the research: Can you have a local history without a community? Was I producing 'a history of place'? Or was it, perhaps, 'a history of a failed venture'?

Local history without community

Graeme Davison has noted that it 'seems almost self-evident that a local history is the history of a community'.[6] The concept of 'community' has been central to modern sociological analysis, despite difficulties in establishing a stable definition. The idea of community possesses two attributes. At the most objective level, it refers to a group of people occupying a specific space. More subjectively, it refers to a set of interlinked institutions and associations engendering a sense of belonging.[7]

Frank Bongiorno and Erik Eklund have emphasised this latter attribute, noting that, methodologically, local history usually involves a 'vernacular take on personal experience, knowledge and subjectivity'.[8] Batemans Bay is blessed with a wealth of histories fitting this description, including those of Frank Johnson, Allison James, Stuart Magee and Ken Odgers. Among other techniques, they draw on local memory and folklore, providing insight into the lives, lifestyles and livelihoods of Batemans Bay residents over the years. Among their many virtues, these local histories help recover a 'lost past' on which the 'shared present' has been built. In this way, these local histories can perform a role in articulating and reinforcing a local 'collective consciousness' beyond the networks of people whom residents know personally.[9]

The research I conducted could not claim such a virtue. In 1841 Batemans Bay was close to the southern limits of location. While there were clusters of settlers further south at Moruya and Broulee, and a few homesteads along the Clyde River, land on the northern shore of Batemans Bay had just been

---

6   Davison, 'Community', 208.
7   For the history and use of the concept of community, see Greig, *The Australian*, ch. 14.
8   Bongiorno and Eklund, 'The Problem', 40. See also Darian-Smith, 'Up the Country', 93.
9   The term *conscience collective* was employed by the French sociologist Emile Durkheim in many of his most famous works, including *The Division of Labour in Society* (1893), *The Rules of Sociological Method* (1895), *Suicide* (1897), and *The Elementary Forms of Religious Life* (1912).

10. CONCLUSION

opened by the government and the new landowners resided in Sydney or the Hunter Valley. There was no settler community to speak of, in either the more objective or the subjective sense.[10]

The northern shore of Batemans Bay was Walbanja Country and, as noted in Chapter 1, the Walbanja formed the community that drew on Cullendulla Creek and its environs for their lifestyle and livelihood in the 1840s, at the time my research was set.[11] Recognition of their attachment to Country, along with the Walbanja community's protection, defence and use of their land, is an essential part of any local history that aspires towards reconciliation. The local Indigenous population also performed an important role after settlers arrived on the north shore of Batemans Bay and established modern industries. This is part of what has been called 'contested country: the problem of writing about a "place" with starkly different meanings and significance for Indigenous and non-Indigenous peoples'.[12] It is a crucial part of the local history of Batemans Bay, with all its methodological challenges.

However, the questions posed in my research (namely, explaining the nature of the St Vincent scheme at Long Beach) did not involve any direct contact between this community and those who planned to introduce a new community into their Country. Those who purchased the land from the government remained absent and the form of community they envisaged in their plan lay in the future—sketched out in Plan 359(A) and on Raphael Clint's lithographic map promoted by the auctioneer Thomas Stubbs. They speculated on the possibility of a community being formed on the northern shore of Batemans Bay as a result of their real estate venture. It was an 'envisaged community' or an 'anticipated community'.[13]

Unlike the people who populate the local histories written by Johnson, James, Magee and Odgers, the feats and the legacy of the main characters who appear in my story will not resonate with the memories, experiences or

---

10 In this sense it resembled the social conditions McKenna researched in *Looking for Blackfellas' Point*: 'In the 30-year period between 1820 and 1850, there is very little evidence of a "community" taking shape in Eden-Monaro" (McKenna, *Looking*, 106). He refrains from calling his book a 'local history'.
11 The significance of the area for the Walbanja people has been touched on in oral histories collected by Eurobodalla Shire Council. See NSW National Parks and Wildlife Service, *Cullendulla Creek*, 14–15; Donaldson, 'Stories about the Eurobodalla by Aboriginal People'.
12 Bongiorno and Eklund, 'The Problem', 41.
13 I would call it an 'imagined community', but this term is used in a very different sense by Benedict Anderson. See Anderson, *Imagined Communities*.

subjectivities of Batemans Bay residents and property owners. The dramatis personae were not earlier members of the community and the only trace they left behind was on parish maps as first land-title holders.

Having been closely involved in updating Bruce Hamon's book *They Came to Murramarang*, I was conscious of the difference between his local history and my research on Long Beach, where no significant engagement or conflict between the main characters and local Indigenous people, nor between settlers and their surrounding environment, occurred; where no early buildings or estates, and no remnants of early livelihood activity, such as old road markers, homesteads, sawmills or wooden tram tracks, remained to explore.[14]

These comparisons led me to question whether a local history could be written without a community, given that a study of the Walbanja people was beyond the scope of my research. In such circumstances, would it be more accurate to call the story of St Vincent a 'history of place'?[15]

A history of place

Ann Curthoys and John Docker defined local history as the 'historicity of place'. Likewise, Davison stated that local history 'links our aspiration for community to a sense of place'.[16] Bongiorno and Eklund concurred that 'the desire to know one's own "place," to uncover its hidden stories, and to gain a greater appreciation of what makes it distinctive' seems to be a 'powerful impulse' in the production of local history.[17] Lennon has also argued that appreciating 'the specifics of place' is vital to 'unmask the complexity and layering of our social foundations'.[18]

The existing local histories of Batemans Bay again fit this definition, uncovering a range of colourful stories about the lives of local people who shaped the social and economic history of the bay area. Many relics of their

---

14   Hamon, *They Came*.
15   McKenna (*Looking*) subtitles his research and reflections on the far South Coast 'An Australian History of Place'; Bongiorno, 'From Local'.
16   Curthoys and Docker, *Is History Fiction?*; Davison, 'Community', 197.
17   Bongiorno and Eklund, 'The Problem', 39–40. Davison ('Community', 210) also notes this importance of distinctiveness in local histories.
18   Lennon, *Across Bass Strait*, 3.

lives still exist, and the combination of the production of history and the visual proximity to these 'monuments' helps enliven the appreciation of the uniqueness of the place.

While the story presented in my research also explores a 'hidden' or 'lost' story (the proposed township of St Vincent), there are three features that diminish it as a history of place: first, there are no 'place markers'; second, the primary action occurs away from the place where the story is set; and, third, the story relies on St Vincent being part of a set of township projects and routes, rather than a distinct place.

On the role of 'place markers' that 'become triggers for the sharing of memories',[19] a distinction can be made between my book and Peter Reynolds's research on land sales around 1840.[20] Reynolds's research on Balmain had a place-bound centripetal tendency, in the sense that, even though it is strengthened by his advocacy of the wider economic history of the colony and the biographies of landholders, his evidence keeps returning to Balmain. The subsequent development of individual subdivisions helped shape the nature of the local landscape and the community over time, reinforcing the uniqueness of place: the lots were sold to specific identifiable individuals; they were transformed through specific building processes; the buildings had unique functions in the neighbourhood; they had subsequent sales; a series of renovations, additions or rebuilds took place; and they were 'repurposed' to reflect changes in local suburban community development. All this 'makes up' Balmain. These markers in time help ground Reynolds's history in place.

No such development of place occurs in my story at Long Beach because the plan for St Vincent never 'got off the ground'. There were none of those 'activities indispensable to foundation'.[21] The landowners and planners involved in the project soon abandoned it, leaving no trace in the place they originally intended to transform.

Local histories often reveal how lifestyles and livelihoods interacted with landscape to make places. Bongiorno and Eklund have cited Queenstown as an exemplary case where extractive activities made a spectacular impact on

---

19 Davison, 'Community', 201.
20 Reynolds, 'From Johnson'. Another example from colonial Sydney is the study of Good Hope Estate in Kelly, 'Eight Acres'.
21 Carter, *The Road*, xv.

the landscape.²² For many locals, the shaping of the landscape is something to be defended or recalled because it shaped the community in turn. Glowrey's environmental history of Corner Inlet is another example of the value of a history of place, revealing different views of community, belonging and understandings of time and space. Lennon's description of how Port Albert squatters, merchants and mariners transformed their landscape also deepens local understanding and intelligibility.²³ Yet, my research on St Vincent explores the landscape before it was transformed by settler livelihoods and lifestyles. The action is centred elsewhere—in Sydney, the Hunter Valley, Jervis Bay, Broulee and the southern interior—even if Long Beach is the object of attention, planning, negotiation, 'puffing', money and title transfers, insolvencies and eventually lotteries.

All places have their distinctiveness and Long Beach retains its unique physical characteristics (the specificity of its headlands, rocks, beaches, creeks, lagoon, gullies, hills and cliffs, spotted gums and burrawangs, birds, marsupials and marine life, among other features). However, the distinctiveness to which Reynolds, Glowrey, Lennon, Davison, Bongiorno and Eklund refer in the production of local history involves capturing an appreciation of the dynamic relationship between people and place. John Blay describes this relationship in his philosophical journeys through the south-east of NSW, noting that 'as the early settlers wrestled to change their land into something they could regard as hospitable, it also changed them'.²⁴

For the reasons alluded to above, the story of Long Beach in 1841 could only have engaged in this dynamic relationship between people and nature if it focused on the land-management practices of the Walbanja people. However, the focus on the St Vincent scheme drew my attention in a different direction. Indeed, the evidence presented in this story retreats from the distinctiveness of place. The proposed township eventually becomes representative of two broader phenomena: the speculative land boom immediately prior to the depression of the 1840s and the search for a means of transporting produce from the southern interior to Sydney.

---

22 Bongiorno and Eklund, 'The Problem', 47.
23 Glowrey, *South of the Strzelecki Ranges*; Lennon, *Across Bass Strait*, 163.
24 Blay, *On Track*, 241. Blay follows a long line of social thinkers on this dialectical relationship between humanity and nature. Karl Marx argued that, through labour, humanity 'acts upon external nature and changes it, and in this way simultaneously changes its own nature'. See Marx, *Capital*, 283. See also Lockie, 'Social Nature'.

10. CONCLUSION

The more I explored the reasons for the scheme at St Vincent, the more I began to realise that the centre of the story was not its distinctiveness but, rather, its role as part of a broader set of ventures and hopes to reorganise southern transport routes. Batemans Bay makes sense in this story, not as a bounded place and a community with a demographic composition, not even as a place with unique geographical features (its own climate, mineral wealth, pastoral conditions), but as a possible conduit linking two different zones of activity: regional producers and city merchants (often represented by the same person). The plan involved turning a place on the periphery of the 19 counties into a point on a continuum of commercial activity, connecting the furthest regions of the southern settled interior with the colony's mercantile metropolis.

From this perspective, my research was not principally a history of place: more broadly, it evolved into a history of a 'quest for a route' or, simultaneously, an analysis of the competition for dominance between ports.[25] This transforms Long Beach (along with the other schemes to develop a port on the South Coast) into a point on a line, a trajectory[26] or a vector, rather than a place.

This analogy distances my research from local history. The action in my research possessed a centrifugal tendency to move away from the location of St Vincent towards other points on the vector. This vector gave the idea of St Vincent its purpose.

However, this does not mean my research did not feed off and engage with local history. Indeed, Bongiorno and Eklund, like Reynolds, refer to 'the new local history' in which 'people enact dramas that are, at once, personal, local, national and human', evoking the 'particularity of "place" at the same time as demonstrating the relevance of the local to larger and more abstract "imagined communities"'.[27] While my story might not possess the local drama often encountered in local history, it nevertheless links a specific vision for Batemans Bay with national (at least colonial) and human dramas, including recounting many personal dramas experienced by individuals who purchased land at Long Beach.

---

25   Rimmer, 'The Search for Spatial Regularities'. See also Blainey, *Tyranny*, 70.
26   Lambert and Lester, 'Introduction', 13–14. This edited collection employs biography to chart the geography of colonialism.
27   Bongiorno and Eklund, 'The Problem', 46.

A history of a failed venture

In the end, there was no township of St Vincent, no community was founded and neither Batemans Bay nor any other southern harbour became the anticipated 'Great Southern Township'. If the absence of settlement makes it difficult to call the research a 'local history' and the lack of distinctiveness makes it a dubious 'history of place', then perhaps the book can best be referred to as 'the story of a failed speculative venture'.

A successful speculative venture, by its very definition, will form part of a local history because it initiates a process whereby human effort transforms nature, and a community emerges from, and is defined by, the process. Some ventures, such as Hughes & Hosking's and J.J. Peacock's Balmain subdivisions in 1841, were considered failures from a financial perspective in 1841, but still initiated sufficient building activity and circulation of capital to generate a new community, or at least an extension of one (as was the case in Balmain). Other failed speculative ventures also left monuments to their effort, like Henry Halloran's relics outside Queanbeyan,[28] or the ruins of Benjamin Boyd's Boyd Town on the south of Twofold Bay.[29] These material markers later become part of the definition and distinctiveness of a place, reminding those who come later that it was once the site of a 'folly'.

However, many failed speculative ventures leave no such traces, including the township of St Vincent. After the advertisements for Edward Lord's subdivisions in June 1842 there was no further mention of St Vincent in the press, no building has ever been uncovered, no boundary markers ever revealed and no settlers handed down stories of their endeavours. Had it not been for the 1907 and 1917 Benandra parish maps, the proposed streets would have been unidentifiable.

While such ventures might appear ephemeral—castles in the air—they can have wider impacts and consequences. They involve human agency, plans, choices and decisions, and can prompt the circulation and disappearance of a lot of money. For some, they lead to financial windfalls, and for others they involve business and individual insolvencies, legal proceedings, personal hardships and tragedies. The story of this speculative venture at St Vincent

---

28 Mortlock and Anderson, *Undiscovered Canberra*, ch. 9.
29 See McKenna, *Looking*, 107–9.

suggests much about the hopes and aspirations, and subsequent fears and regrets, of many within the colony of NSW at the beginning of the 1840s as the 'badness of the times' recalibrated the value of property.

Yet, while St Vincent was a speculative failure, it rested on a set of calculations that were both rational and purposeful at the time. The fact that landowners in similar harbours, such as Jervis Bay and Broulee, were also investing money in, or seeking investment for, a dray road and harbour was testimony to the enthusiasm and demand for such schemes. Further, the government, through Governor Gipps's dispatch of September 1840 (see Chapter 4), had posited the opening of a route to Batemans Bay.

Edward Lord had already joined together many pieces of the jigsaw using the speculative logic germane to such a vector: squatting runs in the High Country, a store in Goulburn, land at Bungendore, cattle runs at Batemans Bay and the Clyde River, land surrounding Long Beach, investment in a steamship company and a merchant house in Sydney (see Chapter 2). The vision of a southern port appealed most to vertically integrated merchant farmers like Edward Lord, but also to woolgrowers in Argyle, Murray, King and the Maneroo. It was a venture that reflected a compelling need for many settlers within the colony in the early 1840s and, therefore, was a vision that attracted speculators.

This is not to deny that undue hope was placed in the possibility of a serviceable road to Batemans Bay and/or the efficacy of steamships. Even before the railway to Goulburn was discussed in 1846,[30] there were signs that the steamship era remained beyond the horizon of hope for the southern townships. The *Clonmel* was an inauspicious start and, while Benjamin Boyd's steamships lasted a few years longer, they too ultimately failed to transform the market or alter settlement patterns (see Chapter 9 and also below). The later steamship trade along the coast was on a much more modest littoral scale.

Nor is it to be denied that certain actors such as Hughes & Hosking as well as Raphael Clint were out to make a quick profit, or that the plans and surveys 'misrepresented' the land being auctioned. As noted in Chapter 5, the rectilinear-gridded township plan of St Vincent seemed oblivious to

---

30   The first reported public meeting proposing a rail line to Goulburn was held in Samuel Lyons's rooms in Sydney on 6 May 1846 (*Morning Chronicle*, 9 May 1846, 2). By 1848, the *Sydney Daily Advertiser* (4 September 1848, 2) was arguing: 'The introduction of Railways into the colony is now the desideratum for prosperity.'

the topography of Long Beach, rendering many blocks unsuitable for building. Almost all the advertising space in the press relating to St Vincent was devoted to the maritime possibilities of Batemans Bay (its convenient contact by steamship to Sydney) and the discovery of a dray road to Batemans Bay through the mountains from the counties of Murray and Argyle. A description of the town itself seemed incidental in the sale of the town lots.

How did the new owner of Long Beach, Raphael Clint, feel when he disembarked from the *Star* in early February 1841, armed with his two-dimensional, rectilinear grid plan of the township (see Chapter 5)? As he stared at the cliff face, he must have questioned whether he had alighted at the right place. We can only imagine. But it did not stop him acting as an agent for Edward Lord's adjacent Stubley Park in April (see Chapter 3) or requesting in June that purchasers decide how they were going to pay him for the residue outstanding on their town allotments (see Chapter 6). What it almost certainly did was persuade him to abandon his plan to purchase land west of Macleod's Creek on the southern side of Batemans Bay or the block on the eastern bank of Cullendulla Creek. He never responded to the surveyor-general's request that he choose more modest portions of land.

Did this mark the St Vincent venture as a swindle? During this period, the British public and Britain's colonial subjects were prey to adventurers and swindlers offering land in emigration and other property schemes. The public had few means of ascertaining the veracity of such real estate claims.

In the early 1820s, Sir Gregor MacGregor had perpetrated one of the most audacious land-sale swindles in history and this was still cited in the colonial press in the 1830s and 1840s.[31] Following a career in the British Army, and after serving in Latin American armies of independence, MacGregor reappeared in London, self-styling himself the ruler (or Cazique) of Poyais, a Central American country on the Miskito Coast. MacGregor was seeking investment and emigrants. He appointed a trusted plenipotentiary in London, who was subsequently introduced to King George IV (the monarch who bore an uncanny resemblance to Thomas Stubbs). For the inquisitive, a book with scientific pretensions was published that provided convincing and encouraging details of the land, its harbours, mountains, climate and people (who were 'attached' to the British). Gold was said to tumble out of its rivers. The capital, St Joseph, was portrayed as a peaceful, temperate

---

31 Sinclair, *The Land*.

and well-governed port with full municipal services, tree-lined boulevards, a domed cathedral, opera house, royal palace and headquarters of the Bank of Poyais. Along with land titles, MacGregor offered Poyais bonds for investors and Poyais banknotes for emigrants.

Some 270 emigrants, mainly from Scotland, set sail for Poyais in 1822 only to find that no such country existed, let alone the capital city and port, and that the land they had purchased was unhealthy and barely habitable. MacGregor had been so convincing that many of the settlers refused to believe their eyes. Despite efforts to make something of their investment, two-thirds of the emigrants eventually perished. One, an Edinburgh cobbler whom MacGregor had appointed the official shoemaker to the Princess of Poyais, 'lay down in his hammock and fired a pistol into his head'.[32]

While Alexander Marjoribanks might have been astonished that auctions in NSW were not conducted on site (see Chapter 3), pointing out that this exposed potential buyers to swindles (lubricated by champagne lunches), similar conditions often prevailed in Britain, especially in ventures associated with emigration. Given these conditions of imperfect knowledge, the public were prey to unscrupulous swindlers such as 'Sir' Gregor McGregor, Cazique of Poyais.

In the colonial press, Poyais came to symbolise a land-sale swindle, or the 'over-puffing' of a scheme that ruined innocent families with 'exaggerated statements'.[33] In NSW during the early 1840s, swindles were not as audacious as MacGregor's. (The NSW press was quick to point to Western Australian and South Australian cases, such as the 1830s Swan River scheme—a worthy cautionary tale.)[34]

As noted in Chapter 3, the press condemned 'puffing' as one of the scourges of the colony, even though auctioneers' advertisements were an important source of revenue. The public was also conscious of the fine line that auctioneers walked between puffing and fraud. As Marjoribanks and the *Sydney Herald* pointed out, speculators accepted buying land sight unseen. Yet, as the case of Berkley Estate revealed, the public was also prepared to call on the power of the state to take legal action against sales agents who

---

32 Sinclair, *The Land*, 230. In London, the future chief protector of Aborigines at Port Phillip, George Augustus Robinson, received news of the tragic fate of MacGregor's victims not long before he was about to embark for Poyais. He decided instead to buy a ticket to Hobart. See D'Arcy, *On His Majesty's*, ch. 3.
33 *Sydney Monitor*, 7 August 1830, 2.
34 *Sydney Monitor*, 21 July 1830, 2. See also the complaint about 'incessant puffers' in Smith, Elder & Co., *Twenty Years*, 78.

made false claims about the attributes of properties. In November 1841, the well-respected auctioneer Samuel Lyons was found guilty in the case of Berkley Estate, brought forward by the plaintiffs George Dent and others. While Dent also purchased lots at St Vincent (see Chapter 6), he made no similar claim that St Vincent 'was not of the description advertised' (see Chapter 3).

There is no record that anyone took Stubbs to court over St Vincent in the same way Lyons was called before the civil side of the Supreme Court for misrepresenting Berkley Estate on Chittaway Bay. The other private towns discussed in previous chapters (such as Broulee, Jervis Town, New Bristol and South Huskisson) could be criticised for puffing and misrepresentation, but no more or no less than St Vincent.

St Vincent was not a deception on the scale of Poyais. The land on offer existed and there was merit to the claims being made about the potential of Batemans Bay. The town plan itself might have been ill conceived, and the auctioneer Thomas Stubbs might have engaged in some puffery, despite his protestations to the contrary, but Stubbs's defence would have been that he left his description of the township in a state of obscurity.[35] He said very little about the lots themselves. The attraction of the land was, first and foremost, its location, which articulated a link between the pastoral interior and the Sydney market. As Thomas Stubbs was fond of saying, it was 'superfluous to make any lengthened comment'.

Boyd Town at Twofold Bay was another venture that failed to live up to expectations. Initiated by Benjamin Boyd two years after St Vincent was planned, the scheme followed the same logic as those at Batemans Bay, Broulee and Jervis Bay.[36] Boyd sought a road through to the Maneroo, where he held squatting runs, and built a whaling station on Twofold Bay. As late as 1845, the *Colonial Times* predicted that Boyd Town would become 'the entrepôt port of New South Wales', serving the southern run from Sydney to Port Phillip, Hobart and other southern settlements, and suggested that it could compete with Port Albert's livestock trade.[37]

---

35 His main acts of puffery involved his January 1841 claim about the thickly settled district and the March 1841 claims that buyers had been 'settled' at the bay and building had commenced.
36 Waitt and Hartig, 'Grandiose Plans'.
37 *Colonial Times*, 18 February 1845, 3; Diamond, *Ben Boyd*, 101–3.

10. CONCLUSION

By 1849, Boyd's scheme was all but abandoned, yet, towards the end, he increasingly made misleading claims for the port to bolster the town's 'factitious prosperity'.[38] Boyd was a subscriber to the 1848 *Geographical Dictionary or Gazetteer of the Australian Colonies: Their Physical and Political Geography: Together with a Brief Notice of All the Capitals, Principal Towns, and Villages* published by one of Raphael Clint's bêtes noires, W.H. Wells (see Chapter 5). While the book devoted a couple of lines to each colonial town and village, with as many as four pages to the great metropolis of Sydney, 17 pages eulogised Boyd Town and the political views of Benjamin Boyd, ranging from the high cost of labour to colonial navigation laws. A review in the *Sydney Morning Herald* suggested that a future edition should relegate Boyd Town to the end of the book as an advertisement, while the *Maitland Mercury and Hunter River General Advertiser* regretted that Wells had 'consented' to allow the 'puffs respecting Boyd Town'.[39]

Despite this, in December 1848 the emigration commissioners agreed to disembark 111 assisted migrant labourers from Britain at Boyd Town. While many found employment within the region, the Immigration Board afterwards described the migrants' reaction as one of 'very great disappointment' and admitted that 'it is hardly a matter of surprise that they should consider themselves at least partially deceived'.[40] Waitt and Hartig's assessment of Twofold Bay as 'grandiose plans, but insignificant outcomes' can be extended to capture all the South Coast ventures in the 1840s discussed in this book.[41]

As noted in Chapter 1, Joseph Phipps Townsend spent four years in the colony between 1842 and 1846. While he appeared to be oblivious to the fact that he was travelling through the site of the township of St Vincent when journeying from Ulladulla to Moruya, he did view the forlorn townships that had been puffed by auctioneers around Jervis Bay in 1841–43 (see Chapter 4). He apportioned the blame for their failure on a combination of circumstances:

---

38 Sidney, *The Three Colonies*, 275.
39 *Sydney Morning Herald*, 28 January 1848, 3; *Maitland Mercury and Hunter River General Advertiser*, 26 February 1848, 4.
40 Diamond, *Ben Boyd*, 82–3. In 1854, William Henry Wells received a two-year jail sentence for fraud associated with a real estate transfer of one of the Bank of Australia lottery prizes. See Chapter 7; *Goulburn Herald and County of Argyle Advertiser*, 19 August 1854, 4. The sentence was commuted after a year.
41 Waitt and Hartig, 'Grandiose Plans'.

> The architects of these aerial towns were often greedy 'land sharks', who richly deserved the pillory; but the originators of others were sometimes themselves as much deceived as those they gulled, and really believed that, if a place had natural advantages, it would and must go a-head, by some strange means or other ... But in what category are we to place the Government? It was surely its duty to discourage in the young colony, which it had at nurse, a mania for speculation in land, which reduced it to a state of syncope. Its policy was the reverse of this. It carried on the auctioneering business to the utmost of its power.[42]

Townsend's assessment is a helpful guide to the venture at St Vincent. Like Jervis Bay, St Vincent is of interest to researchers not because it was a swindle or an exaggerated piece of real estate 'puffing' that 'gulled' buyers, but because it illustrates the temper of the times. Land mania had taken hold at the height of the 1830s wool boom, the population was expanding and money was circulating freely. Under these circumstances, the puffing of auctioneers appeared more credible and the government benefited from the high auction prices for Crown land, using the windfall to support more immigration. Many colonists—from merchants to emigrants—were enchanted by the soaring speculative bubble. When the bubble burst, the consequences included a cascade of insolvencies. The St Vincent venture, along with Broulee and Jervis Bay, was conceived on the eve of the calamity, and vanished as quickly as it appeared.

Yet, the ephemeral nature of these ventures should not detract attention from their functional underpinnings. At a time when wool exports were expanding in importance and Argyle, Murray, King and Maneroo woolgrowers faced dilemmas over carting costs, it was a scheme that had sufficient plausibility for serving the colony's emerging economic needs. Purchasers of land at St Vincent might not have appraised the land by sight before purchasing—as Marjoribanks would have expected them to do—and some might have been 'gulled', but most would have understood the nature of the speculative venture on which they were staking their capital.

There was sufficient rationale behind the St Vincent scheme to allow us to 'recover the possibility of another history'—to use Jane Lennon's phrase. We can reflect on what might have happened if an accessible dray road to Batemans Bay had been established from Braidwood during the early 1840s, if the depression had not withdrawn available capital from the colony, if

---

42 Townsend, *Rambles and Observations*, 143.

high-tonnage steamships had realised their promise and if the Jervis Bay alternative had not been promoted at the same time with such powerful support from pastoralists beyond the mountain.

In the end, however, all the South Coast schemes examined in this book, along with those that came later, could not overcome 'the environmental limitations of the hinterland, the dominance of Sydney, nor changes in the organisation of maritime space and improved internal accessibility'.[43] Another factor that should be added was the growing centralisation of the wool-auctioning system in Sydney, which scuttled hopes of direct wool shipping to London from southern ports.

Ultimately, the competition for southern coastal primacy was historically contingent upon the sentiments and conditions that prevailed in NSW immediately before the depression. By the 1850s, what southern woolgrowers and farmers desired was that the railway would be laid close by their property, not the road to Batemans Bay, nor Broulee or Jervis Bay (see Chapter 9). By the late 1850s, after the Clyde Mountain road was opened and the townships of Nelligen and Batemans Bay were laid out, the future was even clearer: a railroad would connect Goulburn with Sydney, making the road to Batemans Bay less necessary and, therefore, Batemans Bay itself less alluring to the woolgrowers in the southern interior.[44]

Once this future had entered the consciousness of the southern population, the flow of the colony's produce—as well as its capital and investment—would be dependent on what H.J. Gibbney called the 'web of state transport radiating from Sydney'.[45] Yet, it remains legitimate to speculate how an alternative path to the coast might have affected the demographic distribution of NSW settlers, and how this affected the balance between centralisation and regionalisation within the colony.[46]

---

43 Waitt and Hartig, 'Grandiose Plans', 215.
44 According to Jackson (*Australian Economic Development*, 88), it was estimated that:
    in 1869 when the rail connection between Goulburn and Sydney first operated, rail freights per ton were under half the average for road haulage that had been charged five years previously and the time for the journey had been cut to fourteen hours from the previous average of five to ten days.
While transport costs would represent a larger proportion of costs for growers, Jackson cautions that land transportation costs were only a small part of the *total* value of wool. See also Chapter 4, this volume.
45 Gibbney, 'The South Coast', 256. See also Spillman, *Queensland Lords*, 37; Waitt and Hartig, 'Grandiose Plans', 203, 212–13.
46 Rimmer, 'The Search for Spatial Regularities'; Jackson, *Australian Economic Development*, 86.

The speculative venture of St Vincent was undermined even before the railway was built, leaving no material trace whatsoever, despite the space devoted to it in the Sydney press in 1841 and despite the transactions at auctions. The impact of the 'badness of the times' on its promoters and purchasers ensured its demise.[47] Those promoting South Coast schemes had either become insolvent or turned their interest to other speculative ventures. However, this does not render it unintelligible. Apart from the hypothetical question of what might have happened if economic, technological and topographical conditions had not conspired against its backers, the venture also sheds light on the wider competitive environment that existed on the South Coast to create a great township rivalling Sydney.

As Port Phillip was expanding, and as the Van Diemen's Land Commissariat sought 'foreign' supplies, such a southern entrepot port appealed to many merchants and shipowners. The opening of New Zealand added another trading opportunity for such a harbour. Indeed, it is telling how many characters appearing in this story of Batemans Bay had interests in New Zealand: J.J. Peacock, J.W. MacNee, W.B. Rhodes and G.D. Browne.[48] Edward Lord in 1840 was a member of the New Zealand Association and a shareholder in the Bank of New Zealand. At this stage of colonisation, Australia's 'Pacific Frontier' was still a lure for many commercial traders and adventurers, including the ill-fated Benjamin Boyd.[49]

The call for the road to Batemans Bay was briefly revived in the 1850s as the Clyde Road slowly progressed, hampered by a shortage of labour as workers succumbed to gold mania and/or the demand for labour on the encroaching southern rail line. Yet, eventually, Batemans Bay was articulated into the colonial economy through its local forest and maritime resources, neither of which relied on the Clyde Road.

---

47   According to Birch ('The Sydney Railway Company', 53), the colony's 'first major crisis' in the early 1840s meant that 'the economic reasons for railway construction fixed themselves more forcibly upon the public mind'.
48   Gordon Davies Browne was a merchant who explored Batemans Bay in 1827 and established a farm on the Clyde River under an overseer, David Paton. He abandoned the project shortly after and increasingly devoted his attention to New Zealand. His story forms part of the local history of Batemans Bay, which included a shipwrecked crew who walked from Twofold Bay to his farm and the case of an Indigenous man killed by a surveying party.
49   Young, 'Australia's Pacific Frontier'. For Edward Lord, see *Australasian Chronicle*, 23 June 1840, 3; Spillman, *Queensland Lords*, 36. Thomas Stubbs regularly targeted New Zealand buyers, and W.B. Rhodes also targeted his Broulee cattle at New Zealand markets, making multiple trips on his barque, the *Eleanor* (see Ch.3). Captain Oldrey, in his tireless promotion of Broulee, also documented the brisk trade between the port and New Zealand as 'proof of the capabilities of the Port of Broulee'. See *New South Wales Examiner*, 15 August 1842, 3. For the fate of Benjamin Boyd, see Diamond, *Ben Boyd*.

10. CONCLUSION

The failure of these southern ventures reinforced Sydney's magnetic pull. While the focal property of this book was situated on the northern shore of Batemans Bay, most of the action took place in Sydney. More specifically, most of the action in this book takes place within a small area in the centre of Sydney running north along George Street to Bridge Street, west to Elizabeth Street, south past King Street to Market Street, then back along to George Street, or straight ahead to the smouldering Albion Wharf. This was another reason why I hesitated to call the book a 'local history', but it does offer an example of how the histories of urban and rural Australia have been 'mutually constitutive'.[50]

The 1840s depression reverberated down to the southernmost parts of the 'limits of location', while at the same time these areas competed to shape the future settlement patterns and demographic distribution of the colony. This book has traced these links between the experiences of those involved in the St Vincent venture and the broader colonial community at a significant and traumatic point in the history of NSW. It took advantage of an opportunity of constructing biographies of the main players in the venture at St Vincent, making it possible to explore the interconnections between 'the personal troubles of milieu' and 'the public issues of social structure'.[51]

Local histories benefit from engaging with this wider context, be it regional, national, colonial or global.[52] According to Richard Waterhouse,

> there is a continuing need both for national history and for local studies whose findings are relevant to larger subjects and themes, for our understandings of what was different and what was shared in Australia's past depend on both these kinds of history.[53]

Local histories, histories of place and histories of ventures can have a symbiotic relationship. Indeed, it is sometimes difficult to distinguish between them. My initial orienting questions were primarily locally focused and this broader research can still resonate with and speak to local history.

---

50 Morgan, 'Rural History', 554.
51 Mills, *The Sociological Imagination*, 14.
52 Bongiorno and Eklund, 'The Problem', 41; Reynolds, 'Peacock'.
53 Waterhouse, 'Locating', 13. Carter (*The Road*, xxi) adopts a critical approach to local history, defining it as 'the cult of places', but, as Waterhouse suggests, this does not preclude it being 'converted' into wider social research. As Etzioni-Halevy (*Social Change*, 83) argues, researchers not only have to decide how to cut into social reality but also have to choose 'the social reality into which they wish to cut'.

Conclusion

In the end, the township of St Vincent did not leave any trace on Long Beach. Nevertheless, today, when people make their way towards Loma's Seat along the clifftop reserve on their walk towards Maloneys Beach, they might like to envisage the magnificent paddle-steamer *Clonmel* waiting for more firewood to be loaded from Long Beach before making its way back to Sydney on its maiden Australian return voyage (Chapter 9). Or they might look further along Long Beach and catch sight of a lone man, whom they might imagine as Raphael Clint crushing a map in his fist while lamenting that the world had once again conspired against him (Chapter 5). Or else, in the far distance, on the slopes of Longbeach Estate above Higgins Park, a mob of kangaroos might appear to be the grazing horned cattle that Thomas Stubbs imagined being tended by Glengarry's blue-bonneted men (Chapters 3 and 9).

This book suggests that these visions from the past were not implausible, even though the hopes of the participating dramatis personae vanished in a puff of smoke. While no trace of St Vincent exists apart from Raphael Clint's lithographic map, this relic reminds the viewer that the plan for St Vincent was an impractical colonial grid superimposed upon a mode of living that the Walbanja people had practised for tens of thousands of years. This mode of economy, culture and land management proved to be far more enduring than the one envisaged for St Vincent and thus will have its own rich narratives that connect the northern shore of Batemans Bay with other storylines in the locality and beyond. These narratives will be very different from the storylines in this book, which relate to the brief but extraordinary 'bad times' of the 1840s, linking land gamblers with Sydney merchants and connecting southern woolgrowers with the road to Batemans Bay.

Bibliography

ACT Government. *Canberra's Suburb and Street Names: Belconnen—Origins and Meanings*. Canberra: Department of the Environment, Land and Planning, 1992.

Alexander, Isabella. 'Cartography, Empire and Copyright Law in Colonial Australia'. *Law and History* 5 (2018): 24–53.

A.L.F. *Samuel Terry in Botany Bay*. London: J. Pattie, 1838.

Anderson, Benedict. *Imagined Communities*. London: Verso Press, 1991.

Aplin, Graeme, S.G. Foster and Michael McKernan, eds. 'South Coast and Southern Tablelands'. In *Australians 1988*, vol. 6 of *Australians: A Historical Library*, edited by Graeme Aplin, S.G. Foster, Michael McKernan, 258–65. Broadway, NSW: Fairfax, Syme & Weldon, 1988.

Australia Post. 'Shipwrecks: Capturing Our Maritime Past—Part 3'. 20 August 2017. australiapostcollectables.com.au/articles/shipwrecks-capturing-our-maritime-past-part-3.

Australian Highland Cattle Society. 'The History of Highland Cattle in Australia'. Accessed 20 January 2023. www.australianhighlandcattle.org.

Balfour, J.O. *A Sketch of New South Wales*. London: Smith, Elder & Co., 1845.

Barton, Paul. 'Thomas Bluett, Lithographer'. *Australiana* 28, no. 2 (May 2006): 20–6.

Bayley, William Alan. *Behind Broulee: A History of the Central South Coast of New South Wales*. Moruya, NSW: Eurobodalla Shire Council, 1973.

Bennett, J.M. 'The Office of Sheriff: Historical Notes on its Evolution in New South Wales'. *Sydney Law Review* 7, no. 3 (1976): 360–74.

Biosis. 'Batemans Bay Bridge Replacement: Heritage Assessment and Statement of Heritage Impact. Report for Aurecon on Behalf of Roads and Maritime Services'. Wollongong Project no. 24611, 2017.

Birch, Alan. 'The Sydney Railway Company, 1848–1855'. *Royal Australian Historical Society Journal and Proceedings* 43, part 2 (1957): 49–92.

Bishop, Catherine. *Minding Her Own Business: Colonial Businesswomen in Sydney*. Sydney: NewSouth Books, 2015.

Blackley, Roger. *Stray Leaves: Colonial Trompe L'Oeil Drawings*. Wellington: Victoria University Press, 2001.

Blainey, Geoffrey. *The Tyranny of Distance*. Melbourne: Sun Books, 1966.

Blay, John. *On Track: Searching Out the Bundian Way*. Sydney: NewSouth Books, 2015.

Bongiorno, Frank. 'From Local History to the History of Place: A Brief History of Local History in Australia'. Victoria County History International Symposium Institute of Historical Research, 6–8 July 2009.

Bongiorno, Frank and Erik Eklund. 'The Problem of Belonging: Contested Country in Australian Local History'. *New Scholar: An International Journal of the Humanities, Creative Arts and Social Sciences* 3, no. 1 (2014): 39–53.

Boyce, James. *1835: The Founding of Melbourne and the Conquest of Australia*. Melbourne: Black Inc., 2013.

Braim, Thomas. *A History of New South Wales from its Settlement to the Close of the Year 1844*. Vols 1 and 2. London: Richard Bentley, 1846.

Broadbent, James. 'Aspects of Domestic Architecture in New South Wales 1788–1843'. PhD thesis, The Australian National University, 1985.

Brodribb, William Adams. *Recollections of an Australian Squatter: 1835–1883*. Sydney: John Ferguson, 1978. Originally published 1883.

Brown, Nicholas. *A History of Canberra*. Melbourne: Cambridge University Press, 2014.

Bryan, Michael. *Bryan's Dictionary of Painters and Engravers*. Vol. 1. New York: Macmillan, 1903.

Burke, Peter. *Sociology and History*. London: George Allen & Unwin, 1980.

Burroughs, P. 'The Fixed Price Experiment in New South Wales, 1840–1841'. *Australian Historical Studies* 12, no. 47 (1966): 389–404. doi.org/10.1080/10314616608595337.

Burrows, P. *Britain and Australia 1831–1855*. Oxford: Clarendon Press, 1967.

Butlin, N.G., J. Ginswick and P. Statham. 'Colonial Statistics before 1850'. *Source Papers in Economic History*, no. 12. Canberra: Economic History Department, Research School of Social Sciences, The Australian National University, 1986.

Butlin, S.J. *Foundations of the Australian Monetary System: 1788–1851*. Sydney: University of Sydney Library, 2002.

Byrne, J.C. *Emigrant's Guide to New South Wales Proper, Australia Felix, and South Australia*. London: Effingham Wilson, 1848.

Caldow, Wayne. 'The Early Livestock Trade between Gippsland and Van Diemen's Land: Insights from Patrick Coady Buckley's Journal of 1844'. *La Trobe Journal*, no. 86 (December 2010): 23–36.

Caldow, Wayne. 'Gippsland and Van Diemen's Land Livestock Trade: Log of The Dew Drop 1847–49'. *The Great Circle* 34, no. 2 (2012): 19–43.

Campbell, Enid. 'The Quit-Rent System in Colonial New South Wales'. *Monash University Law Review* 35, no. 1 (2009): 32–44.

Cannon, Michael. *The Land Boomers: The Complete Illustrated History*. Melbourne: Lloyd O'Neil, 1986.

Carter, Paul. *The Road to Botany Bay: An Exploration of Landscape and History*. Chicago: University of Chicago Press, 1989.

Clark, Manning. *History of Australia*. Melbourne: Melbourne University Press, 1997. Abridged by Michael Cathcart.

Clement, J.A. and W.H. Richmond. 'Port Albert and Gippsland Trade, 1840–66'. *Australian Economic History Review* 8, no. 2 (January 1968): 129–38. doi.org/10.1111/aehr.82004.

Cohen, Stanley. *Folk Devils and Moral Panics*. Oxford: Martin Robertson, 1980.

Cooper, Ian. 'Bridgewater Bridge, Tasmania'. Department of Infrastructure, Tasmania, and Engineering Heritage Tasmania, April 2018.

Cottrell, W.R. 'Patterns and Impressions: An Investigation into the Copying of British Furniture Designs, the Cabinetmaker's Pattern Book and Trade Catalogue in New Zealand 1820–1920'. PhD thesis, University of Canterbury, 2016.

Cumpston, J.H.L. *Thomas Mitchell: Surveyor General and Explorer*. London: Oxford University Press, 1954.

Curr, Edward M. *Recollections of Squatting in Victoria from 1841 to 1851*. Melbourne: George Robertson, 1883.

Curthoys, Ann and John Docker. *Is History Fiction?* Sydney: UNSW Press, 2010.

D'Arcy, Jacqueline. *On His Majesty's Service: George Augustus Robinson's First Forty Years in England and Van Diemen's Land.* Kibworth Beauchamp, UK: Troubador Press, 2019.

Darian-Smith, Kate. 'Up the Country: Histories and Communities'. *Australian Historical Studies* 3, no.118 (2002): 90–9. doi.org/10.1080/10314610208596 182.

Davison, Graeme. 'Community: The Uses of Local History'. In *The Uses and Abuses of Australian History*. Sydney: Allen & Unwin, 2000.

Davison, Graeme. *The Unforgiving Minute: How Australia Learned to Tell the Time.* Melbourne: Oxford University Press, 1993.

Decker, Frank. 'Monetary Recovery Measures in the New South Wales 1840s Depression—A New Assessment'. Asia Pacific Economic and Business History Conference, Wellington, February 2010.

Design and Art Australia Online. 'Raphael Clint'. 1992. www.daao.org.au/bio/raphael-clint/biography/.

Deutscher and Hackett, 'Important Women Artists + Selected Australian and International Fine Art, Auction, Melbourne, 10 November 2021', www.deutscherandhackett.com/65-important-women-artists, 2021, pp. 300.

Diamond, Marion. *Ben Boyd of Boydtown*. Melbourne: Melbourne University Press, 1995.

Dictionary of Sydney. 'Albion Mills, Darling Harbour'. Accessed 20 January 2023. dictionaryofsydney.org/structure/albion_mills_darling_harbour.

Donaldson, James. *Colonial Mandarin: The Life and Times of Alexander Macleay.* London: Austin Macauley Publishers, 2017.

Donaldson, Susan Dale. 'Stories about the Eurobodalla by Aboriginal People'. Report for Eurobodalla Aboriginal Heritage Steering Committee, Eurobodalla Shire Council, July 2006.

Drown, J.M. 'An Apparatus of Empire: The Construction of Official Geographic Knowledge in the Survey Departments of New South Wales and Van Diemen's Land, 1788–1836'. PhD thesis, University of Sydney, 2012.

Dyster, Barrie. 'The Depression of the 1840s in New South Wales'. *Australian Dictionary of Biography*, National Centre of Biography, The Australian National University, 2022. adb.anu.edu.au/essay/29/text40594.

Dyster, Barrie. 'The 1840s Depression Revisited'. *Australian Historical Studies* 25, no. 101 (1993): 589–607. doi.org/10.1080/10314619308595938.

Dyster, Barrie. 'Inventing the Suburbs and Making a Fortune'. *Leichhardt History Journal*, no. 11 (1982): 6–12.

Earl, George Windsor. *Enterprise in Tropical Australia*. London: Madden & Malcolm, 1846.

Earnshaw, John. 'A Further Note on Billy Barlow'. *Meanjin* (December 1956): 422–3.

Eaton, Karen. 'John Black Carmichael 1803–1857'. *Australiana* 37, no. 4 (November 2015): 6–18.

Edwards, George W. *History of Violet Town and the Anglican Church of St Dunston*. 1984 (n.p.).

Egan, Paul and Philip Soos. *Bubble Economics: Australian Land Speculation 1830–2013*. Melbourne: Prosper Australia, 2013.

Elbourne, Elizabeth. 'The Bannisters and Their Colonial World'. In *Within and Without the Nation*, edited by Karen Dubinsky et al., 49–75. Toronto: University of Toronto Press, 2015.

Eldershaw, M. Barnard. *A House Is Built*. Windsor, NSW: Lloyd O'Neil, 1972. Originally published 1929.

Etzioni-Halevy, Eva. *Social Change*. London: Routledge Kegan Paul, 1981.

Fahey, Warren. 'Billy Barlow in Australia'. 2014. www.warrenfahey.com.au/billy-barlow-in-australia/ (page discontinued).

Fernyhough, W.H. *Album of Portraits, Mainly of New South Wales Officials*. Sydney: Austin & Co., c. 1836.

Fitzpatrick, Brian. *The British Empire in Australia 1834–1939*. Melbourne: Macmillan, 1969.

Fowles, Joseph. *Sydney in 1848: Illustrated by Copper-Plate Engravings of the Principal Streets, Public Buildings, Churches, Chapels, etc.* Sydney: J. Fowles, 1848.

Franklin, Jane. *This Errant Lady: Jane Franklin's Overland Journey from Port Phillip to Sydney, 1839*. Canberra: National Library of Australia, 2002.

Galbraith, J.K. *The Affluent Society*. London: Penguin, 1973.

'Garryowen'. *The Chronicles of Melbourne 1835 to 1851*. Vol. 2. Melbourne: Ferguson & Mitchell, 1888.

Ghosh, Amitav. *The Nutmeg's Curse: Parables for a Planet in Crisis*. London: John Murray, 2021. doi.org/10.7208/chicago/9780226815466.001.0001.

Gibbney, H.J. *Eurobodalla: A History the Moruya District*, Sydney, Library of Australian History, 1980.

Gibbney, H.J. 'The South Coast and Southern Tablelands'. In *Australians 1988*, vol. 6 of *Australians: A Historical Library*, edited by Graeme Aplin, S.G. Foster and Michael McKernan, 255–7. Broadway, NSW: Fairfax, Syme & Weldon, 1988.

Gill, Samuel Thomas. *The Australian Sketchbook*. Melbourne: Hamel & Ferguson, 1865.

Glowrey, Cheryl. *South of the Strzelecki Ranges: An Environmental History of Corner Inlet*. Melbourne: Anchor Books, 2018.

Golder, Hillary. *Politics, Patronage and Public Works: 1840–1900*. Sydney: UNSW Press, 2005.

Goulding, Megan and Kate Waters. 'Eurobodalla Aboriginal Cultural Heritage Study, South Coast, New South Wales'. Report for Eurobodalla Shire Council, March 2005.

Gray, Nancy. 'Raphael Clint (1797–1849)'. *Australian Dictionary of Biography*, National Centre of Biography, The Australian National University, 1966. adb.anu.edu.au/biography/clint-raphael-1904/text2251.

Greig, Alastair. *The Australian Way of Life: A Sociological Introduction*. Melbourne: Palgrave, 2013.

Hamey, Kath. 'John Hosking'. *Peninsula Observer*, December 1992, 3.

Hamon, Bruce. *They Came to Murramarang*, 2nd edition, edited by Alastair Greig and Sue Feary. Canberra: ANU Press, 2015. doi.org/10.22459/TCM.10.2015.

Hancock, W.K. *Discovering Monaro*. Cambridge: Cambridge University Press, 1972.

Hancock, W.K. 'A Note on Mary Kingsley'. In *Politics in Pitcairn and Other Essays*. London: Macmillan, 1947.

Henzel, Ted. *Australian Agriculture: Its History and Challenges*. Melbourne: CSIRO Publishing, 2007. doi.org/10.1071/9780643094659.

Hewitt, William. *Land, Labour and Gold, or, Two Years in Victoria*. London: Longman, Brown, Green, Longmans, & Roberts, 1858.

Historic Houses Trust of NSW. *Annual Report 2015–2016*. www.parliament.nsw. gov.au/tp/files/69842/Historic%20Houses%20Trust%20SLM%20Annual%20 Report%202015-16.pdf.

Hodder, Edwin. *A History of South Australia from Its Foundation to Its Jubilee*. Vol. 1. London: Sampson Low, Marston & Co. Ltd, 1893.

Hodgson, Christopher Pemberton. *Reminiscences of Australia, with Hints on the Squatter's Life*. London: W.N. Wright, 1846.

Holcomb, Janette. 'Opportunities and Risks in the Development of the NSW Shipping Industry, 1821–1850'. PhD thesis, University of New England, 2008.

Horsburgh, James. *The India Directory, or Directions for Sailing*. London: Wm. H. Allen and Co., 1841.

Hoskins, Ian. *Coast: A History of the New South Wales Edge*. Sydney: NewSouth Books, 2013.

Huf, Benjamin. 'The Capitalist in Colonial History: Investment, Accumulation and Credit-Money in New South Wales'. *Australian Historical Studies* 50, no. 4 (2019): 418–40. doi.org/10.1080/1031461X.2019.1637444.

Huf, Benjamin. 'Making Things Economic: Theory and Government in New South Wales, 1788–1863'. PhD thesis, The Australian National University, 2018.

Irwin, Frederick Chidley. *The State and Position of Western Australia: Commonly Called the Swan-River Settlement*. London: Simpkin, Marshall and Co., 1835.

Jackson, R.V. *Australian Economic Development in the Nineteenth Century*. Canberra: Australian National University Press, 1977.

James, Allison. *Batemans Bay: Story of a Town*. Batemans Bay, 2001.

J.B.M. *Reminiscences*. Camden: A.J. Doust, 1884.

Johnson, Frank. *Where Highways Meet: A History of Bateman's Bay and the Clyde & Tomakin Rivers*. Batemans Bay, NSW: Clyde River and Batemans Bay Historical Society, 1980.

Kelly, M.J. 'Eight Acres: Estate Sub-Division and the Building Process, Paddington, 1875 to 1890'. *Australian Economic History Review* 10, no. 2 (1970): 155–68. doi.org/10.1111/aehr.102003.

Kercher, Bruce. *An Unruly Child: The History of Law in Australia*. Abingdon: Routledge, 2020. doi.org/10.4324/9781003114857.

Lamb, Rebecca. *Macquoid of Waniassa: Portrait of a Colonial Sheriff.* Canberra: Waniassa Publications, 2006.

Lambert, David and Ian Lester. 'Introduction: Imperial Spaces, Imperial Subjects'. In *Colonial Lives across the British Empire: Imperial Careering in the Long Nineteenth Century*, edited by D. Lambert and I. Lester, 1–32. Cambridge: Cambridge University Press, 2006.

Lennon, Jane L. *Across Bass Strait: Inter-Colonial Trade in Meat and Livestock.* Melbourne: Anchor Books, 2022.

Leski Auctions. *Australian & Historical.* 28–29 November 2020. www.leski.com.au/auction/australian-historical-a463/.

Lockie, Stewart. 'Social Nature: The Environmental Challenge to Mainstream Sociology'. In *Controversies in Environmental Sociology*, edited by Rob White, 26–42. Cambridge: Cambridge University Press, 2004. doi.org/10.1017/CBO9780511804434.003.

Lost Christchurch. 'John Peacock and His Controversial Fountain'. 2014. lostchristchurch.wordpress.com/2012/08/04/john-peacock-and-his-fountain/.

Low, D.A. 'Introduction'. In *Keith Hancock: The Legacies of an Historian*, edited by D.A. Low, 1–14. Melbourne: Melbourne University Press, 2001.

Maclehose, J. *Picture of Sydney and Stranger's Guide in New South Wales for 1838.* Sydney: J. Spilsbury, 1838.

Magee, Stuart. *All Broulee and Mossy.* Canberra: Stuart Magee, 2003.

Mann, W. *Six Years Residence in the Australian Provinces.* London: Smith, Elder & Cornhill, 1839.

Marjoribanks, Alexander. *Travels in New South Wales.* London: Smith, Elder & Co., 1847.

Marx, Karl. *Capital.* Vol. 1. London: Penguin Books, 1976. Originally published 1867.

McCombie, Thomas. *Arabin, Or, the Adventures of a Colonist in New South Wales.* London: Simmonds and Ward, 1845.

McDonald, John and Eric Richards. 'The Great Emigration of 1841: Recruitment for New South Wales in British Emigration Fields'. *Population Studies* 51, no. 3 (1997): 337–55. doi.org/10.1080/0032472031000150096.

McKenna, Mark. *Looking for Blackfellas' Point: An Australian History of Place.* Sydney: UNSW Press, 2002.

McMichael, Philip. 'Crisis in Pastoral Capital Accumulation: A Re-Interpretation of the 1840s Depression in Colonial Australia'. In *Essays in the Political Economy of Australian Capitalism*. Vol. 4, edited by E.L. Wheelwright and K. Buckley, 17–40. Sydney: Australia and New Zealand Book Company, 1980.

Melville, Herman. *Omoo*. Boston: L.C. Page and Co., 1925. Originally published 1847.

Merton, Robert K. *Social Theory and Social Structure*. Glencoe, IL: Free Press, 1964.

Mills, C. Wright. *The Sociological Imagination*. London: Penguin, 1970.

Mills (nee White), Maud. 'The Story of the Whites of Bluff Downs'. [Unpublished manuscript]. University of Queensland, n.d.

Morgan, Ruth. 'Rural History and Environmental History'. *Australian Historical Studies* 48, no. 4 (2017): 554–68. doi.org/10.1080/1031461X.2017.1326956.

Morrissey, Sylvia. 'The Pastoral Economy'. In *Essays in Economic History of Australia*, edited by James Griffin, 51–112. Milton, Qld: Jacaranda Press, 1970.

Mortlock, Allan and Bernice Anderson. *Undiscovered Canberra*. Canberra: Australian National University Press, 1978.

Mossman, Samuel and Thomas Banister. *Australia Visited and Revisited: A Narrative of Recent Travels and Old Experiences in Victoria and New South Wales*. London: Addey and Co., 1853.

Moyal, Ann. 'Surveyors: Mapping the Distance, Early Surveying in Australia'. *Australian Dictionary of Biography*, National Centre of Biography, The Australian National University, 2017. adb.anu.edu.au/essay/22/text34969.

Mundy, Godfrey C. *Our Antipodes, or Residence and Rambles in the Australasian Colonies: With a Glimpse of the Gold Fields*. London: Richard Bentley, 1857.

Murphy, Peter. 'James Sprent and the Trigonometrical Survey of Tasmania'. FIG Congress 2010, Facing the Challenges—Building the Capacity, Sydney, 2010.

Museums of History NSW. 'Raphael Clint Sundial'. Accessed 20 January 2023. mhnsw.au/stories/general/raphael-clint-sundial/.

Neville, R.A.J. 'Printmakers in Colonial Sydney 1800–1850'. MA thesis, University of Sydney, 1988.

NSW National Parks and Wildlife Service. *Cullendulla Creek Nature Reserve Plan of Management*. 2004. www.environment.nsw.gov.au/-/media/OEH/Corporate-Site/Documents/Parks-reserves-and-protected-areas/Parks-plans-of-management/cullendulla-creek-nature-reserve-plan-of-management-040133.pdf.

Odgers, Kim. *Our Town, Our People—Batemans Bay: A Tribute to the Men and Women Who Have Shaped Our Town*. Vol. 1. Batemans Bay, 2014.

Parsons, Vivienne. 'Hosking, John (1806–1882)'. *Australian Dictionary of Biography*, National Centre of Biography, The Australian National University, 1966. adb.anu.edu.au/biography/hosking-john-2200/text2843.

Paterson, A.B. *Old Bush Songs*. Sydney: Angus & Robertson, 1905.

Pearson, Michael and Jane Lennon. *Pastoral Australia: Fortunes, Failures & Hard Yakka: A Historical Overview, 1788–1967*. Collingwood, Vic.: CSIRO Publishing, 2010. doi.org/10.1071/9780643100503.

Perry, T.M. *Australia's First Frontier: The Spread of Settlement in New South Wales, 1788–1829*. Melbourne: Melbourne University Press, 1963.

Philo-Palinurus. *Land Gambling: New South Wales—Its Present Social and Political Condition*. London: Palmer and Clayton, 1842.

Prebble, John. *The Highland Clearances*. London: Penguin, 1969.

Reynolds, Peter. 'From Johnson Street to Cameron's Cove'. *Leichhardt Historical Journal*, no. 14 (1986): 23–53.

Reynolds, Peter. 'Peacock Weston, Pearson and Paul: How "Suburbanisation" Began in Balmain'. *Leichhardt Historical Journal*, no. 11 (1982): 13–27.

Reynolds, Robert, Vernice Gillies and Murray Arnold. 'Restoring Menang Noongar Names Project'. Report CCS 357, City of Albany, March 2021.

Rimmer, P. 'The Search for Spatial Regularities in the Development of Australian Seaports: 1861–1961/2'. *Geografiska Annaler. Series B, Human Geography* 49, no. 1 (1967): 42–54. doi.org/10.1080/04353684.1967.11879303.

Roberts, S.H. *History of Australian Land Settlement*. Abingdon: Frank Cass, 1969.

Roberts-Thomson, Peter J. 'The Search for the Highest Mountain Peak in Tasmania'. *THRA P&P* 56, no. 1 (2009): 71–80.

Robinson, Frederick W. *Canberra's First Hundred Years and After*. Sydney: W.C. Penfold & Co., 1927.

Rubenstein, William. *The All-Time Australian 200 Rich List: From Samuel Terry 'The Convict Rothschild' to Kerry Packer*. Sydney: Allen & Unwin, 2004.

Sandercock, Leonie. *The Land Racket*. Canberra: Silverfish Books, 1979.

Sandercock, Leonie. *Property, Politics and Urban Planning*. London: Transaction Publishers, 1990.

Scott, Ernest. *A Short History of Australia*. Melbourne: Oxford University Press, 1930.

Seddon, George. 'The Suburban Landscape in Australia'. In *Landprints: Reflections on Place and Landscapes*, 149–52. Cambridge: Cambridge University Press, 1997.

Sewell, John. 'Captain William Oldrey RN'. *Journal of the Moruya and District Historical Society Inc.* (September 2017): 18–20.

Shoobert, Joanne, ed. *Western Australian Exploration, 1826–1835*. Vol. 1. Carlisle: Hesperian Press, 2005.

Shumack, Samuel. *Tales and Legends of Canberra Pioneers*. Canberra: Australian National University Press, 1977.

Sidney, Samuel. *The Three Colonies of Australia*. London: Ingram, Cooke & Co., 1853.

Sinclair, David. *The Land That Never Was: Sir Gregor MacGregor and the Most Audacious Fraud in History*. Cambridge, MA: Da Capo Press, 2003.

Skinner, Graeme. 'Thomas Stubbs and His Descendants'. *Australharmony*. Accessed 20 January 2023. sydney.edu.au/paradisec/australharmony/stubbs-thomas-and-descendents.php.

Skinner, Graeme. 'Toward a General History of Australian Musical Composition: First National Music, 1788–c.1860'. PhD thesis, University of Sydney, 2011.

Smith, Elder & Co., ed. *Twenty Years Experience in Australia; Being the Evidence of ... Residents and Travellers in Those Colonies ... the Whole Demonstrating the ... Advantage of Emigration to New South Wales*. London: Smith, Elder & Co., 1839.

Smith, Peter. *The Clarke Gang: Outlawed, Outcast and Forgotten*. Sydney: NewSouth Books, 2015.

Spillman, Janet. *Queensland Lords: Edward and Eliza Lord's Colonial Family*. Salisbury, Qld: Boolarong Press, 2015.

Stancombe, G.H. 'The Early Surveyors of Tasmania'. *Tasmanian Historical Research Association, Papers and Proceedings* (9 September 1959): 8–15.

Sykes, Trevor. *Two Centuries of Panic: A History of Corporate Collapses in Australia*. Sydney: Allen & Unwin, 1998.

Tegg, James. *Tegg's New South Wales Pocket Almanac and Remembrancer, 1842*. Sydney: James Tegg Bookseller and Publisher, 1842.

Toms, K.N. and P.M. Plunkett. 'Crown Land Survey Administration in Van Diemen's Land'. *Australian Surveyor* 31, no. 2 (1982): 72–83. doi.org/10.1080/00050326.1982.10434955.

Townsend, Joseph Phipps. *Rambles and Observations in New South Wales*. London: Chapman & Hall, 1849.

Turner, J.W. *Thematic History of Eurobodallashire*. Newcastle, NSW: Hunter History Consultants, 1996.

Waitt, Gordon and Kate Hartig. 'Grandiose Plans, but Insignificant Outcomes: The Development of Colonial Ports at Twofold Bay, New South Wales'. *Australian Geographer* 28, no. 2 (1997): 201–18. doi.org/10.1080/00049189708703193.

Ward, Russel. 'Jemmy Green and Billy Barlow'. *Meanjin* 14, no. 2 (June 1955): 249–54.

Waterhouse, Richard. 'Locating the New Social History: Transnational Historiography and Australian Local History'. *Journal of the Royal Australian Historical Society* 95, no. 1 (2009): 1–17.

Watson, Don. *Caledonia Australis: Scottish Highlanders on the Frontier of Australia*. Melbourne: Vintage, 1997.

Watson, Frederick, ed. *Historical Records of Australia*. Series 1, vol. 19. Sydney: Library Committee of the Commonwealth Parliament, 1923.

Watson, Frederick, ed. *Historical Records of Australia*, Series 1, vol. 20. Sydney: Library Committee of the Commonwealth Parliament, 1923.

Watson, Frederick, ed. *Historical Records of Australia*, Series 3, vol. 6. Sydney: Library Committee of the Commonwealth Parliament, 1923.

Wegman, Imogen. 'Understanding Colonial Maps'. *Traces* 13 (2020): 1–5.

Wilson, G. *Murray of Yarralumla*, Canberra, Tabletop Press, 2001.

Worms, Laurence and Ashley Baynton-Williams. 'Raphael Clint'. *British Map Engravers: A Dictionary of Engravers, Lithographers and Their Principal Employers to 1850—A Supplement*. 2011. britishmapengravers.net/entries/e-entries/raphael-clint/.

Young, J.M.R. 'Australia's Pacific Frontier'. *Australian Historical Studies* 12, no. 74 (1966): 373–88. doi.org/10.1080/10314616608595336.

BIBLIOGRAPHY

Newspapers, magazines and journals (with years cited)

Albany Advertiser (WA), 1930
Argus (Vic.), 1849
Art Journal, 1854
Australasian (Vic.), 1878
Australasian Chronicle (NSW), 1840–43
Austral-Asiatic Review (VDL), 1833–34
Austral-Asiatic Review, Tasmanian and Australian Advertiser (VDL), 1843
Australian (NSW), 1830–47
Bell's Life in Sydney and Sporting Reviewer (NSW), 1845–51
Citizen (NSW), 1847
Colonial Magazine and Commercial-Maritime Journal, 1842
Colonial Observer (NSW), 1841–42
Colonial Times (VDL), 1833–47
Colonist (NSW), 1835–40
Colonist and Van Diemen's Land Commercial and Agricultural Advertiser (VDL), 1832–34
Commercial Journal and Advertiser (NSW), 1838–40
Commercial Journal and General Advertiser (NSW), 1845
Cornwall Chronicle (VDL), 1848
Courier (VDL), 1851
Daily News and Evening Chronicle (NSW), 1848
Daily Telegraph (NSW), 1899
Dispatch (NSW), 1843
Empire (NSW), 1854–60
Fife Herald (Scotland), 1840
Fisher's Colonial Magazine and Commercial Maritime Journal, 1842
Free Press and Commercial Journal (NSW), 1841
Geelong Advertiser (Vic.), 1840–48
Golden Age (NSW), 1862
Goulburn Herald and Chronicle (NSW), 1869
Goulburn Herald and County of Argyle Advertiser (NSW), 1852–54
Hobart Town Advertiser (VDL), 1849
Hobart Town Courier (VDL), 1834–36

Hunter River Gazette; and Journal of Agriculture, Commerce, Politics, and News (NSW), 1842
Illawarra Mercury (NSW), 1858
Inquirer and Commercial News (WA), 1898
Launceston Advertiser (VDL), 1836
Launceston Courier (VDL), 1841
London Illustrated News (England), 1845
Maitland Mercury and Hunter River General Advertiser (NSW), 1843–57
Melbourne Times (Vic.), 1842–43
Monmouthshire Merlin (England), 1848
Moreton Bay Courier (Qld), 1850
Morning Chronicle (NSW), 1844–46
Morning Star and Commercial Advertiser (VDL), 1835
New South Wales Examiner (NSW), 1841–42
New South Wales Government Gazette (NSW), 1838–99
New Zealand Gazette and Wellington Spectator (NZ), 1842
Omnibus and Sydney Spectator (NSW), 1841
Parramatta Chronicle and Cumberland General Advertiser (NSW), 1844
Parramatta Messenger and Cumberland Express' (NSW), 1847
People's Advocate and New South Wales Vindicator (NSW), 1850–56
Perth Gazette and Western Australian Journal (WA), 1833–39
Pittwater Online News (NSW), 2011–21
Port Phillip Gazette (Vic.), 1844
Port Phillip Gazette and Settler's Journal (Vic.), 1846
Port Phillip Patriot and Melbourne Advertiser (Vic.), 1841–42
Port Phillip Patriot and Morning Advertiser (Vic.), 1848
Queenslander (Qld), 1887
Sentinel (NSW), 1845–47
Shipping Gazette and Sydney General Trade List (NSW), 1851
South Australian (SA), 1847
South Australian Gazette and Colonial Register (SA), 1837
Sun and New South Wales Independent Press (NSW), 1843
Sydney Chronicle (NSW), 1847
Sydney Daily Advertiser (NSW), 1848
Sydney Free Press (NSW), 1841–42
Sydney Gazette and New South Wales Advertiser (NSW), 1821–42

Sydney Gazette (NSW), 1835
Sydney Gazette and NSW Monitor (NSW), 1839–41
Sydney Herald (NSW), 1832–42
Sydney Monitor and Commercial Advertiser (NSW), 1836–41
Sydney Monitor and NSW Advertiser (NSW), 1840–41
Sydney Monitor (NSW), 1830–38
Sydney Morning Herald (NSW), 1842–82
Sydney Record (NSW), 1843
Sydney Times (NSW), 1835–38
Tasmanian (VDL), 1833–34
Teetotaller and General Newspaper (NSW), 1842
Transactions of the Society, Instituted at London, for the Encouragement of Arts, Manufactures, and Commerce, 1824–25
True Colonist Van Diemen's Land Political Dispatch and Agricultural and Commercial Advertiser (VDL), 1836
Trumpeter General (VDL), 1834
Weekly Register of Politics, Facts and General Literature (NSW), 1843
Yass Courier (NSW), 1859

Index

Note: Page numbers in italics indicate illustrations or maps. Page numbers with 'n' indicate footnotes.

A House Is Built 168, 188n.61
Albion, trade name 154
    see also Hughes, John Terry
Albion House 154–5, *155*, 164
Albion Wharf fire 15, *16*, 26n.12, 43, 134, 151n.22, 195
auctioneering system 7, 23, 30–1, 32n.30, 33n.31, 46
    blamed for economic depression 135
    fraud/misrepresentation 31, 36, 205
    puffing 23–47, 62, 69, 113, 200, 205–6, 208
Australian Steam Navigation Company 53n.11, 58

Bank of Australia 15, 45, 127, 129, 136n.16, 137n.18, 141, 149n.12, 153, 207
    collapse, 133–6, 168
    lottery, 8, 136–140, *137*, 140n.33, 152, 152n.27
Batemans Bay, township of xiii, 5, 6, 192, 193–4, 196, 197–8, 199, 209
Benandra 12, 115, *115*, 117, 163, 177, *178*, 178n.30, 202
Benandarah, *see* Benandra
Berry, Alexander 53, 56
'Billy Barlow in Australia' 156–7, 165

Blair, Augustus Edmund 112, 112n.3, 118, 142
Bluett, Thomas 96n.91, 107, 108n.144
boundaries of location, *see* limits of location
Boyd, Benjamin 4, 57, 69, 187, 188, 188n.61, 206–7, 210
Boyd Town 57, 187, 202, 206, 207
Brataualong 182
    see also Indigenous
Broughton, William 155, 155n.41
Broulee 48–65, 66, 67, 173, 175, 189
Browne, Gordon Davies 210, 210n.48
Burdekin, Thomas 157, 157n.49, 157n.50, 168

cadastral maps 76, 93
    Indigenous presence, erasure 93, 109
Campbell, Archibald 53
Campbell, Robert 53
Chapple, Mary Ann, *see* Clint, Mary Ann
Clint, Mary Ann 73, 75, 99, 105–7, 106n.140, 106n.142, 108n.144, 108n.146, 165, 168n.79
    alleged sly grog seller 79n.34, 107
    estrangement 101–2
    marriage 73n.4

229

Clint, Raphael 26, 35, 71–109, *72*, 114, 151n.21, 165, 203
  agent for Edward Lord/Stubley Park 39, 71, 204
  biography ix, 73
  cadastral maps 76–7, 77n.22
  controversy 78–9, 79n.34, 80–2, 95, 102
  cooperation with Hughes & Hosking 26, 26n.12
  death 105–6
  elevated social and moral position 83–5
  enigmatic and mercurial 8
  horseshoe punt 79, 79n.36
  hydrographer 8, 81, 96, 96n.94, 101
  insolvency 102–3, 133
  jury duty 124n.38
  land purchase, Long Beach 15, 45, 71, 96, 112, 142, 167
  land sale, Long Beach 45, 48, 71, 96, 112
  lithographer 71, 76, 85–99, 90n.70, 95n.89, 96n.92, 97n.95, 98n.102, 104, 111
  lithographic plan, 1841 St Vincent 26, 39, 71, *87*, 88–93, 115–16, 177, 193–4, 197, 212
  marriage breakdown 101–2
  New Zealand lithographs 95
  piracy 82–3, 82n.52, 97n.95
  relations with John Hosking 146n.5
  runaway apprentices/servants 81–2, 81n.44, 84
  seal engraver 26, 73–7, 77n.23, 85, 94–6, 98–100
  soundings 91–2
  surveyor 71, 73–4, 74n.5, 76
  visit to St Vincent 38, 93, 109, 204, 212
  well-known public figure 7, 99
  see also Peacock, John Jenkins

Clonmel, the x, 34, 48, 171–81, 175n.16, 185, 203, 212
  wreck 9, *172*, 181, 185, 187–8, 194
Clyde Road, the 67, 68n.77, 68n.78, 189–91, 210
Coghill, John 53
Conmel Wharf 178–9, *178*
Connell, Michael 179

dray road, hope of 4, 19, 37, 50–3, 59, 67, 88, 186, 188–9, 203–4, 208
  Kinghorne–Green 35, 52, 67
  Larmer 52
  Nicholson 61, 63
  see also Wool Road
Dent, George 31, 114, 114n.10, 117–18, 129, 133, 206

economic conditions
  badness of the times 7, 43–6, 44n.64, 48, 67, 94, 203, 210
  expansionist/optimistic 5, 6
  depressed market 56, 130, 135, 137
  over-speculation 43, 135, 142
  see also 'land mania'
Evans, George 125, 125n.42, 126–7, 128

Fletcher, Eliza, *see* Lord, Eliza
Foss and Lloyd, auctioneers 55, 64, 85n.62
Frazer, James 64–5

Gipps, George 23, 24n.3, 51, 51n.5, 69, 124, 203
Glengarry x, 179–83, 180n.35, 182n.40, 182n.42, 187, 212
Goddard, William 125, 127, 127n.50, 128, 158
Great Southern Township, competition 4, 48
  see also St Vincent
Grose, Joseph Hickey 187, 188

INDEX

Hosking, John 19, 24n.5, 48, 58, 145, *148*, 154, 158, 163
  alderman, City of Sydney 166
  Balmain landholding 24, 26, 134, 149
  biography ix, 13
  Carrara, Vaucluse mansion 149, 149n.13, 164
  death 150
  director, Hunter River Steam Navigation Company 173n.6
  insolvency 146–50
  mayor of Sydney *13*, 14, 14n.12, 29, 146
  mercantile elite 14
  relations with John Hughes 150
  relations with Raphael Clint 146n.5
  second bankruptcy 149
  well-known public figure 7, 146
Hosking, Martha 13, 149n.13, 150
Hughes, Esther 13, 154
Hughes, John Terry 15n.15, 19, 29, 134n.7, 141, 143n.37, 145–6, 150–8, 163
  biography ix, 13
  death 154
  executor of Samuel Terry's will 14
  granted certificate of insolvency 154
  Jervis Bay Wool Road subscriber 57, 61
  land conspiracy case 12n.4, 14n.10, 150
  mercantile elite 14
  refused certificate of insolvency 152, 152n.26, 152n.30, 153n.31
  relations with John Hosking 150
  scapegoat for depression ix, 9, 152–3, 156
Hughes, Samuel Terry 154
Hughes & Hosking 25–6, 38, 40, 57n.31, 88, 141, 152, 166, 168, 179, 202–3

1840s depression 15, 134n.4
Bank of Australia mortgage 45, 127, 129, 136
  block, St Vincent *115*, 117n.16
  insolvency 8, 133–6
  Jervis Bay Wool Road subscriber 57
  land purchase, Long Beach *10*, 11–12, 15, 45, 45n.67, 48, 71, 96, 112–13
  land sale, Long Beach 14, 33, 142
  large landholder 7, 12–13
  over speculation 21, 143n.37
  Port Phillip landholdings 13
Hunter River Steam Navigation Company 58n.35, 173, 173n.6

Indigenous
  conflict, Gippsland 47n.75, 182
  dispersal 143
  dispossession 47, 186
  guides 1, 73
  placenames 12n.5, 73
  roads 4–5, 35n.36
  see also Brataualong; Walbanja
Insolvency Act 9, 130, 137n.18, 146–7, 147n.6, 147n.7, 159n.55, 164, 164n.70
insolvency law reform 147, 147n.6, 159n.55

Jervis Bay Road 53, 55, 59–60, 67, 191
Jervis Bay Wool Road consortium 60
  see also Wool Road

Kinghorne, Alexander 11, 12n.4, 35, 52, 67, 90n.72
Keele, William 91–2

land
  boom 144, 200
  minimum price 12, 12n.4, 20n.27, 23, 24n.3

231

speculation 5, 8, 126, 133, 142–3, 144n.42, 165
land gambling, land-jobbing, land quackery, land racket, *see* land mania
land mania 8, 20, 24n.3, 135, 135n.11, 143–4, 143n.41, 168, 208
Lang, John Dunmore 44, 77
Langley, Charles E. 91, 91n.73, 97, 97n.96, 105n.139, 108, 123n.35
Larmer, James 12, 25n.7, 36n.40, 52, 59, 67, 88n.66, 90, 157n.50
limits of location 11, 18, 23, 58, 63, 68, 76, 93, 186, 196, 211
local history, genre 9, 193–202, 197n.10, 211, 211n.53
Lord, Ada 162
Lord, Edward 21, 38–9, 88, 158–64, *160*, 167–8, 202–3
   biography ix, 7, 18
   death 159
   director, Hunter River Steam Navigation Company 173
   insolvency 133, 145
   interests in New Zealand 210
   investments on the Clyde River 19
   land grant, Long Beach 16, *17*
   petition for wharf at Broulee Harbour 58
   well-known public figure 7
   see also Stubley Park
Lord, Eliza 18, 159, 159n.59, 161, 164
Lord, James 18, 161, 161n.63
Lyons, Samuel 26–7, 27n.13, 45, 45n.68, 53–5, 64–5, 118n.19, 130, 139–41, 173
   Clonmel auction 187
   legal trouble 31, 31n.26, 32, 32n.30, 82n.54, 114, 206

Macarthur, Hannibal Hawkins 136, 136n.13
   see also Bank of Australia

MacDonell, Aeneas Ranaldson, *see* Glengarry
MacGregor, Gregor, *see* Poyais Affair
MacKenzie, John 53
Macleay, Alexander 53, 53n.11, 66n.69, 130n.58
MacNee, John Whitehead 167, 167n.77, 175n.16, 210
Macquoid, Thomas x, 120n.26, 121–4, 121n.28, 121n.29, *122*, 123n.34, 124n.38, 155n.41
   suicide 123, 130, 194
   Wool Road 53, 130, 130n.48
Mallon, John 46n.70, 86n.64
Marjoribanks, Alexander 30–1, 33, 33n.31, 37, 92, 113, 180, 205, 208
Marsden, Samuel 13
Mitchell, Thomas 49n.2, 52, 68n.78, 74, 181
Mort, Thomas 57n.29, 138
Mudie, Forbes 95, 107
Murray, Terence 53, 56n.24
Myles, Lawrence 16

Nelligen, 190–1, 192, 209
Nicholson, Charles 59–61

Office of the Sheriff 112, 118, 121, 121n.28, 124, 194
Oldrey, William x, 46n.70, 58, 60–5, 60n.46, 62n.53, 69, 173, 210n.49
Oxley, John 51

Park, Alexander 39, 161, 161n.64, 168
Peacock, John Jenkins x, 39, 45, 45n.67, 117, 117n.16, 168, 202
   alderman, City of Sydney 166
   currency lad 166
   death of son, 15
   declared insolvent 166, 167n.74
   interests in New Zealand 166–7, 210
   joint owner of land at Long Beach 15, 25–6, 33, 86, 112–13, 142, 166

Port Albert 3, 6, 9, 171, 181, 182–7, 191, 200
port hierarchy 4, 171
Poyais affair 204–5, 205n.32
Price, John 81, 82, 83, 85, 107
  see also Clint, Raphael
private towns 2, 7, 23, 25, 25n.7, 56n.28, 92, 118n.19, 206
  Boyd Town 57
  Clyde 162
  Jervis Town 54, 65
  New Bristol 55
  Singleton 125n.39, 157n.49
  South Huskisson 53
  see also St Vincent
Prout, Cornelius 116, 116n.15, 120, 120n.26, 121n.29, 125
puffing, see auctioneering system; Lyons, Samuel; Stubbs, Thomas

railway, promise of 185–6, 188–91, 203, 203n.30, 209–10
Rattray, George 141–2, 166
Royal Bank of Australia 57
Ryan, John 36n.40, 112

Select Committee on Monetary Confusion 135
sociological imagination 3, 169, 195, 211n.53
southern port, dream of 5, 9, 19, 48–9, 58, 68, 70, 130, 171, 203
  see also great St Vincent, Great Southern Township of; Port Albert
Southern Tablelands 3, 4, 19, 65
Sprent, James 74, 74n.8
Staple, John ix, 8, 111–30, 133, 134, 157n.49, 158n.54
  attorney 119, 129n.56
  conveyancer 119–20
  insolvency 116–17, 118n.18, 126–8
  purchased land at St Vincent 115–19

speculatist 118, 129
struck off 128
under sheriff 8, 119–20, 123
steamships, promise of 9, 34, 52, 57, 63, 171–4, 186–8, 190–1, 194, 203–4, 209
  see also Australian Steam Navigation Company; *Clonmel*; Hunter River Steam Navigation Company
Stubbs, Richard 32, 32n.28, 105
Stubbs, Thomas 7, 27, *28*, 105, 117–18, 127, 130, 134n.5, 166, 183
  appearance 29, 30, 204
  Auction Mart 29, 29n.16, 33–4, 86
  biography ix, 27–9
  city auctioneer (Sydney) 104, 104n.134
  Clonmel, reference to 34, 48, 177, 179, 180, 187
  composer 29, 104n.132
  currency lad ix, 166
  George Inn auction 66, 67n.73
  January 1841 advertisement 33, 91n.74, 92, 150n.17, 158, 171, 178–9, 187, 206n.35
  Jervis Town auctions 54, 120
  legal trouble 32
  oratory skills 30, 33n.31, 93, 179
  passive-voiced 40, 179n.34, 181
  puffing 36, 41, 44, 54, 113, 206, 206n.35
  skilled auctioneer 30, 30n.19
  St Vincent auctions 35–42, 45, 47, 71, 86, 88, 93–4, 113–14, 117–18, 206
  targeting New Zealand buyers 210n.49
  witness, Select Committee on Monetary Confusion 135
St Vincent
  County of 11, 12, *25*, 27, 27n.13, 51n.5, *178*

Great Southern Township of 2, 21, 33, 50, 67, 71, 142, 163
Lands Title Plan 359(A) 25–6, 33n.32, 109n.148, 112, 118n.18, 177, 178, 197
Private Town of 115, *115*
street names 116–17, 117n.16
town name 26–7, 27n.13
see also Clint, Raphael, lithographic plan
Stubley Park, 18, 40, 41, 43, 94, 114, 115, 161
auction 20, 25, 26–7, 38–9, 42, 45, 65, 71, 173, 204
subdivision 25, 88, 113, 158, *162*, 163
suburban farms 38, 41, 86
suburbanisation 24, 24n.5
Sydney, population 24n.5

Terry, Martha Foxlowe, *see* Hosking, Martha
Terry, Samuel ix, 13, 14, 14n.12, 152n.27, 152n.29, 163
Botany Bay Rothschild 13
controversy over will 150
Thomson, Edward Deas 53, 53n.11, 55n.22, 94, 118n.19, 130n.58
Thompson, George 53
Tollervey, John S. 174, 176, 187
see also Clonmel
Townsend, Joseph Phipps 1, 2, 56, 66n.69, 109, 207

Ulladulla 66–7, 192

Walbanja 1, 2, 9, 109, 182, 197, 198, 200, 212
Waldron, Francis Charles 64, 65, 159n.57
Walker, Thomas 53
Ward, Joseph Hill 125–7, 125n.39

Wells, William Henry x, 90n.71, 97n.96, 107, 140
insolvent 133
jailed for property fraud 140n.30, 207n.40
rivalry with Raphael Clint 82–3, 82n.52, 97, 103, 138, 207
see also Clint, Raphael
Wentworth, William 136, 136n.16, 140n.33
Wilson, Thomas Braidwood 53
wool drays 49–50, *50*, 50n.3, 53, 55, 191n.75
Wool Road, the 51, 53–7, 55n.22, 56n.24, 59–60, 60n.46, 62, 65, 67, 130, 191
see also Clyde Road, the; dray road; Jervis Bay Road

www.ingramcontent.com/pod-product-compliance
Lightning Source LLC
Chambersburg PA
CBHW070759230426
43665CB00017B/2428